Other Books by Stephen R. Graves and Thomas G. Addington

Clout: Using Spiritual Wisdom to Become a Person of Influence

Behind the Bottom Line: Powering Business Life with Spiritual Wisdom

Daily Focus: Daily Readings for Integrating Faith in the Workplace

The Fourth Frontier: Exploring the New World of Work

The Cornerstones for Life at Work
A Case for Character
A Case for Skill
A Case for Calling
A Case for Serving

Life@Work

on

LEADERSHIP

Life@Work

on

LEADERSHIP

Enduring Insights
for Men *and* Women
of Faith

Stephen R. Graves and Thomas G. Addington

Foreword by Ken Blanchard

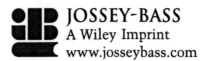

JOSSEY-BASS
A Wiley Imprint
www.josseybass.com

Published by Jossey-Bass
A Wiley Imprint
989 Market Street, San Francisco, CA 94103-1741   www.josseybass.com

Jossey-Bass books and products are available through most bookstores. To contact Jossey-Bass directly call our Customer Care Department within the U.S. at 800-956-7739, outside the U.S. at 317-572-3986 or fax 317-572-4002.

Jossey-Bass also publishes its books in a variety of electronic formats. Some content that appears in print may not be available in electronic books.

Credits are on page 274.

ISBN 0-7879-6420-4

FIRST EDITION
HB Printing   10 9 8 7 6 5 4 3 2

Contents

To our friend and mentor Tom Muccio.
Your intensity, your humor, your wiring to teach,
your faith-walk, and your friendship have shaped us as
businessmen and followers of Jesus. Thanks, "Mooch."

Foreword

Our nation is in the middle of a revival of faith. Although it began before September 11, 2001, the events of that day certainly have stepped up our appetite for more depth and meaning around life and work.

The worlds of leadership and faith were meant to be married. Never separated, never at odds, and never in competition. They were never intended to stand on opposite sides of the room, lonely and isolated, staring at each other. Although rejoining the two spheres is a great goal, most of us would quickly admit it's not always easy to harness faith and leadership together for appropriate and effective application.

Steve Graves and Tom Addington started *Life@Work* four-and-a-half years ago to help stimulate that conversation. I am happy to add a chapter of my work on leadership to this compilation and would enthusiastically encourage you to serve, to lead, and to follow in the footprints that the Master Faith-Leader left.

Ken Blanchard
July 2002

Acknowledgments

A thank you is in order to the authors who first articulated these ideas in the original chapters that we have selected for this "best of" on leadership.

Kristi Reimer, you are a joy to work with. Your writing and editing skills are better than even you realize, and we are looking forward to the next project.

Thanks to Brad Lomenick, still the "head wrangler" of the vast network of friends we've made through *Life@Work*.

Thank you, Kathy Blank. You're not a support person, but you certainly have supported us and this project from start to finish.

A special thanks to our agent, Chip MacGregor, and Andrea Christian of Alive Communication. You guys have become good friends, which makes a project like this even more meaningful.

Sheryl Fullerton and Mark Kerr, we are having a blast working with you. You're helping to make our book projects significant and fun.

And thanks to all the men and women of faith who are leading well.

Introduction

If you walk into a bookstore or library or go online to do a bit of browsing on the subject of leadership, you're likely to be staggered by the amount of material available. As of this writing, Amazon.com offers almost nine thousand books containing the word *leadership* in the title. Seminars, personal coaches, motivational training videos, websites—there seems to be an inexhaustible supply of riches for the leadership-curious.

But are they really all equally valuable? A discriminating reader-viewer-consumer is quick to be skeptical. As is true of any subject, there's quite a bit of chaff to be sifted through in order to uncover the wheat. Some ideas are shallow and poorly thought out at best, and at worst they can be downright wacky and quacky. Titles of value are out there, great ideas and insights are available, but finding them can be a challenge.

Welcome to this book. In the last several years, we have paid close attention to the emerging hunger for spirituality in the workplace as well as the desire for many followers to become leaders and for many leaders to develop their skills in order to become more effective in their current positions. These trends are not really new, but they are reaching such a level of intensity and interest in the marketplace that the need seems more potent than ever.

We launched *Life@Work* four-and-a-half years ago to look at the intersection between faith and work. But we had begun examining the subject in our personal lives and through other endeavors long before that. In that time we have become aware of some of the key players in the arena and some of the best writings available on important subjects—one of the most important being leadership. Because of the sheer volume of information available on leadership, we saw the need for a guide—a primer, if you will—to give interested people an introduction to some of the best ideas and a jumping-off point for them to explore the subject in greater depth.

Leadership is an area where it can be easy to go relatively deep in a certain aspect, but in doing so you may lose the bigger picture. A new book, sermon, or seminar can give you a flash of new insight and excitement about one facet of leadership, but its dazzle may blind you to the entire jewel, and opportunities for growth can slide by unnoticed. We don't want that to happen, so we've compiled sixteen chapters of what we consider to be a great introduction to various contributions on leadership.

Without a doubt, this book is far from exhaustive. There are many more fantastic writings out there, and there is no way we could include every single one. Some readers will feel strongly that we left out a key thinker—or two or three or eight. We accept that. What we want to do is begin the conversation: introduce you to some of our favorites, give an overview of the best practices of leadership in a spiritual context, and let you take it from there.

Here's how it works. Each of the sixteen chapters is organized around a key word, the kernel of truth at the heart of that writer's insights. That word is intended to guide you through the chapter and help you glean the richness of it. At the end of each chapter is a place for you to take action based on what you've read. We've come up with a couple of questions to help form a bridge between what you've read and your own life. They are captured in the box following the selected material. If you find yourself asking "So what?" then take a hard look at these questions, interact with the text a little, and see if the relevance isn't there after all.

One of the reasons we're so excited about leadership, and why we think it so significant, is that we find so many examples of leadership done right in Scripture. And probably one of the greatest examples in our minds is King David, of whom it is said, "He chose David His servant and took him from the sheep pens; from tending the sheep he brought him to be the shepherd of His people Jacob, of Israel his inheritance. And David shepherded them with integrity of heart; with skillful hands he led them" (Psalm 78:70–72).

If we had to choose one Old Testament passage that describes a successful leader, this would be the one. In that final sentence resides a two-pronged formula for leadership that no current business bestseller on the subject (including the ones excerpted in this book) has been able to top. King David wasn't a soft-side guru who was great at relationships but a little lacking when it came to business expertise. Nor was he a hard-side genius who came up short in the people-skills department. He was a holistic leader. He led with integrity of heart *and* with skillful hands. He was both left-brained and right-brained. He'd visited both Mars and Venus.

We don't need to inform you that David wasn't perfect, but he led so well that all the kings who followed were compared to him. None scored higher. The impact of David's leadership was felt for centuries to come. In Acts 13:36, the Apostle Paul says that David served God's purpose in his own generation and then he died. To further explain it, David had an enormous amount of influence in the Kingdom of God. He hit a home run in the ball game of life. Then, when his nine innings were up, he died.

The key to David's success in leadership was simple. He served God's purpose—with integrity of heart and with skillful hands—in his own generation. The application for us is equally simple. Today is our chance to be the leaders God wants us to be. We can't control how we're remembered, but we can control how we live today.

So as you read through this book, we hope you'll gain many valuable, practical insights into leadership. But we also hope you'll remember—as many of our writers point out—that at the end of the day, leadership isn't about us. It's about the people under our stewardship and about the God we serve.

Life@Work

on

LEADERSHIP

Promises

THERE IS SIMPLY NO BETTER WAY
to begin a book on leadership than with a selection by Max De Pree. From the publication of
Leadership Is an Art, the book that identified him
as a key participant in the leadership conversation,
to the establishment of the De Pree Leadership
Center in California, De Pree's voice has been one
of the most clear and compelling on the subject.
He stands apart not only because of his ability to
translate vision into day-to-day reality but also
because of his emphasis on values—how a leader
must cultivate a moral quality that transcends success of the organization to bring about success of
the individual.

> The best leaders promise only what's worth defending.

This chapter from *Leadership Jazz,* "A Key
Called Promise," discusses what a leader must pledge
to his or her followers—both the making and carrying out of promises. De Pree emphasizes that in
most cases, the leader cannot be responsible for the
day-to-day maintenance that keeps an organization
running. What the leader must do instead is promise certain things to the followers and ensure that
those promises are kept. One of the most significant

The promises that come from a leader tell the story of her mettle. How those promises are carried out reveals the position a leader will occupy in the history of the organization.

reasons we selected this chapter is De Pree's inclusion of eleven expectations an organization should count on its leader to fulfill. Without the realization of those expectations, an organization flounders.

De Pree, now retired, was with Herman Miller for years, most recently as chairman emeritus, and has been elected to *Fortune*'s National Business Hall of Fame. As the following chapter illustrates, he is able to cut through the noise and chatter with sharp-edged clarity. It's impossible to read his work and not come away with a new perspective on what leadership is all about.

A Key Called Promise

• • •

Max De Pree

I have a key in my bosom, called Promise, that will, I am
persuaded, open any lock in Doubting Castle.

—The Pilgrim's Progress

Leadership may be good work, but it's also a tough job. There is always more to do than time seems to allow. Measuring out both time to pursue one's own responsibilities and time to respond to the needs of others can be difficult. And leaders are constantly under pressure to make promises.

Though I'm still learning things about being a leader, I can tell you at least two requirements of such a position: the need to give one's witness as a leader—to make your promises to the people who allow you to lead; and the necessity of carrying out your promises. It sounds easier than it is.

One day Pat McNeal, a scheduler in the plant whom I'd known for a good many years, called me to say that Valerie from the second shift wanted to talk to me about a very serious matter. At the time I was CEO. Not knowing me, she had asked Pat to pave the way into my office. Pat said, "I want you to know that Valerie's a very dependable person. You would be wise to listen to what she has to say."

A date was set and Valerie appeared. She began by asking me if I knew that a vice president had fired the relatively new manager of the second shift without following the prescribed procedures. I told her that no, I wasn't aware of this. She then gave me the entire story of the abrupt and unwarranted dismissal of not one, but two fine young managers of the second and third shifts by this vice president, who seemed to have lost his bearings.

Valerie then handed me a beautifully written petition outlining the qualifications of the second-shift manager, his performance, and his relationship with all the people on the shift. Every person on the second shift had signed.

Those of you who have had experience managing in manufacturing plants will understand the risk Valerie ran in circulating the petition and in coming to me. The careful investigation that followed proved Valerie and her co-workers entirely correct and demonstrated that Valerie was serving Herman Miller (our company) well by protesting the firings. Valerie—not her superior in the hierarchy—was honoring corporate values and policies. She had put me and other senior managers in the position of living up to policies the company had clearly promised. Valerie was helping the leaders of the company to connect voice and touch.

Many of us privately make promises. We promise ourselves to lose weight, work harder, or finish a book. If we don't keep this kind of promise, we can usually find a reason, sometimes even a good reason. But followers can't afford leaders who make casual promises. Someone is likely to take them seriously. Leaders make public promises. They put themselves on the line to the people they lead. An enormous chasm separates the private world, where we often smile indulgently at broken promises, from the public one, where unkept promises do great harm. Leaders constantly look out across the distance. For no leader has the luxury of making a promise in a vacuum.

At no time is the gap between individual needs and organizational needs more painfully obvious than in times of cutbacks or difficult business conditions. Leaders must balance sensitively the needs of people and of the institution. A leader's promises come under critical examination at these times. A leader who backs away from her promises under duress irreparably damages the organization and plants the seeds of suspicion among her followers.

What would happen if the President of the United States were to visit an inner-city Chicago elementary school, tell the teachers and administration that she was publicly taking accountability for improving that school, and promise that she would hold the administration and teachers accountable? And, the President would continue, "I will visit this school exactly one year from now to see what progress has been made. Call me for help." Does anyone doubt that the quality of education in the school would rise?

There is great power in the public promise of a true leader, power to strengthen and enable people. One of the great dangers to organizations arises when a leader's private and public promises contradict each other. Then the expectations of followers are liable to go beyond the reality delivered. Especially in lively, exciting institutions and corporations, when the private and public worlds of the leaders become confounded or contradictory, the mix-up can be deadly. At this point, we begin to question the leader's integrity.

Another of the great problems of leadership is what exactly to promise. The clarity and appropriateness of a leader's promises bear directly on the effectiveness and maturity of the institution and the performance of the people in it. What should a leader take from the private and personal bouts of concentrated thinking about the institution's future and make public as a promise?

The best leaders promise only what's worth defending.

With this in mind, before looking at what a leader may promise, I would like to discuss a few givens essential when thinking about leadership.

It's important to understand that good work means something a little different these days. In today's workplace, where the great majority of people are well prepared and thoroughly motivated, individual involvement through an open, participative structure or system of management most often elicits good performance. Every vital organization thrives because it depends more on commitment and enthusiasm than on the letter of the contract.

Because of the variety of gifts and skills that people bring to the workplace, the need for good people, and their willingness to move, we should treat the great majority of people as volunteers. They don't have to stay in one place. They don't have to work for one company or for one leader. They follow someone only when she deserves it. Thus leaders and followers don't sit on parallel lines, always close but never meeting. Leaders and followers are all parts of a circle.

Whether formally or informally, it's important to recognize that practically everything we accomplish happens through teamwork. We are not on our own. Everyone works within a loop of social account-abilities—a family, a congregation, a business. Ours is an arm-in-arm accountability. The highest-risk leader is the one who thinks she works alone.

It's important to understand that leadership is a posture of indebt-edness. The process of leading is the process of fulfilling commitments made both to persons and to the organization. A leader's promises are her commitments. Keeping these promises and the way in which they are kept are parts of the mystery and the art of leadership. Knowing what not to do is fully as important as knowing what to do.

Followers can really determine how successful a leader will be. And so I would like to propose some ways of thinking about followership. What are the rights and needs of followers? Remember to think of fol-lowers as volunteers. Remember, too, that the goals of the organization are best met when the goals of people in the organization are met at the same time. These two sets of goals are seldom the same. While teaching at night school, I used to ask my classes, "Why do you go to work?" No one ever answered, "To make profit for the company."

Any follower has a right to ask many things of her leader. Here are several questions that leaders should expect to hear. The answers to these questions, you see, are some of the promises leaders will make.

- What may I expect from you?
- Can I achieve my own goals by following you?
- Will I reach my potential by working with you?
- Can I entrust my future to you?
- Have you bothered to prepare yourself for leadership?
- Are you ready to be ruthlessly honest?
- Do you have the self-confidence and trust to let me do my job?
- What do you believe?

Some time ago, shortly after the board of directors had elected Ed Simon president and chief operating officer of Herman Miller, I was out in one of our plants. A longtime worker stopped me and wanted to talk about the reasons for, and the implications of, this important decision. He had a number of well-thought-out questions, and I could tell that he had been waiting for me to come by. Without thinking, I started to answer some of his questions. I was foolish enough to think that the chairman of the board knew all the answers! He interrupted me. "I don't want to hear you answer these questions, I need to hear Ed's answers. I already know that Ed is our president, but what I need to know is, *who is Ed?*" And he wasn't asking what Ed looked like.

This person needed to know what kind of a leader he was following and what this new leader would promise.

What a leader promises to the institution can be developed by thinking in a certain way about the needs of the institution. Just as individuals have a right to expect certain things of a leader, an institution (as a corporate body of many groups of people) expects and demands certain things from its leaders. I will list a few to stimulate your thinking.

(You'll notice that I haven't listed the promises leaders should make. I can't tell you that. The promises that come from a leader tell the story of her mettle. How those promises are carried out reveals the position a leader will occupy in the history of the organization.)

The organization expects the leader to define and express both in writing and, especially, through behavior the beliefs and values of the institution. This may not be easy, but like many disciplines, it's essential. Writing down what an institution values makes everyone come clean. It can also make people uncomfortable. The safety of vaguely known beliefs will disappear pretty fast.

To carry out its work, the organization needs from a leader a clear statement of its vision and its strategy. Of course, a leader may not be the only author of these, but she is primarily accountable for expressing them and making them understood.

A leader is accountable for the design of the business. A business or institutional structure, the bones and muscle of any organization, needs always to be kept in sync with the strategy and aimed at the future. The design of the organization should never be gerrymandered to serve the politicians or the bureaucracy of the insiders.

A leader is responsible for lean and simple statements of policy consistent with beliefs and values, vision and strategy. Policy gives practical meaning to values. Policies must actively enable people whose job it is to carry them out. I'm not talking about rules here. Leaders who live by rules rather than by principles are no more than dogs in mangers.

Equity is the special province of a leader. There is more than the financial side of equity, and I do not mean control. A leader is responsible for equity in the assignment of all resources, tangible and intangible, in relation to agreed-on priorities. I hope that you will allow me to include in the meaning of equity the chance to advance in the organization and the chance to reach one's potential. I would also put in this definition communication, recognition, and reward. Any organization accrues to itself these three kinds of equity. It is incumbent on a leader to protect them.

A leader focuses not on her own image as leader, but on the tone of the body of the institution. Followers, not leaders, accomplish the work of the organization. We need to be concerned, therefore, with how the followers deal with change. How do they handle a customer's need for good service and good quality? How do the followers deal with conflict? How do they measure and respond to their results? These are questions that will help us evaluate the tone of the body; these are the ways in which the work of a leader comes under scrutiny. Just how lithe is your organization?

Appearance follows substance; the message subordinates the medium. A leader gets good results by leading, not by appearing to lead. The Marquis de Custine, a French traveler, was crossing with a group of Russian nobles from Sweden to St. Petersburg in the nineteenth century. The Russians were discussing the burdens of attending at the Czar's court, among which was the obligation to listen politely to all sorts of trivial and boring conversation. They were trying to determine the best way of appearing to listen, since we all admire attentiveness. The Frenchman made a simple observation. "The best way of appearing to listen," he said, "is to listen."

A leader ensures that priorities are set, that they are steadfastly communicated and adhered to in practice. This can be accomplished only if the leader halts the endless negotiation of the politicians in the group, the negotiators' waltz, as I sometimes call it. The participative process stimulates contrary opinion, as it should, but no organization can survive endless negotiation. At some point, public acceptance of a direction must appear.

A leader ensures that the planning for the organization at all levels receives the necessary direction and approvals. The benefits of a good plan are three-fold. It sets a clear direction. It makes the necessary objectives and goals visible and understandable. It serves as a road map for all the people in the organization who need to know where and with whom to make a connection.

A leader reviews and assesses results primarily in three areas: key appointments and promotions, results compared to the plan, the connections to key publics. Promotions, key appointments, and succession planning are the most crucial elements in the organization's future. These activities are a leader's true domain. The organization has a right to understand the criteria used in these decisions, and each one must be examined carefully.

One of the many pacts of love that a leader upholds is to make the organization accountable for results compared to the plan. Not to be accountable for results is to be seriously out of touch with reality. Only leaders can stand up to the organization and hold it to its goals and to its required performance.

Institutions must never be permitted to operate in isolation. It is a matter of survival that we stay in touch with reality by opening ourselves to key groups: students and faculty, followers and customers, constituents and stockholders. Perhaps only success is more fragile in institutional life than the condition of being truly in touch with what's real.

Leaders are accountable for the continuous renewal of the organization. Renewal, I think, results directly when a leader understands and communicates opportunities, constraints, and reality. The understanding without communication is futile; communication without understanding is fruitless. Leaders need a solid understanding, and they owe pellucid explanation. We also need to remember that the unexamined message is not worth giving. The leader who opens her communication to question and debate brings about a much more promising result. If you believe this, it's easy to see that video reports are not communications.

Renewal also requires that leaders be alive in a special way to innovation and be hospitable to the creative person. This brings an ability to solve problems, to deal constructively with change, and to enable and encourage continual personal growth.

A leader ought never to embarrass followers. What is it exactly that embarrasses one's followers? Just ask them.

Leaders can only do so much. In very small organizations, leaders can sometimes have a hand in everything. This soon changes. In larger organizations, leaders simply can't do the work that moves the group day to day. Nor should they. Leaders remain responsible, perhaps more so than anyone else, for making the future promising and making promises for the future.

Businesses and institutions, like nature, abhor a vacuum. A leader who makes no promises leaves a vacuum soon to be filled by promises made by other people for her or by politicians trying to manipulate the organization. The best leaders make their promises under the scrutiny of their followers. Then they keep them. This is one way to connect voice and touch.

Reflecting on the
Promises of My Leadership

1. My "Promises" report card would look as follows:
   - I am aware that I am making promises to those under my stewardship.
   - I have maintained a "promises made–promises kept" philosophy.
   - I am helping those on my team take promises seriously.
   - I am keeping my unwritten, nonpublic, small promises as faithfully as I keep my big, high-profile, costly promises.

2. What are some promises I have made to my followers? How did I succeed or fail in carrying them out, and what were the results?

3. De Pree lists eleven things an organization has a right to expect from its leader: beliefs and values, vision and strategy, design, policy, equity, tone, priorities, planning, review and assessment, renewal, and no embarrassment. In which of these areas have I excelled as a leader? Which need some more work?

4. Who is a leader I have watched make and keep promises well?

Politics

The truth of the
matter is, *politics*
isn't always a
dirty word; it's
the means using
our sphere of
interpersonal
relationships in
ways that enable
us to accomplish
our goals.

*P*OLITICS PROBABLY ISN'T THE FIRST
word you would associate with leadership—at
least not healthy leadership. Outside of a civic context, the idea of a leader engaging in political activity brings to mind shady deals behind closed doors,
underhanded maneuvers that harm innocent people,
and compromises that diminish personal integrity.
In a business context, politics often refers to the
petty intrigue among coworkers that undercuts
morale and wreaks havoc with productivity.

Calvin Miller, author of *The Empowered Leader,*
approaches the idea of politics differently, breathing
new life into the concept. In "The Politics of Grace
and the Abuse of Power," he points out that in its
original sense, the word *politics* simply meant the
establishment of a system that sought the greatest
good for members of a public body. Achieving this
goal is just as necessary now as it was when Aristotle
brought the term into common use. All leaders,
regardless of the size and nature of the organization over which they preside, find themselves at the
hub of relational dynamics—moderating conflict,

The key to the whole issue is this: Are you using deference, courtesy, and public relations to get others to grant you power, or are you using these things to create a wider sphere of influence for God?

building support, leveraging relationships. Politics is simply part of the landscape of leadership.

Drawing on the history of King David of Israel, Miller illustrates how political actions can be grounded in grace, as when David befriended Mephibosheth, the relative of his great friend Jonathan, to bring peace between warring factions. But politics can also be self-serving and destructive, as in the case of David's interference in the lives of Uriah and Bathsheba. Miller shows us that although the temptation to use people for personal gain is immense, the potential to change people's lives for their good—which ultimately leads to the good of the organization—is even greater.

Miller is familiar to many readers. A longtime pastor and author of more than forty books, he is now a professor at Beeson Divinity School at Samford University in Birmingham, Alabama. Also a poet, artist, and novelist, Miller is able to infuse creativity and theological substance into the discussion of any topic. The following pages are no exception.

The Politics *of* Grace *and* *the* Abuse *of* Power

...

Calvin Miller

Politics is often a word of contempt for people in the church. Church politics somehow seem more ungodly than civil politics. "We must keep politics out of the church," say the offended.

Mark this!

In every organization, including the church, the leader must be somewhat of a politician. He or she must learn how to motivate various people by making commitments, side deals, complimenting, remonstrating, and bargaining in order to get things done. In 2 Samuel 9, David demonstrated the political overtones of his leadership. Do not think David unspiritual for behaving as he does toward Mephibosheth. The truth is, he is being especially effective.

I remember being terribly incensed some years ago when a friend of mine suggested that every successful pastor was a politician. I determined that even if he spoke the truth, I would rather not succeed than use politics in any aspect of my ministry. I actually held some resentment toward him until I later read a similar statement in a book by a pastor-writer whom I had always admired. At that time I tried to convince myself that I was living free of the whole issue. But in later moments of honest thought, I realized that politics need not be a dirty word when used in the context of ministry.

Our distaste for church politics swelters in the aftermath of national scandals like Watergate and those of cable television evangelists. The truth of the matter is, *politics* isn't always a dirty word; it's the means using our sphere of interpersonal relationships in ways that enable us to accomplish our goals. *Politics* is defined in the dictionary as the "art and science of government . . . the art of influencing policy or winning control." There's a secondary meaning of *politics* that emphasizes competition between groups or individuals for power and leadership.

Of course, the very suggestion that pastors or churches ought to be locked in egoistic power struggles is unworthy of the cross of Christ. But let us remember that the word *politics* derives from the same term as the word polity and polite. *Polity* is the word for cooperation in and understanding within the community. *Polite* refers to any action that is marked by courtesy, consideration, or correct social usage.

I would like us to focus on the use of the word *politics* as it regards courtesy and correct social usage. Jesus certainly did not encourage power struggles in the church. He did say that kindness and courtesy were to be the laws of His kingdom. He said that the Christian was to be wise, knowing his world, but harmless as far as the desire for power or control was concerned (see Matt. 10:16). He even went so far as to compliment an unjust steward by saying that the children of this world are wiser in their generation than the children of light (see Luke 16:8). Is Jesus condoning a "Watergate" in the church? Of course not! But He is saying the kind of diplomacy and courtesy employed in the world might be of benefit in the kingdom of God.

Practically, this means you are not free as a Christian to compete with selfish power in the church. Sadly, there are many who have made the church a forum for political abuse. Warren Bennis speaks for churches as well as secular society when he says that too often we don't want leaders anymore; we want conspirators.[1] It isn't just the conspirators that Christians admire; they also admire superstar believers. We evangelicals often elevate our superstars to idol status. We gape at them and hunger for their autographs. Why? Because they are great leaders? No! Because they give us a feeling of touching greatness with none of the demands that great leaders endure. We elevate them to marquis status because they flatter us in allowing us to know them while they require nothing of us. We sometimes create non-content neurotics by our adulation, knowing that it is a lot easier to live with stars than leaders.[2]

Leaders can make us feel uncomfortable for our small commitments. Christians in many cases avoid their kingdom responsibilities and snuggle into an affirming and undemanding community. Christians should seek to promote God's kingdom in the hearts of men and to establish the church of Jesus. If by courtesy, deference, or kindness you cause enemies to love each other or the power-prone to submit to Christ, then politics is good. The key to the whole issue is this: Are you using deference, courtesy, and public relations to get others to grant you power, or are you using these things to create a wider sphere of influence for God?

It is wise to remember that Jesus was victimized by civil politics at His trial. Although He had all power, He succumbed to the political machinery of the Romans, Pharisees, Sadducees, and Zealots. His life was crushed. Much harm is done in the church because we forget the corrupting nature of power. It is easy to want to control others for our own advantage. We easily degenerate to tit-for-tat administration. We quickly learn the spiteful art of battling politics with politics. The cross always reminds us that we are not here to control others in the interests of building our own empires.

Peter Koestenbaum recognized that the best use of power contains at least one element of altruism. "Leadership is the use of power. But power, to be ethical, must never be abused. To ensure that, one rule cannot be broken: Power is to be used only for the benefit of others, never for yourself. That is the essential generosity and self-sacrifice of the leader."[3] Remember, self-sacrifice, like that Paul charges in Galatians 2:20, is not only the key to holiness, it is the door to Christian leadership.

In 2 Samuel, David of Israel used his old friendship with Jonathan to promote goodwill between warring political camps. David used deference and courtesy in a splendid way. He befriended Mephibosheth, Jonathan's crippled son. The result of his kindness to Jonathan's son produced a new harmony and better relationships in Israel. With this kindness, David practiced the politics of grace.

The politics of grace is built upon an understanding that wherever human beings gather they form a community of need. The politics of grace explains their attractions. The grace that lies at the center of the Christian community should be marked with a special kind of politics. This politic of relationships should be fueled by a New Testament ethic.

Themes That Empower Christian Leadership

- Make people feel significant
- Teach all that learning and competence matter
- Inspire community
- Incite vision

Warren Bennis gives to my whole view of leadership four themes that should empower Christian leadership. First, people must feel significant. Second, learning and competence matter. This is important in Christian leadership, for one sometimes gets the feeling that Christians feel that merely the adjective *Christian* makes every value superior. How wrong! Christian leadership must also touch these sound bases of competence and learning. Incompetence and ignorance cannot sanctify what is shoddy and unstructured, even if it wears the word *Christian*. Third, people are and must be part of a community. Hopefully this community endows its constituents with largesse. Sometimes the Christian community cannot produce great leaders, because it builds only little souls nourished on stingy dogma and legalisms. Fourth, vision should make work exciting. Growing churches may be hard work but its people never complain. Excitement sanctifies work.[4]

The POLITICS *of* LEADERSHIP

Moderating Conflict

In 2 Samuel 2–4, David and his supporters killed all of the house of Saul to keep any claimants to that dynasty from rising in revolt. Doubtless there were deep grudges throughout the kingdom because of this purge. In 2 Samuel 9:1, we see David looking for new ways to bring those diehards, still loyal to the house of Saul, into orbit with his own goals.

Did David do anything illicit in looking for political answers to resolve this quarrel between the two families? No. Unfortunately, his blood-drenched military purge against Saul's clan had resolved the matter. However, his bloody constraint was succeeded by the politics of grace.

I have never known a pastor who did not seek to make decisions that would make the greatest number of people happy. In no church is it always possible to make everybody happy. But harmony must prevail at a reasonable level to keep the church moving ahead.

Gaining Support

Patronage refers to the use of special-interest actions to gain support. Jesus' final words in the parable of the dishonest steward are, "Use worldly wealth to gain friends for yourselves" (Luke 16:9, NIV). Jesus' statement is almost the dictionary definition of *patronage*. Does Jesus' statement imply that it is good to use patronage to provide people with future security? In certain instances Jesus seemed to say it is acceptable. Jesus had another parable in which He endorsed the right to spend money in political ways that we might be received into eternal habitations (Luke 16:10).

In what ways did David exercise good leadership in his patronage of Mephibosheth (2 Sam. 9:3–7)? In the kindness that he showed, was he only buttering him up to collect patronage? With so many people in the house of Mephibosheth and Ziba, it must have taken quite a bit of the king's resources to feed and clothe them. A real leader can sometimes see, however, that money must be spent to change discord into harmony.

All of us can remember a time when we saw our pastor (or other church leaders) take special-interest action to bring a sense of harmony and peace to the whole church. The actions of a good pastor would harmonize such special-interest action with the beatitude, "Blessed are the peacemakers" (Matt. 5:9, NIV). Every notable leader, from Abraham to the present time, has tried to work out political compromises that would harmonize hostilities without war.

The key issue is that in playing politics, a leader does not begin to use power abusively. It is dehumanizing—even ungodly to exercise abusive power over others. Rollo May writes, "No human being can stand the perpetually numbing experience of his own powerlessness."[5] The problem is that no matter how we struggle to be free of being abusive, we are all tempted to want to control others. One gets the feeling in watching so many abusers of power that this desire to be king of the world is no laughing matter. So many evangelical power magnets seem possessed of an ungodly desire to build video empires at any cost. It is hard to tell how far they want to go with this, but they develop movements that have almost cult-like status.

Myron C. Madden warned us that seemingly God-filled people may, in reality, be agents of evil. "Evil, which is at the core of all temptations, seems to reside near the centers of power. That power may be political, religious, financial, intellectual or social, and it can change channels without high conversion costs."[6] Warren Bennis, like Madden, agrees about the dangers of evil always inherent in such cult-like leaders. He says that when cults develop around leaders, they get a God-complex, believing themselves infallible. Further, says Bennis, such idolatry of leadership can turn those who do the idolizing into drones who are so content to worship a corporate idol they no longer develop their own creative powers.[7]

How Christianity longs for a new Elijah to come and state the plan of God without using his proclamations to become rich.

The path to abusive power is easily traceable. It begins simply in our need for appreciation. From there the path winds upward to self-esteem, which—when it takes itself too seriously—moves toward arrogance. Arrogance often disparages others and leads to abusive power.

The current culture has made power a god. Its sole religious quest is how to achieve this power. The new heroes of culture are not the creative achievers but merely the powerful. Warren Bennis describes Americans well. He says that we have changed heroes. We used to admire people who achieved in theater or sports or human service. Now, however, we are in a mindset that admires tycoons, entrepreneurs, and CEOs. We no longer have heroes who do things, only heroes who occupy spotlights of wealth and visibility. We show we are infatuated with the rich and famous.[8] I wish I could say the church was free of these delusions, but alas, there seems to be an admiration of America's "religious names," not for what they believe or how they minister, but almost totally for the strength of their control or the size of their church or media empires.

How far we have gone since people like Carey or Judson were icons of evangelical respect!

The roots of abusive power are often found in the very men and women who were once victimized by power. For this reason Rollo May, in his book *Power and Innocence,* says that it is not always power that corrupts; indeed, powerlessness may be the corrupter. Powerlessness may be a prison for the unconquered spirit—a prison from which cellmates dream of being free and, once free, create the same abusive cells of powerlessness in which they force others to live.

Sigmund Freud noticed that most boys had psychological vendettas against their fathers. In early life these vendettas can lead them to begin vying with their fathers for power. Such vendettas produce powerful men who wield great, and sometimes abusive, power. James MacGregor Burns, in his Pulitzer Prize–winning book *Leadership,* says that Adolph Hitler is rumored to have been born with an undescended testicle. Such a child in a male-oriented world may struggle to achieve power in order to compensate for his deformity.[9]

The shift in those whom secular America lionizes is lamentable. Warren Bennis says that eighteenth-century America was famous for its geniuses, nineteenth-century America for its adventurers and creative discoverers. But what of twentieth-century America? Alas, we are defined only by our drudges, bureaucrats, and corporate machine tenders.[10] Is it possible that in the world of religion we must be labeled with the same spurious admiration? Do our young pastors too much admire the spiritual giants or the new video icons of power? Our own spiritual deformity may be so twisted as to make Mephibosheth look like a marathon titlist.

When examining David's role in history, it is futile to speak of his character as the result of an oppressive father or a physical deformity. The truth is, God placed David in a leadership role in order to forge a disorganized, tribal government into a nation. David clearly was not crushed by feelings of powerlessness, but he must have had such feelings from time to time.

Any condition of powerlessness, such as not being esteemed in childhood, may cause a person to strive extra hard to become an influential adult. Comedian Rodney Dangerfield has popularized the idea of how the lack of our esteem can cripple us. "I don't get no respect," he laments for everyone who feels the impact of powerlessness.

Did David ever feel that he "got no respect?" In the case of David's anointing (see 1 Sam. 16), his father Jesse appeared to esteem him least of all his sons. David's menial job of shepherding suggested—if only by reason of his youth—that he was not esteemed competent to go to war. If so, David's powerlessness may have become a springboard into the center of attention and national leadership.

We cannot assume that David tried to show the world that he "got no respect" and thus became a political superachiever. Nor did David exhibit after his rise to the throne very many abuses of power. The growth of personal authority can be a platform for effective leadership, but it can also be the threshold of exploitation and power abuse. Most of David's life was marked by effective leadership, but in 2 Samuel 11 we see power abuse.

Leaders whom James MacGregor Burns would call "moral leaders" are those whose motivation is to produce changes in the world that will be of real value to both the leader and those he leads.[11] However, abusive power fails to see the followers and makes decisions in which the welfare of others is not a real concern. In such a "pro-me" use of others, the universe becomes a "you-niverse" in which others exist solely to supply the advance of the power abuser.

I suspect that most power-mad leaders never define themselves that way. Their erosion to the abusive use of power was so gradual that they may not have seen it. On their way up the ladder of control, they may well have served those they led; they were moral leaders. But once they gained the pinnacle of control, the power they had once been willing to share became their sole pursuit.

The pinnacle of position that power-mad leaders occupy often causes people around them to admire, and even envy, them. Admiration often feeds our cancerous self-esteem until we, in Muhammad Ali fashion, can say with little embarrassment that we really are the greatest. Arrogance, when well fed, begins to believe that the world owes it whatever it can seize.

This was apparently David's philosophy in 2 Samuel 11. How did it develop? We cannot know exactly when and where David's sinful abuse of power began. We can see that by 2 Samuel 11 the king's heart had turned from servant leadership toward scandalous power. Servant leadership is that all-important checkpoint that bridles demonic power. Max De Pree said: "The first responsibility of a leader is to define reality, the last is to say 'thank you'. In between the two, the leader must become a servant and a debtor. That sums up the progress of an artful leader."[12]

As long as we follow Christ, we are safe! It is impossible to live out Christian servanthood and wield the mace of abusive power. He who tries to rule from the throne of Christ is a usurper, and not a servant. David learned this truth as a consequence of his evil deeds. In Psalm 51 we see that David had learned the beauty of the words that close the Lord's Prayer: "Thine is the kingdom and the power" (Matt. 6:13, KJV).

We are servants as long as we remember what Jesus said to Pilate: "You would have no power over me if it were not given to you from above" (John 19:11, NIV). We need to repeat this truth in every area of leadership to ensure that we truly are servant leaders.

Power Abuse Evidence #1: Giving Up Those Disciplines We Demand *of* "Underlings"

"At the time when kings go off to war," David stayed home (2 Sam. 11:1, NIV). No reason is offered for his failure to go with the army. He did not seem to be ill or incapacitated. War is dangerous, but David was no coward. War is hard, but David had always thrived on what was difficult. Why didn't David go to war? It appears as though he had excused himself from the war solely on the basis that he was king and could do as he wished. His self-excusing reason may have been, "Even though it is customary, I owe this to me." We have already said that power abuse is rooted in selfishness. David, as some see it, killed Uriah to take his wife. David must have viewed dying as the duty of underlings while he had the right to enjoy the more exalted status of being king! It is a fault of power abusers that they come to overvalue their own lives as they devalue others. Some men, they feel, are created more equal than others. Is such a degenerate view of human dignity common in all power abuse?

Power Abuse Evidence #2: Believing That Others Owe Me Whatever Use I Can Make *of* Them

In 2 Samuel 11:2–3, Bathsheba and her husband became objects for David's personal use. Power abuse is always characterized by the use of people. Some pastors and religious workers have found ladders to their own personal success right within church. They rise to power using those they were called to serve. Even as they use others, they falsely quote Philippians 2, which speaks of the Christ who humbled Himself and became nothing. They do not always realize what they are doing. When confronted with their abuse, they deny it. They wish for the more humbling image of themselves that they prefer. Is it possible that David continued writing psalms while using Bathsheba and plotting her husband's death? Is it possible that he was even faithful in his attendance at temple worship during this season of power abuse?

Years ago I had a friend whose life I longed to emulate. She seemed to have such a successful walk with Christ. More than anything, she seemed to long for Christlikeness. Just when I had nearly canonized her as a saint, she snapped her fingers, wrote her family off, and acknowledged her adulterous affairs with several men. She had grown so powerful in her company that she seemed to feel that her wealth and influence gave her a right to live any way she chose.

POWER ABUSE EVIDENCE #3:
TRYING *to* FIX THINGS UP RATHER
THAN MAKE THINGS RIGHT

This evidence of power abuse shows the art of manipulating circumstances without moral conscience. David's sin in 2 Samuel 11:6 was that he didn't start to mend his ways by confessing his sin. Instead, he engineered the course of his life to a favorable end. It allowed him to retain his kingly image rather than face the hard moral and spiritual work of getting right with God.

So often in life we find ourselves making a mess of our circumstances. Yet we often think in terms of how to fix things up rather than to make things right. This tendency is common with power abusers. David ultimately gets things right with God, but his attempt was to fix things up. It usually doesn't occur to us to ask God to make things right while we are trying to fix things. Fixing mess-ups falls short of being mended by the atoning work of Christ.

POWER ABUSE EVIDENCE #4:
CLOSING MY MIND *to* EVERY SUGGESTION
THAT I COULD BE OUT *of* GOD'S WILL

If King David had been sensitive to walking with God, he would have heard Uriah's counsel as a rebuke; the men of Israel were dying in the field and therefore Uriah would not live at home in selfish ease (2 Samuel

11:11). Are we so involved in selfish indulgence that we are blind to the signposts that God puts in our way to call us to Himself? How we need to keep our eyes open to the lessons God sends our way. Second Samuel 11:11 is evidence that power blinds us to God's rebuke. Other incidents in David's story allow us to see that God had to nudge David toward repentance. How often like David we pursue pleasure while others die in pain or live under great hardship. How often the American church lives it up while Christian brothers in other cultures are dying in need. Even if we do not in such moments see ourselves as indulgent, we are called the "ugly Americans" or even the "ugly Christians" because we are blind to our own narcissism and power hungry egoism.

POWER ABUSE EVIDENCE #5: BELIEVING THAT PEOPLE *in* MY WAY ARE EXPENDABLE

In 2 Samuel 11:14, Uriah refused to return home for even one night. Just one visit would have made Bathsheba's illicit pregnancy appear to be the natural result of their fidelity. But Uriah's stand for truth became an embarrassment to his cheating king. David took steps to eliminate Uriah. At last he married Uriah's widow and legitimized her pregnancy. The only reason David could consider this denigration was that he had depersonalized Uriah as a Gentile. Could David ever have arranged the tidy elimination if he had admitted Uriah's worth to God? So often our own personal agenda has caused us to forget how much God loves our antagonists. Uriah's Gentile status let David see him as expendable. How ugly must be those hidden prejudices that cause us to see our own socioethic status as more esteemed than that of others.

CONCLUSION

God made us to love people and use things. Why is it that we so often love things and use people? God longs to raise up those rare Christ-filled leaders who use their might to create right rather than claim that their might is right. How He longs for leaders who wield the politics of grace rather than those who become graceful politicians. God wants to raise up leaders who, united with Christ, become in all issues of decision-making indistinguishable from Christ.

> ## Reflecting on the
> ## *Politics* of My Leadership
>
> 1. My "Politics" report card would look as follows:
>   - I keep a double standard.
>   - I am a closed leader.
>   - I use people unfairly and inappropriately.
> 2. To what degree is power abuse related to psychological wiring and personality, personal insecurity, or the leadership that was modeled for me?
> 3. How can I revitalize the terms *politics* and *power* in my organization and turn them into positive tools?

Notes

1. Warren Bennis, *Why Leaders Can't Lead* (San Francisco: Jossey-Bass Publishers, 1989), 41.

2. Ibid., 35.

3. Peter Koestenbaum, *Leadership: The Inner Side of Greatness* (San Francisco: Jossey-Bass Publishers, 1991), 94.

4. Bennis, 22–23.

5. Rollo May, *Love and Will* (New York: Dell Publishing Co., Inc., 1969), 13.

6. Myron C. Madden, *Blessing: Giving the Gift of Power* (Nashville: Broadman Press, 1988), 58.

7. Bennis, 72–73.

8. Ibid., 36.

9. James MacGregor Burns, *Leadership* (New York: Harper & Row, 1979), 61–62.

10. Bennis, 33.

11. Burns, 41.

12. Max De Pree, *Leadership Is an Art* (New York: Dell Publishing, 1989), 11.

Roles

For leadership,
achieving a
vision requires
*motivating and
inspiring*—keep-
ing people mov-
ing in the right
direction, despite
major obstacles
to change, by
appealing to
basic but often
untapped human
needs, values, and
emotions.

A TTENTION: IF YOU'RE LOOKING
for fluff, skip this chapter. You're not going
to find ten easy steps or the latest pop psychology
buzzwords in these pages. But if you're looking for
depth and substance—if you really want to learn
something—then grab a cup of coffee, turn the
music down, and pay attention. Because John P.
Kotter is not for the trivial minded.

Kotter, a former Harvard Business School professor, is a universally recognized authority on leadership. His best-selling books on the topic have
been translated into seventy languages, and the
Harvard Business Review has sold millions of his
reprints—more than any other writer in the last
twenty years. Kotter brings freshness and creativity
to the subject and invokes enthusiasm on the part
of readers, not unlike that favorite college professor
who made you actually want to sit in the front row
so you wouldn't miss a word.

Reading Kotter can be deceptive, as you'll find
in this chapter, "What Leaders Really Do." His
style, rather than being convoluted and tedious like
some academic writing, is clear and forceful. He

Corporations that do a better-than-average job of developing leaders put an emphasis on creating challenging opportunities for relatively young employees.

explains concepts lucidly so that you can understand them easily. But later, after you've absorbed and digested his ideas and tumbled them around in your brain, don't be surprised if their potency and force rise up in your awareness—you may find yourself in your office saying, "Aha! This is what Kotter meant by the difference between management and leadership!" At that moment you'll realize just how deeply Kotter has studied the world of leadership and how thoroughly he understands it. Which is why this chapter was essential to include in this book.

So roll your sleeves up, dive in, and learn from the professor.

What Leaders Really Do

• • •

John P. Kotter

Leadership is different from management, but not for the reasons most people think. Leadership isn't mystical and mysterious. It has nothing to do with having "charisma" or other exotic personality traits. It is not the province of a chosen few. Nor is leadership necessarily better than management or a replacement for it.

Rather, leadership and management are two distinctive and complementary systems of action. Each has its own function and characteristic activities. Both are necessary for success in an increasingly complex and volatile business environment.

Most U.S. corporations today are overmanaged and underled. They need to develop their capacity to exercise leadership. Successful corporations don't wait for leaders to come along. They actively seek out people with leadership potential and expose them to career experiences designed to develop that potential. Indeed, with careful selection, nurturing, and encouragement, dozens of people can play important leadership roles in a business organization.

But while improving their ability to lead, companies should remember that strong leadership with weak management is no better, and is sometimes actually worse, than the reverse. The real challenge is to combine strong leadership and strong management and use each to balance the other.

Of course, not everyone can be good at both leading and managing. Some people have the capacity to become excellent managers but not strong leaders. Others have great leadership potential but, for a variety of reasons, have great difficulty becoming strong managers. Smart companies value both kinds of people and work hard to make them a part of the team.

But when it comes to preparing people for executive jobs, such companies rightly ignore the recent literature that says people cannot manage *and* lead. They try to develop leader-managers. Once companies understand the fundamental difference between leadership and management, they can begin to groom their top people to provide both.

The DIFFERENCE BETWEEN
MANAGEMENT *and* LEADERSHIP

Management is about coping with complexity. Its practices and procedures are largely a response to one of the most significant developments of the twentieth century: the emergence of large organizations. Without good management, complex enterprises tend to become chaotic in ways that threaten their very existence. Good management brings a degree of order and consistency to key dimensions like the quality and profitability of products.

Leadership, by contrast, is about coping with change. Part of the reason it has become so important in recent years is that the business world has become more competitive and more volatile. Faster technological change, greater international competition, the deregulation of markets, overcapacity in capital-intensive industries, an unstable oil cartel, raiders with junk bonds, and the changing demographics of the work force are among the many factors that have contributed to this shift. The net result is that doing what was done yesterday, or doing it 5% better, is no longer a formula for success. Major changes are more and more necessary to survive and compete effectively in this new environment. More change always demands more leadership.

Consider a simple military analogy: a peacetime army can usually survive with good administration and management up and down the hierarchy, coupled with good leadership concentrated at the very top. A wartime army, however, needs competent leadership at all levels. No one yet has figured out how to manage people effectively into battle; they must be led.

These different functions—coping with complexity and coping with change—shape the characteristic activities of management and leadership. Each system of action involves deciding what needs to be done, creating networks of people and relationships that can accomplish an agenda, and then trying to ensure that those people actually do the job. But each accomplishes these three tasks in different ways.

Companies manage complexity first by *planning and budgeting*—setting targets or goals for the future (typically for the next month or year), establishing detailed steps for achieving those targets, and then allocating resources to accomplish those plans. By contrast, leading an organization to constructive change begins by *setting a direction*—developing a vision of the future (often the distant future) along with strategies for producing the changes needed to achieve that vision.

Management develops the capacity to achieve its plan by *organizing and staffing*—creating an organizational structure and set of jobs for accomplishing plan requirements, staffing the jobs with qualified individuals, communicating the plan to those people, delegating responsibility for carrying out the plan, and devising systems to monitor implementation. The equivalent leadership activity, however, is *aligning people*. This means communicating the new direction to those who can create coalitions that understand the vision and are committed to its achievement.

Finally, management ensures plan accomplishment by *controlling and problem solving*—monitoring results versus the plan in some detail, both formally and informally, by means of reports, meetings, and other tools; identifying deviations; and then planning and organizing to solve the problems. But for leadership, achieving a vision requires *motivating and inspiring*—keeping people moving in the right direction, despite major obstacles to change, by appealing to basic but often untapped human needs, values, and emotions.

A closer examination of each of these activities will help clarify the skills leaders need.

SETTING *a* DIRECTION VS. PLANNING *and* BUDGETING

Since the function of leadership is to produce change, setting the direction of that change is fundamental to leadership.

Setting direction is never the same as planning or even long-term planning, although people often confuse the two. Planning is a management process, deductive in nature and designed to produce orderly results, not change. Setting a direction is more inductive. Leaders gather a broad range of data and look for patterns, relationships, and linkages that help explain things. What's more, the direction-setting aspect of leadership does not produce plans; it creates vision and strategies. These describe a business, technology, or corporate culture in terms of what it should become over the long term and articulate a feasible way of achieving this goal.

Most discussions of vision have a tendency to degenerate into the mystical. The implication is that a vision is something mysterious that mere mortals, even talented ones, could never hope to have. But developing good business direction isn't magic. It is a tough, sometimes exhausting process of gathering and analyzing information. People who articulate such visions aren't magicians but broadbased strategic thinkers who are willing to take risks.

Nor do visions and strategies have to be brilliantly innovative; in fact, some of the best are not. Effective business visions regularly have an almost mundane quality, usually consisting of ideas that are already well known. The particular combination or patterning of the ideas may be new, but sometimes even that is not the case.

For example, when CEO Jan Carlzon articulated his vision to make Scandinavian Airline System (SAS) the best airline in the world for the frequent business traveler, he was not saying anything that everyone in the airline industry didn't already know. Business travelers fly more consistently than other market segments and are generally willing to pay higher fares. Thus focusing on business customers offers an airline the possibility of high margins, steady business, and considerable growth. But in an industry known more for bureaucracy than vision, no company had ever put these simple ideas together and dedicated itself to implementing them. SAS did, and it worked.

What's crucial about a vision is not its originality but how well it serves the interests of important constituencies—customers, stockholders, employees—and how easily it can be translated into a realistic competitive strategy. Bad visions tend to ignore the legitimate needs and rights of important constituencies—favoring, say, employees over customers or stockholders. Or they are strategically unsound. When a company that has never been better than a weak competitor in an industry suddenly starts talking about becoming number one, that is a pipe dream, not a vision.

One of the most frequent mistakes that overmanaged and under-led corporations make is to embrace "long-term planning" as a panacea for their lack of direction and inability to adapt to an increasingly competitive and dynamic business environment. But such an approach misinterprets the nature of direction setting and can never work.

Long-term planning is always time consuming. Whenever something unexpected happens, plans have to be redone. In a dynamic business environment, the unexpected often becomes the norm, and long-term planning can become an extraordinarily burdensome activity. This is how most successful corporations limit the time frame of their planning activities. Indeed, some even consider "long-term planning" a contradiction in terms.

In a company without direction, even short-term planning can become a black hole capable of absorbing an infinite amount of time and energy. With no vision and strategy to provide constraints around the planning process or to guide it, every eventuality deserves a plan. Under these circumstances, contingency planning can go on forever, draining time and attention from far more essential activities, yet without ever providing the clear sense of direction that a company desperately needs. After awhile, managers inevitably become cynical about all this, and the planning process can degenerate into a highly politicized game.

Planning works best not as a substitute for direction setting but as a complement to it. A competent planning process serves as a useful reality check on direction-setting activities. Likewise, a competent direction-setting process provides a focus in which planning can then be realistically carried out. It helps clarify what kind of planning is essential and what kind is irrelevant.

ALIGNING PEOPLE VS. ORGANIZING *and* STAFFING

A central feature of modern organizations is interdependence, where no one has complete autonomy, where most employees are tied to many others by their work, technology, management systems, and hierarchy. These linkages present a special challenge when organizations attempt to change. Unless many individuals line up and move together in the same direction, people will tend to fall all over one another. To executives who are overeducated in management and undereducated in leadership, the idea of getting people moving in the same direction appears to be an organizational problem. What executives need to do, however, is not organize people but align them.

Managers "organize" to create human systems that can implement plans as precisely and efficiently as possible. Typically, this requires a number of potentially complex decisions. A company must choose a structure of jobs and reporting relationships, staff it with individuals suited to the jobs, provide training for those who need it, communicate plans to the work force, and decide how much authority to delegate and to whom. Economic incentives also need to be constructed to accomplish the plan, as well as systems to monitor its implementation. These organizational judgments are much like architectural decisions. It's a question of fit within a particular context.

Aligning is different. It is more of a communications challenge than a design problem. First, aligning invariably involves talking to many more individuals than organizing does. The target population can involve not only a manager's subordinates but also bosses, peers, staff in other parts of the organization, as well as suppliers, governmental officials, or even customers. Anyone who can help implement the vision and strategies or who can block implementation is relevant.

Trying to get people to comprehend a vision of an alternative future is also a communications challenge of a completely different magnitude from organizing them to fulfill a short-term plan. It's much like the difference between a football quarterback attempting to describe to his team the next two or three plays versus his trying to explain to them a totally new approach to the game to be used in the second half of the season.

Whether delivered with many words or a few carefully chosen symbols, such messages are not necessarily accepted just because they are understood. Another big challenge in leadership efforts is credibility—getting people to believe the message. Many things contribute to the credibility: the track record of the person delivering the message, the content of the message itself, the communicator's reputation for integrity and trustworthiness, and the consistency between words and deeds.

Finally, aligning leads to empowerment in a way that organizing rarely does. One of the reasons some organizations have difficulty adjusting to rapid changes in markets or technology is that so many people in those companies feel relatively powerless. They have learned from experience that even if they correctly perceive important external changes and then initiate appropriate actions, they are vulnerable to someone higher up who does not like what they have done. Reprimands can take many different forms: "That's against policy" or "We can't afford it" or "Shut up and do as you're told."

Alignment helps overcome this problem by empowering people in at least two ways. First, when a clear sense of direction has been communicated throughout an organization, lower level employees can initiate actions without the same degree of vulnerability. As long as their behavior is consistent with the vision, superiors will have more difficulty reprimanding them. Second, because everyone is aiming at the same target, the probability is less that one person's initiative will be stalled when it comes into conflict with someone else's.

MOTIVATING PEOPLE VS. CONTROLLING *and* PROBLEM SOLVING

Since change is the function of leadership, being able to generate highly energized behavior is important for coping with the inevitable barriers to change. Just as direction setting identifies an appropriate path for movement and just as effective alignment gets people moving down that path, successful motivation ensures that they will have the energy to overcome obstacles.

According to the logic of management, control mechanisms compare system behavior with the plan and take action when a deviation is detected. In a well-managed factory, for example, this means the planning process establishes sensible quality targets, the organizing process builds an organization that can achieve those targets, and a control process makes sure that quality lapses are spotted immediately, not in 30 or 60 days, and corrected.

For some of the same reasons that control is so central to management, highly motivated or inspired behavior is almost irrelevant. Managerial processes must be as close as possible to fail-safe and risk-free. That means they cannot be dependent on the unusual or hard to obtain. The whole purpose of systems and structures is to help normal people who behave in normal ways to complete routine jobs successfully, day after day. It's not exciting or glamorous. But that's management.

Leadership is different. Achieving grand visions always requires an occasional burst of energy. Motivation and inspiration energize people, not by pushing them in the right direction as control mechanisms do but by satisfying basic human needs for achievement, a sense of belonging, recognition, self-esteem, a feeling of control over one's life, and the ability to live up to one's ideals. Such feelings touch us deeply and elicit a powerful response.

Good leaders motivate people in a variety of ways. First, they always articulate the organization's vision in a manner that stresses the values of the audience they are addressing. This makes the work important to those individuals. Leaders also regularly involve people in deciding how to achieve the organization's vision (or the part most relevant to a particular individual). This gives people a sense of control. Another important motivational technique is to support employee efforts to realize the vision by providing coaching, feedback, and role modeling, thereby helping people grow professionally and enhancing their self-esteem. Finally, good leaders recognize and reward success, which not only gives people a sense of accomplishment but also makes them feel like they belong to an organization that cares about them. When all this is done, the work itself becomes intrinsically motivating.

The more that change characterizes the business environment, the more that leaders must motivate people to provide leadership as well. When this works, it tends to reproduce leadership across the entire organization, with people occupying multiple leadership roles throughout the hierarchy. This is highly valuable, because coping with change in any complex business demands initiatives from a multitude of people. Nothing less will work.

Of course, leadership from many sources does not necessarily converge. To the contrary, it can easily conflict. For multiple leadership roles to work together, people's actions must be carefully coordinated by mechanisms that differ from those coordinating traditional management roles.

Strong networks of informal relationships—the kind found in companies with healthy cultures—help coordinate leadership activities in much the same way that formal structure coordinates managerial activities. The key difference is that informal networks can deal with the greater demands for coordination associated with nonroutine activities and change. The multitude of communication channels and the trust among the individuals connected by those channels allow for an ongoing process of accommodation and adaptation. When conflicts arise among roles, those same relationships help resolve the conflicts. Perhaps most important, this process of dialogue and accommodation can produce visions that are linked and compatible instead of remote and competitive. All this requires a great deal more communication than is needed to coordinate managerial roles, but unlike formal structures, strong informal networks can handle it.

Of course, informal relations of some sort exist in all corporations. But too often these networks are either very weak—some people are well connected but most are not—or they are highly fragmented—a strong network exists inside the marketing group and inside R&D but not across the two departments. Such networks do not support multiple leadership initiatives well. In fact, extensive informal networks are so important that if they do not exist, creating them has to be the focus of activity early in a major leadership initiative.

CREATING *a* CULTURE *of* LEADERSHIP

Despite the increasing importance of leadership in business success, the on-the-job experiences of most people actually seem to undermine the development of attributes needed for leadership. Nevertheless, some companies have consistently demonstrated an ability to develop people into outstanding leader-managers. Recruiting people with leadership potential is only the first step. Equally important is managing their career patterns. Individuals who are effective in large leadership roles often share a number of career experiences.

Perhaps the most typical and most important is significant challenge early in a career. Leaders almost always have had opportunities during their twenties and thirties to actually try to lead, to take a risk, and to learn from both triumphs and failures. Such learning seems essential in developing a wide range of leadership skills and perspectives. It also teaches people something about both the difficulty of leadership and its potential for producing change.

Later in their careers, something equally important happens that has to do with broadening. People who provide effective leadership in important jobs always have a chance, before they get into those jobs, to grow beyond the narrow base that characterizes most managerial careers. This is usually the result of lateral career moves or of early promotions to unusually broad job assignments. Sometimes other vehicles help, like special task-force assignments or a lengthy general management course. Whatever the case, the breadth of knowledge developed in this way seems to be helpful in all aspects of leadership. So does the network of relationships that is often acquired both inside and outside the company. When enough people get opportunities like this, the relationships that are built also help create the strong informal networks needed to support multiple leadership initiatives.

Corporations that do a better-than-average job of developing leaders put an emphasis on creating challenging opportunities for relatively young employees. In many businesses, decentralization is the key. By definition, it pushes responsibility lower in an organization and in the process creates more challenging jobs at lower levels. Johnson & Johnson, 3M, Hewlett-Packard, General Electric, and many other well-known companies have used that approach quite successfully. Some of those same companies also create as many small units as possible so there are a lot of challenging lower level general management jobs available.

Sometimes these businesses develop additional challenging opportunities by stressing growth through new products or services. Over the years, 3M has had a policy that at least 25% of its revenue should come from products introduced within the last five years. That encourages small new ventures, which in turn offer hundreds of opportunities to test and stretch young people with leadership potential.

Such practices can, almost by themselves, prepare people for small- and medium-sized leadership jobs. But developing people for important leadership positions requires more work on the part of senior executives, often over a long period of time. That work begins with efforts to spot people with great leadership potential early in their career and to identify what will be needed to stretch and develop them.

Again, there is nothing magic about this process. The methods successful companies use are surprisingly straightforward. They go out of their way to make young employees and people at lower levels in their organizations visible to senior management. Senior managers then judge for themselves who has potential and what the development needs of those people are. Executives also discuss their tentative conclusions among themselves to draw more accurate judgments.

Armed with a clear sense of who has considerable leadership potential and what skills they need to develop, executives in these companies then spend time planning for that development. Sometimes that is done as part of a formal succession planning or high-potential development process; often it is more informal. In either case, the key ingredient appears to be an intelligent assessment of what feasible development opportunities fit each candidate's needs.

To encourage managers to participate in these activities, well-led businesses tend to recognize and reward people who successfully develop leaders. This is rarely done as part of a formal compensation or bonus formula, simply because it is so difficult to measure such achievements with precision. But it does become a factor in decisions about promotion, especially to the most senior level, and that seems to make a big difference. When told that future promotions will depend to some degree on their ability to nurture leaders, even people who say that leadership cannot be developed somehow find ways to do it.

Such strategies help create a corporate culture where people value strong leadership and strive to create it. Just as we need more people to provide leadership in the complex organizations that dominate our world today, we also need more people to develop the cultures that will create that leadership. Institutionalizing a leadership-centered culture is the ultimate act of leadership.

Reflecting on the
Roles of My Leadership

1. Am I clear in my own mind about what role I do and do not play in my organization?
2. Have I assumed a role that is not mine and that is creating work stress, overcapacity, and blatant misunderstanding?
3. What four words best describe my current role in my job?

Faith

I've observed over
the years that
effective leaders
are those who
have developed
a sturdy faith.

Y EARS AGO, JOHN D. BECKETT
struggled with the question of whether to go
into full-time ministry. God called him instead into
a career in business—specifically, as president of
R. W. Beckett Corp., an oil-burner manufacturing
company. Now, in a twist of divine irony (or, more
likely, providence), Beckett is ministering powerfully to thousands of people through his writing—
perhaps more than he could ever have reached as a
pastor. All because he was faithful to his calling to
a secular industry.

What makes Beckett, a relatively new personality in the leadership lineup, unique? A primary
reason is his passionate dedication to faith as the
underpinning for all successful leadership. For
Beckett, there can be no effectiveness without
faith because nothing built without it will endure
throughout eternity.

With forceful conviction yet gentle humility,
Beckett takes his readers on a journey through
Scripture and his own personal experiences to
illustrate how a life intertwined with faith leads to
the richest reward of all—peace with God and an

I have learned that faith does not develop overnight, although crises can often catapult us to new levels of trust in God.

eternal impact on other people. Many tenets surrounding the faith in leadership dialogue seem to be counterintuitive: instead of seeking to rule, they seek to serve. Instead of striving for power, they embrace humility. Instead of relying on self-confidence, they trust in God.

We believe that every word of this chapter, "Leadership and Legacy" from the compilation *Faith in Leadership,* is worth taking to heart. But the four key principles of personal faith that Beckett lists at the end are as good a summary as any you'll find outside of Scripture on the role of faith in effective leadership for a follower of Christ. Read them and meditate on them. Your leadership will be richer for it.

Leadership *and* Legacy

One Leader's Journey *in* Faith

· · ·

John D. Beckett

For nearly four decades, I have been on a life-changing journey in the development of my personal faith. The growth in my faith has paralleled my professional development as a president of a manufacturing business in northern Ohio. So intertwined have been these two facets of my life that I would be hard pressed to delineate between them, for they have indeed gone hand in hand.

I fully realize that my experience is uniquely my own and may not be directly related to the development of your own faith. But personal lessons learned, I have found, often have broader applications, if only to encourage, affirm and inspire.

CAN WE SUCCEED WITHOUT FAITH?

I've observed over the years that effective leaders are those who have developed a sturdy faith. That kind of faith has taken those leaders beyond a narrow, self-serving perspective and to the realization that they are a vital part of God's greater strategy—uniquely endowed, vested with purpose, and reliant on divine wisdom. For these people, faith has become an essential ingredient of the capacity to lead.

"But," you may protest, "don't we see leadership without faith every day?" Indeed we do: in the self-made business owner who, through grit and determination, has built a thriving enterprise; in the politician who garners sufficient favor among constituents to be returned to office after each election; in the superstar athlete who flaunts a questionable lifestyle. How do we explain these anomalies?

It is possible to achieve much, at least in terms of this world's measures, without an active faith. How can we fail when we are equipped with high-powered education, boundless information, technology, storehouses of conventional wisdom, and reason (including that reliable old standby, common sense)? We see nations governed, fortunes amassed, and empires built without any reference or deference to God.

The pivotal question, however, is this: Can we leave a lasting legacy without deliberately involving God in the process? The writer of the New Testament book of Hebrews contends that we cannot—"Without faith, it is impossible to please Him" (Heb. 11:6)—and the apostle Paul is even more emphatic, "And whatever is not of faith is sin" (Rom. 14:23). These statements suggest that if we are simply operating by our own logic and energy instead of actively employing faith in the exercise of our responsibilities, we are actually placing ourselves at a distance from the Lord and, ultimately, conducting our efforts in opposition to Him. How many leaders are in exactly this position, choosing human modalities rather than embracing a faith-based approach?

Is there a better way? On the basis of my experience, I suggest that there is. My journey in faith has led me to invest my efforts in building carefully on "that foundation already laid, which is Jesus Christ," and my desire intensifies each day to produce results that endure, symbolized by "gold, silver and precious stones," instead of results that are temporal and superficial, symbolized by "wood, hay and stubble," which in the final judgment will be unceremoniously consumed (1 Cor. 3:11–15).

Four Keys *to a* Growing Faith

I have learned that faith does not develop overnight, although crises can often catapult us to new levels of trust in God. Faith develops progressively as we are properly focused, and as we learn from life's challenges through the willingness to change and embrace the process that all growth requires. Four areas have proved pivotal for me:

1. Understanding who God is, and who we are
2. The link between faith and God's word
3. Faith for our calling
4. The release of faith in our work

The "Who" in Our Faith

Most basic to the development of faith is an understanding of who God is and who we are. As we all well know, there is a world of difference.

One of the least common phrases in the Bible is "I saw the Lord." The few who did see God in all His splendor were left completely awestruck. After catching sight of God "high and lifted up" Isaiah could say only, "Woe is me, for I am ruined . . . for my eyes have seen the King, the Lord of Hosts" (Isa. 6:1–5). Similarly, when Job was in the midst of his suffering, God addressed him out of the whirlwind (Job 38), demanding answers to such questions as "Where were you when I laid the foundations of the earth?" Overwhelmed by the impact of this encounter, Job answered, "I have heard of Thee by hearing of the ear; but now my eye sees Thee; therefore I retract, and I repent in dust and ashes" (Job 42:5, 6).

The irony is that this omnipotent God—who spun the universe from His fingertips, who collected a scoop of dust from which to fashion the first human being, whose breath held back the waters of the Red Sea and the Jordan River, who did so much more than even the Bible fully recounts—actually takes note of us, dealing with us so personally and intimately, even numbering the very hairs of our heads. David captures this truth in the Psalms: "O Lord, our Sovereign, how majestic is your name in all the earth. . . . When I look at your heavens, the work of your fingers. . . . What are human beings that you are mindful of them, mortals that you care for them?" (Ps. 9:1, 3–4). How remarkable that God, who superintends the universe, is also involved in every detail of our lives.

An early lesson in my business career taught me something of God's nature and infinite care. My father passed away after I had been working with him for only a year in our small family business. At the age of twenty-six, I felt woefully ill-prepared to take the helm of the R. W. Beckett Corporation. Dad, forty years my senior, had worn all the hats in our business, and I clearly lacked his talents and vast experience. Therefore, I immediately set out to hire a capable colleague to assist me, particularly in the area of marketing.

My first step was a logical one. I began to contact former college classmates and business acquaintances who I thought might be interested—all to no avail. It seemed our fledgling company was too risky a prospect for them. At that stage in my life, I was only beginning to understand the power of prayer; but, faced with the urgent need for help in running the company, I began to pray in earnest. My prayer was a simple one: that God would send the right person for the job.

The answer came quickly and unexpectedly. Bob Cook, a marketing executive for one of our customers, was traveling with me on a business trip to evaluate a potential supplier. As we conversed on the plane, Bob began asking about our company's future. To my surprise, he expressed interest in coming to work for us. It was soon apparent that he had exactly the skills I was looking for and was ready to take on the challenges we were facing. Here was God's answer to my prayer—not in the files of an executive-search firm, but comfortably seated next to me on a business trip.

That providential discussion with Bob marked the beginning of a thirty-five-year working relationship that continues to this day. But, more important, it marked for me the beginning of a new understanding of the primacy and effectiveness of consulting God first on any matter pertaining to my company. It built my faith, especially as I began to understand the Lord's desire for personal involvement in matters pertaining to my work.

The Object of Our Faith

Faith needs an object, but for many, sadly, faith is invested merely in the future, or in the free enterprise system, or in democracy, or in natural law, or even in their own personal abilities. By contrast, Jesus told His followers, "Have faith in God" (Mark 11:22). How wonderful that God so clearly invites us to have faith in Him! How remarkable to have God as the sole object—actually, a very living subject—of our faith! Our faith, if it is true faith, must be in God and in God alone.

Dependence on Ourselves or on God?

The great King David cried out, "But I am a worm" as he considered himself relative to the holy awesome God (Ps. 22:6). We must ultimately decide whether our faith is in God or in ourselves. Self-confidence, where it is legitimate at all, must be in the context of what God imparts.

But there's a wrestling match here. I am sobered as I realize how far I will go into an activity or a project while depending solely on my own skills and abilities, never bothering to invite God's perspective or to lean into His wisdom and His ways. Over the years, I have come to understand that my most responsible posture is not to see how much I can inject of my own will, my own ways, and my own self into the equation but rather to humble myself and acknowledge my utter dependence on God. Only when we look up are we able to see how reliant we are on the Lord for everything of true and lasting value.

The Mind-Set of a Servant

Paul wonderfully describes this state of mind in his letter to the Philippians. "Let this mind be in you," he says, and he goes on to describe Christ's own mind-set as He laid aside his divine prerogative and completely humbled Himself. Here is the full rendering of this idea:

> Let Christ Jesus be your example as to what your attitude should be. For he, who had always been God by nature, did not cling to his prerogatives as God's equal, but stripped himself of all privilege by consenting to be a slave by nature and being born as mortal man. And, having become man, he humbled himself by living a life of utter obedience, even to the extent of dying, and the death he dies was the death of a common criminal. [Phil. 2:5–8]

Here is the most vital lesson in leadership I can give to a business leader or professional person seeking to walk in faith: make it a lifelong habit to embrace the mind-set of a servant. Despite some contemporary attempts at "servant leadership" (Greenleaf, 1977; Spears, 1995), the world's way of thinking largely revolves around rulership—imposing authority, lording it over others. This approach may appear to be effective, and it may actually produce worldly success, but results like these are not the ones we should seek, nor are they the ones that reflect the character of Christ.

Our posture of humility and dependence is also the catalyst to earnest prayer. As we pray, we are acknowledging God as the source of all strength, all wisdom and insight, all grace and mercy. Through our "dialogue" in prayer, we draw from His infinite storehouse and gain the perspective and fortitude—and, yes, the faith—to function in our callings.

The man or woman who walks in humility, prayerfully staying dependent on God, will by no means be ineffective, but the standard will be different. Such a person will reflect God's love, reaching people's hearts, not just their pocketbooks. With such an approach, we will actively resist wrong thinking and wrong activities, not just tolerate them. In humility, we will forgo the quick fixes that bypass the deeper lessons God is trying to teach us. And, because He has promised to do so, God will in due time exalt us.

Thus this is a call for a different way of thinking, whereby God is at the very center of our faith. As we acknowledge Him as majestic Lord, and as we, like Christ, take on the role of a humble servant, God's ways and life-giving energy are practically woven into the fabric of our lives and attitudes. We can relax, resting in a dependence on God for everything of true value. From our repose begins to emerge the kind of solid faith required for effective leadership.

FAITH *and* GOD'S WORD

Our first responsibility, then, in the development of personal faith is to apprehend the overwhelming greatness of God and our need for humble and complete reliance on Him. Next, I would point to the Bible, God's word, as an essential catalyst to the development of personal faith. The apostle Paul describes the connection between faith and God's word this way, in his letter to the church at Rome: "So then faith comes by hearing, and hearing by the word of God" (Rom. 10:17). Hearing biblical truth produces faith.

For nearly thirty years, it has been my practice to read the Bible each day. My decision to do this came initially in response to a challenge put forth by a speaker at a Christian teaching conference. He asked the attendees to commit themselves to reading the Bible daily for at least five minutes. I like challenges, and I took this one. At first it was sheer discipline, but as I dutifully continued my daily Bible reading, the discipline gradually became a delight. Almost imperceptibly, I began looking at things differently as ideas and concepts from the Scriptures began reshaping my thoughts and attitudes.

From that regular practice, faith began to blossom in me as I read the examples of those whose life accounts are recorded in the Old Testament. What faith it took for Noah as he stood alone in his generation and built a strange ship far from the ocean's shore; for Moses as he confronted Egypt's pharaoh and then led a nation out of bondage; for David as he waited patiently for God's timing in the fulfillment of his prophetic destiny to be king; for Daniel, in the vulnerable position of a civil servant to foreign kings, as he stayed unflinchingly true to God.

Scripture's examples also helped me understand the breadth and versatility of faith. As Tozer has so aptly said ([1961] 1996), "Faith in one of its aspects moves mountains; in another it give patience to see promises afar off and wait quietly for their fulfillment."

We can learn much from biblical role models about how to build dependability into our character, a steadfastness that will not be deflected by opposition. The Bible is replete with examples of faith for all seasons. By emulating this kind of faith, God's people can build godly enterprises, lead nations to their righteous destinies, and in the process, inherit an eternal reward.

Faith, *the* Fuel *for* Our Calling

"Come now, therefore, and I will send you to Pharaoh, that you may bring my people, the children of Israel, out of Egypt" was God's clear call to Moses (Exod. 3:10). We see many others in the Bible who were uniquely called: Joseph, Nehemiah, Ruth, and Esther, for example. Each of them at some point encountered God's direction, in a way that clarified their callings. From that point on, their faith developed and held firm as they walked out their calls.

Not all of them succeeded, for it is always left to the individual to obey or disobey God's call. Saul's faith weakened to the point where he sought assistance from a necromancer. Esau, driven by physical hunger, forfeited his faith, his calling, and his birthright for some food. Mark, weakened in faith, decided not to go with Paul on a dangerous mission into central Asia. Jesus prayed for Peter before his act of betrayal, "that your faith should not fail" (Luke 22:32), but Peter, despite his protests to the contrary, found out within hours how weak his faith could be. Perhaps this is why he later wrote to his fellow saints that they should "be even more diligent to make your calling and election sure," prescribing for them several qualities of character that, if embraced and sustained, would keep them from stumbling—and foundational to the connection between those qualities and their callings was faith (2 Pet. 1:5–11).

FINDING OUR WAY *and* OUR CALLING

The development of my capacity for faith has been inextricably linked with my call to business. For many years, it was far from clear that a career in business was God's call for me. Toward the end of high school, as I was considering where to attend college, I struggled with whether to pursue some recognized form of ministry. I had grown up in the Episcopal denomination, and I wondered whether pastoral ministry might be right for me, so I applied to Kenyon College, which had an adjunct Episcopal seminary.

But my heart was elsewhere. My father had trained as an engineer, and, deep down, I wanted to be an engineer, too. So I also applied to the Massachusetts Institute of Technology (MIT), reasoning that the outcome of my application process could also bring clarity to my choice of career.

A letter of acceptance arrived from Kenyon, and I wondered whether it meant that I was headed toward a pastoral vocation; a rejection from MIT would confirm this direction. I waited for what seemed like an eternity, although it was just weeks. And then came the hoped-for letter of acceptance from MIT. It meant that the way had opened toward a vocation in engineering and business; it was as though an invisible hand were steering me.

Later, in college, I went through a similar process, this time wondering whether I should undertake a stint as a military chaplain. Again, this choice sounded more "worthy," a higher calling than simply plunging into a business career. I took counsel with the rector of the Episcopal church I was attending in Boston and was given the straightforward advice that I shouldn't pursue an ecclesial vocation unless I was sure I had a clear call. I couldn't say that I did have one, and when an offer came for me to work as an engineer in an aerospace firm, I again concluded that an invisible hand was pointing me in the direction of business. But the nettling issue of whether I was missing the highest calling for my career was still unsettled.

The question of calling arose again not long after I had been thrust into the leadership of the family business. I took stock. Our business was doing very well. I loved my work. Our family was developing wonderfully. My faith was growing. And yet I was nagged by doubt. Was I really where God wanted me, or was I in business more through personal preference? This time I prayed earnestly about the matter, my mind wrestling week after week, but with no clear answer. But then I felt that I was the one being asked a probing question: Would I be willing to completely give up my family business, change careers, and follow God in a different direction, wherever and whenever?

Finally, I made one of the most difficult decisions of my life. I said, "God, this business can't be yours and mine at the same time. I give it, myself, and my career totally over to you. I will follow you wherever you want me to go." What I heard in response was unexpected but unmistakably clear. I sensed the Lord saying, "John, I needed to know you were completely willing to follow me, and not put other things, including your work, ahead of me. But you are exactly where I want you to be. I have called you to business. For you, there is no higher calling." This understanding was accompanied by a tremendous sense of peace, more that I had ever known. A decades-long struggle was over. I knew I was where God wanted me, and I could pursue business with the same zeal and sense of call that I would have felt in any other kind of ministry.

That decision was made over thirty years ago, and I can now look back on how God has faithfully confirmed this direction for me. My work, heading up a manufacturing company, has been a calling in which I have been able to achieve much that I never could have achieved in a more traditional form of ministry, for one principal reason: I am where God wants me to be. Out of this firm conviction has come the faith to function in this calling. Instead of facing day-to-day situations in timidity and fear, I have my faith, which has instilled boldness, courage, and confidence—not in myself but in Christ. I have found that faith accompanies the call—faith that, by His grace, is always sufficient. A friend of mine once said, "You can't be righteous in Dallas if God has called you to be in Philadelphia," and the converse is equally true and profound, especially in the context of having faith: if we know beyond a doubt that we are where God has called us to be and doing what we've been called to do, then we will have faith to function boldly and effectively, producing results that count for eternity (Diehl, 1987).

FAITH *at* WORK

The full development of one's personal faith never takes place in isolation from the "real" world. God puts us into families, communities, and institutions that become unique classrooms where faith is forged, tested, refined, and enlarged. Sparks has addressed this process:

> You notice that the Apostles got their revelation for the Church in practical situations. They never met around a table to have a Round-Table Conference, to draw up a scheme of doctrine and practice for the churches. They went out into the business and came right up against the desperate situation, and in the situation which pressed them, oft-times to desperation, they had to get before God and get revelation. The New Testament is the most practical book, because it was born out of pressing situations.

Events, relationships, challenges, problems, even crises—the things that continually unnerve and stretch us—are not happening outside the purview of God. They are not random. They are not arbitrary. God is at work in them, pressing us closer into divine purposes.

This pattern was evident even in Jesus' life. He lived in total harmony with the Father, and yet, time after time, things happened that were unplanned and unanticipated. They happened while he was "on the way"—the encounter with the woman at the well, the nighttime visit by Nicodemus, the meeting with the woman who touched the hem of His garment, the call for help from the blind man, the encounter with a tax collector. How did Jesus respond to all that the Father placed before Him? In every situation, Jesus saw His Father at work; then, by faith, He joined in, achieving all that He could redemptively: "'My Father is still working, and I also am working,' Jesus said to them. 'Very truly, I tell you, the Son can do nothing on his own, but only what he sees the Father doing; for whatever the Father does, the Son does likewise'" (John 5:17–19).

Faith is the means by which we see the purposes of God in each situation. Through faith, we step out of the narrow perspective that attends mere human endeavor and reach for the divine insight hidden from our natural view. We are looking for God at work. In faith we join in, and as we employ faith, it grows. The analogy to the muscles in our bodies applies: what is exercised strengthens; what is not, atrophies.

Practical Outworking *of* Faith

In my experience, work and faith are continually intersecting. I recall a time when I was baffled by a technical problem. I had worked most of a Saturday in our development lab, trying to find a solution to a combustion problem with one of our products. With no solutions forthcoming, I decided to leave work and swim with my family, saying a quick prayer as I left our factory that I might somehow soon find the answer.

The key insight into the solution came while I was swimming laps, and it came so clearly that I knew this solution would work. Later that afternoon, back in our lab, I was able to test out the concept I had seen through faith. It was perfect, and I learned a valuable lesson: to think much more broadly about how God wants to be involved in our everyday affairs.

Faith also became the essential ingredient in a business decision some years later, during an international oil crisis, when an embargo in the Middle East threatened to shrink the market for our products by at least half. To add to our worry, we had just completed a major expansion of our plant facilities, putting a strain on our financial resources. Our competitors were taking drastic action. They were cutting sales activity, and some were scaling back and downsizing their entire operations.

After much consternation—and, this time, more systematic prayer—our senior managers and I came to a decision: rather than pull back to a safe position, we would take the opposite course. We would be bold and aggressive and look beyond the current disruption to the long term. To others in our industry, we probably looked somewhat foolish, but faith quite often does. (Remember Noah?) Our strategy turned out to be exactly right, and when the energy crisis abated, the company was in a stronger position than ever. Our expanded facilities had become necessary, more than we had ever imagined.

REVERSING *the* SEQUENCE: HAVING FAITH EARLY

One of the most important lessons I am learning about faith in the "school of Christ" is the principle of having faith early instead of waiting for a crisis that requires me to exercise faith in an extraordinary way. My tendency is to let faith come into play only when I have exhausted my own resources. I do what I can on my own strength, and if I don't get the needed results, then I turn to God in faith—when I reach the end of my rope. But the irony, and the flaw, in this out-of-sequence application of faith is my perception that the more capable I am, the less I need God. After all, why pray if I can handle the situation myself? Why not save the faith walk for when I really need help?

I am endeavoring to reverse this sequence. God's desire, I believe, is that we exercise faith early instead of putting forth our best efforts first and turning to Him only in desperation. With most of us, God has very graciously tolerated this back-to-front sequence, but there is a better way. That better way is to see faith intertwined with every dimension of life and to engage faith from the start. It is to see faith as a vital strand in a robust cord, integrally joined with and supporting our God-given gifts and abilities. That way, we don't come to the end of our rope and only then call for help. Faith becomes an active ingredient in every step along the way.

This is easier said than done, especially for leaders. We often think we are superbly competent, but if we hold to the traditional view of crisis faith in desperate situations instead of undertaking each event of each day in faith, we will stall out in the "school of Christ." Even the mundane things—having our morning toast and coffee, driving to work, greeting people at the office, setting our schedules and priorities for the day, holding meetings, making decisions, letting ourselves be interrupted—can be done in faith, in God's presence, where we find the heart of God and our real reward: our continually increased sense of God's presence and involvement in our lives.

CONCLUSION

Several times, Jesus chided His followers for having so little faith—for example, when His fearful disciples woke Him during the raging storm, and when doubt ended Peter's walk toward Jesus on the Sea of Galilee (Matt. 6:30, 8:26, 14:31). "You of little faith," Jesus said. (My own faith flags before I even get into the boat!)

Fortunately for us, the development of faith is very progressive. By using the words "little faith," Jesus is telling us something very significant: faith can grow, no matter where we are on the growth curve. The disciples, realizing the smallness of their faith, appealed to Jesus directly: "Increase our faith" (Luke 17:5). Jesus responded with the analogy of the mustard seed, the smallest of seeds: faith even that small, he said, could move everything from mulberry trees to mountains, "and nothing will be impossible for you" (Luke 17:6; Matt. 17:20). Likewise, we can ask God to increase our faith to deal with whatever mountains are before us.

I have found four key principles of personal faith, and I want to share them here with other leaders:

1. *Faith is instilled in us as we see God in His vastness, His greatness, His majesty, and His dominion and glory.* It further develops as we humble ourselves and let ourselves be embraced by the oceanic depths of divine love, reminding ourselves how desperately we need God day by day and moment by moment. Truly, without God, we are nothing.

2. *The word of God is the seedbed of true faith.* No investment will bring greater return than study of and meditation on God's word. It is a prime catalyst for faith, and it is worthy of our best attention. It is a life source that endures forever.

3. *Faith helps us make our calling sure.* God's call is unique for each of us. If we are not where God has called us to be, we will have an uphill battle to receive faith in facing our day-to-day challenges. But when we are in God's calling for us, he will be pleased, even zealously eager, to give us faith in every situation.

4. *Our work is a classroom for the development of our faith.* Faith is manifested as we are "on the way." It is dynamic, lively, relevant to where we are. We need to begin in faith and stay in faith instead of expending our best human efforts, hitting the wall, and only then turning to God.

The ultimate reality is that this faith we speak of really isn't our faith at all: like everything else of true value, it is a gift from God. It is bestowed, imparted, given abundantly by the One who is always full of faith: faithful.

Reflecting on the *Faith* of My Leadership

1. Am I bringing my faith life to bear on my work life, or are they polarized entities?

2. Whom do I know in my work or a similar setting who integrates personal faith into his or her job effectively and appropriately?

3. What are the differences between authentic faith in God and empty, self-driven optimism?

References

Diehl, W. *In Search of Faithfulness: Lessons from the Christian Community.* San Francisco: Harper San Francisco, 1987.

Greenleaf, R. K. *Servant Leadership: A Journey into the Nature of Legitimate Power and Greatness.* New York: Paulist Press, 1977.

Spears, L. (ed.). *Reflections on Leadership: How Robert K. Greenleaf's Theory of Servant Leadership Influenced Today's Top Management Thinkers.* New York: Wiley, 1995.

Sparks, T. A. *The School of Christ.*

Tozer, A. W. *The Knowledge of the Holy: The Attributes of God: Their Meaning in the Christian Life.* New York: Walker, 1996. (Originally published 1961.)

CHAPTER 5

SuperLeaders

Leading others to lead themselves is the key to tapping the intelligence, the spirit, the creativity, the commitment, and most of all the tremendous unique potential of each individual.

WHEN YOU SAW THE TITLE OF this chapter, did your heart sink a little? Did you say to yourself, "Oh, no. It's not enough to be a good leader; now I have to be a SuperLeader?" We wouldn't be surprised if you pictured yourself as a comic book hero, hand on hip, cape fluttering, with a great big *L* emblazoned on the front of your standard-issue superhero uniform.

That's what we did when we first saw this essay by Charles C. Manz and Henry P. Sims Jr. But the more we read, the more intrigued we grew. We're pretty sure you'll be intrigued too. What these authors have to say has the potential to radically transform our ideas about—and practice of— effective leadership.

First, Manz and Sims take us through what effective leadership is *not,* at least not any longer. It is not the strong man who imposes his will on his followers, underlings who must do his bidding or suffer the consequences. Nor is it the transactor, who trades rewards for positive performance. It isn't even the visionary hero who emotionally inspires followers to join in the crusade. These types have all

It is time to transcend the notion of leaders as heroes and to focus instead on leaders as hero-makers. Is the spotlight on the leader, or on the achievements of the followers?

been dominant at one time or another throughout recent history, and we tend to be drawn to them for a number of reasons—our conditioning, a skewed idea of who will get the job done, or an unbalanced view of the value of that elusive and overrated quality of charisma.

Rather, say Manz and Sims, a SuperLeader is a leader who enables others to lead themselves. An ideal leader is someone who provides followers with the right tools, training, and empowerment to make decisions, set goals, and achieve success on their own. Only through this process, the authors say, is the power of the individual released and true progress accomplished.

Manz is a speaker, consultant, and best-selling business author; he holds a chaired teaching position at the University of Massachusetts. Sims has held management positions at Ford, U.S. Steel, and Amoco and is currently teaching at the University of Maryland.

SuperLeadership

Beyond *the* Myth *of* Heroic Leadership

• • •

Charles C. Manz & Henry P. Sims Jr.

When most of us think of leadership, we think of one person doing something to another person. This is "influence," and a leader is someone who has the capacity to influence another. Words like "charismatic" and "heroic" are sometimes used to describe a leader. The word "leader" itself conjures up visions of a striking figure on a rearing white horse who is crying "Follow me!" The leader is the one who has either the power or the authority to command others.

Many historical figures fit this mold: Alexander, Caesar, Napoleon, Washington, Churchill. Even today, the turnaround of Chrysler Corporation by Lee Iacocca might be thought of as an act of contemporary heroic leadership. It's not difficult to think of Iacocca astride a white horse, and he is frequently thought of as "charismatic."

But is this heroic figure of the leader the most appropriate image of the organizational leader of today? Is there another model? We believe there is. In many modern situations, *the most appropriate leader is one who can lead others to lead themselves.* We call this powerful new kind of leadership "SuperLeadership."

Our viewpoint represents a departure from the dominant and, we think, incomplete view of leadership. Our position is that true leadership comes mainly from within a person, not from outside. At its best, external leadership provides a spark and supports the flame of the true inner leadership that dwells within each person. At its worst, it disrupts this internal process, causing damage to the person and the constituencies he or she serves.

Our focus is on a new form of leadership that is designed to facilitate the self-leadership energy within each person. This perspective suggests a new measure of a leader's strength—one's ability to maximize the contributions of others through recognition of their right to guide their own destiny, rather than the leader's ability to bend the will of others to his or her own. The challenge for organizations is to understand how to go about bringing out the wealth of talent that each employee possesses. Many still operate under a quasi-military model that encourages conformity and adherence rather than one that emphasizes how leaders can lead others to lead themselves.

WHY IS SUPERLEADERSHIP *an* IMPORTANT PERSPECTIVE?

This SuperLeadership perspective is especially important today because of several recent trends facing American businesses. First, the challenge to United States corporations from world competition has pressured companies to utilize more fully their human resources. Second, the workforce itself has changed a great deal in recent decades—for instance, "baby boomers" have carried into their organization roles elevated expectations and a need for greater meaning in their work lives.

As a consequence of these kinds of pressures, organizations have increasingly experimented with innovative work designs. Widespread introduction of modern management techniques, such as quality circles, self-managed work teams, Japanese business practices, and flatter organization structures, has led to the inherent dilemma of trying to provide strong leadership for workers who are being encouraged and allowed to become increasingly self-managed. The result is a major knowledge gap about appropriate new leadership approaches under conditions of increasing employee participation. The SuperLeadership approach is designed to meet these kinds of challenges.

Before presenting specific steps for becoming a SuperLeader, it is useful to contrast SuperLeadership with other views of leadership.

Viewpoints on what constitutes successful leadership in organizations have changed significantly over time. A simplified historical perspective on different approaches to leadership is presented in Table 1. As it suggests, four different types of leader can be distinguished: the "strong man," the "transactor," the "visionary hero," and the "SuperLeader."

TABLE 1. *Four Types of Leaders*

	Strong Man	Transactor	Visionary Hero	SuperLeader
Focus	Commands	Rewards	Visions	Self-leadership
Types of power	Position authority	Rewards	Relational/ Inspirational	Shared
Source of leader's wisdom and direction	Leader	Leader	Leader	Mostly followers (self-leaders) and then leaders
Followers' response	Fear-based compliance	Calculative compliance	Emotional commitment based on leader's vision	Commitment based on ownership
Typical leader behaviors	Direction command	Interactive goal setting	Communication of leader's vision	Becoming an effective self-leader
	Assigned goals	Contingent personal reward	Emphasis on leader's values	Modeling self-leadership
	Intimidation	Contingent material reward	Exhortation	Creating positive thought patterns
	Reprimand	Contingent reprimand	Inspirational persuasion	Developing self-leadership through reward and constructive reprimand
				Promoting self-leading teams
				Facilitating a self-leadership culture

The *strong-man view* of leadership is perhaps the earliest dominant form in our culture. The emphasis with this autocratic view is on the strength of the leader. We use the masculine noun purposely because when this leadership approach was most prevalent it was almost a completely male-dominated process.

The strong-man view of leadership still exists today in many organizations (and is still widely reserved for males), although it is not as highly regarded as it once was.

The strong-man view of leadership creates an image of a John Wayne type who is not afraid to "knock some heads" to get followers to do what he wants done. The expertise for knowing what should be done rests almost entirely in the leader. It is he who sizes up the situation and, based on some seemingly superior strength, skill, and courage, delivers firm commands to the workers. If the job is not performed as commanded, inevitably some significant form of punishment will be delivered by the leader to the guilty party. The focus is on the leader whose power stems primarily from his position in the organization. He is the primary source of wisdom and direction—strong direction. Subordinates simply comply.

The second view of leadership is that of a *transactor*.

As time passed in our culture, the dominance of the strong-man view of leadership lessened somewhat. Women began to find themselves more frequently in leadership positions. With the development of knowledge of the power of rewards (such as that coming from research on behavior modification), a different view of influence began to emerge. With this view, the emphasis was increasingly placed on a rational exchange approach (exchange of rewards for work performed) in order to get workers to do their work. Even Taylor's views on scientific management, which still influence significantly many organizations in many industries, emphasized the importance of providing incentives to get workers to do work.

With the transactor type of leader, the focus is on goals and rewards; the leader's power stems from the ability to provide rewards for followers doing what the leader thinks should be done. The source of wisdom and direction still rests with the leader. Subordinates will tend to take a calculative view of their work. "I will do what he (or she) asks as long as the rewards keep coming." . . .

The next type of leader, which probably represents the most popular view today, is that of the *visionary hero*. Here the focus is on the leader's ability to create highly motivating and absorbing visions. The leader represents a kind of heroic figure who is somehow able to create an almost larger-than-life vision for the workforce to follow. The promise is that if organizations can just find those leaders that are able to capture what's important in the world and wrap it up into some kind of purposeful vision, then the rest of the workforce will have the clarifying beacon that will light the way to the promised land.

With the visionary hero, the focus is on the leader's vision, and the leader's power is based on followers' desire to relate to the vision and to the leader himself or herself. Once again, the leader represents the source of wisdom and direction. Followers, at least in theory, are expected to commit to the vision and the leader.

The notion of the visionary hero seems to have received considerable attention lately, but the idea has not gone without criticism. Peter Drucker, for example, believes that charisma becomes the undoing of leaders. He believes they become inflexible, convinced of their own infallibility, and slow to really change. Instead, Drucker suggests that the most effective leaders are those not afraid of developing strength in their subordinates and associates. One wonders how Chrysler will fare when Iacocca is gone.

The final view of leadership included in our table represents the focus of this article—the *SuperLeader*. We do not use the word "Super" to create an image of a larger-than-life figure who has all the answers and is able to bend others' wills to his or her own. On the contrary, with this type of leader, the focus is largely on the followers. Leaders become "super"—that is, can possess the strength and wisdom of many persons—by helping to unleash the abilities of the "followers" (self-leaders) that surround them.

The focus of this leadership view is on the followers who become self-leaders. Power is more evenly shared by leaders and followers. The leader's task becomes largely that of helping followers to develop the necessary skills for work, especially self-leadership, to be able to contribute more fully to the organization. Thus, leaders and subordinates (that are becoming strong self-leaders) together represent the source of wisdom and direction. Followers (self-leaders) in turn experience commitment and ownership of their work.

The Transition to Self-Leadership

Three basic assumptions underlie our ideas on self-leadership. First, everyone practices self-leadership to some degree, but not everyone is an effective self-leader. Second, self-leadership can be learned, and thus is not restricted to people who are "born" to be self-starters or self-motivated. And third, self-leadership is relevant to executives, managers, and all employees—that is, to everyone who works.

Few employees are capable of highly effective self-leadership the moment they enter a job situation. Especially at the beginning, the SuperLeader must provide orientation, guidance, and direction. The need for specific direction at the beginning stages of employment stems from two sources. First, the new employee is unfamiliar with the objectives, tasks, and procedures of his or her position. He or she will probably not yet have fully developed task capabilities. But more pertinent, the new employee may not yet have an adequate set of self-leadership skills. For the SuperLeader, the challenge lies in shifting employees to self-leadership. Thus the role of the SuperLeader becomes critical: He or she must lead others to lead themselves.

Throughout the entire process of leading others to lead themselves, aspects of SuperLeadership are involved that do not necessarily represent a distinct step but that are nevertheless quite important. For example, *encouragement* of followers to exercise initiative, take on responsibility, and to use self-leadership strategies in an effective way to lead themselves, is an important feature that runs through the entire process. Also, a feature we call *guided participation* is very important to SuperLeadership. This involves facilitating the gradual shifting of followers from dependence to independent self-leadership through a combination of initial instruction, questions that stimulate thinking about self-leadership (e.g., What are you shooting for? What is your goal? How well do you think you're doing?), and increasing participation of followers.

Consider the goal setting process as an example of how the transition to self-leadership unfolds. Teaching an employee how to set goals can follow a simple procedure: First, an employee is provided with a model to emulate; second, he or she is allowed guided participation; and finally, he or she assumes the targeted self-leadership skill, which in this case is goal setting. Once again modeling is an especially key element in learning this skill. Because of their formal position of authority, SuperLeaders have a special responsibility to personally demonstrate goal setting behavior that can be emulated by other employees. Furthermore, goals need to be coordinated among the different levels of the hierarchy. Subordinate goals, even those that are self-set, need to be consistent with superior and organizational goals.

A SuperLeader takes into account the employee's time and experience on the job, as well as the degree of the employee's skill and capabilities. For a new employee, whose job-related and self-leadership skills may yet be undeveloped, an executive may wish to begin with assigned goals, while modeling self-set goals for himself or herself. Within a short period of time, the SuperLeader endeavors to move toward interactive goals. Usually the best way to accomplish this is by "guided participation," which includes asking the employee to propose his or her own goals. At this stage, the SuperLeader still retains significant influence over goal setting, actively proposing and perhaps imposing some of the goals. Usually, this is the give and take that is typical of the traditional MBO approach.

Finally, for true self-leadership to develop and flourish the Super-Leader will deliberately move toward employee self-set goals. In this situation, the SuperLeader serves as a source of information and experience, as a sounding board, and as the transmitter of overall organizational goals. In the end, in a true self-leadership situation, the employee is given substantial latitude to establish his or her own goals.

We have found that sharing goal setting with subordinates is frequently one of the most difficult transitions for traditional leaders to understand and accept on their road to effective SuperLeadership. Often, an executive is reluctant to provide the full opportunity for a subordinate to lead himself or herself because it seems the executive is losing control.

Good leaders intuitively understand the effects on performance of "knowing where they are going." During subordinate employees' critical transition from traditional external leadership to self-leadership, previous dependency on superior authority needs to be unlearned. In its place, employees must develop a strong sense of confidence in their own abilities to set realistic and challenging goals on their own.

Frequently this transition is not very smooth, leaving the employee wondering why "the boss" is not providing more help, and the executive biting his lip to avoid telling the employee to do the "right thing." Employees need to have some latitude in making mistakes during this critical period.

Reprimand takes on special importance during the critical transition phase, when the superior-subordinate relationship is very delicate. Careless use of reprimand can seriously set back the employee's transition to self-leadership. The issue becomes especially salient when employees make mistakes—sometimes serious mistakes. In our experience, during the transition to self-leadership, some mistakes are inevitable and should be expected as an employee reaches out. The way the SuperLeader responds to the mistakes can ensure or thwart a successful transition.

Andrew Grove, CEO of chip maker Intel Corporation, discussed the issue of how to react when an employee seems to be making a mistake. Reacting too soon or too harshly can result in a serious setback in efforts to develop employee self-leadership. According to Grove, the manager needs to consider the degree to which the error can be tolerated or not. For example, if the task is an analysis for internal use, the experience the employee receives may be well worth some wasted work and delay. However, if the error involves a shipment to a customer, the customer should not bear the expense of boosting the employee further down the learning curve.

Sometimes the SuperLeader might *deliberately* hold back goals or decisions that, at other times, in other places, he or she would be more than willing to provide. Self-led employees must learn to stand on their own.

Once through this critical transition phase, the effects on the self-led employee's performance can be remarkable. Effectively leading themselves produces a motivation and psychological commitment that energizes employees to greater and greater achievements. SuperLeaders who have successfully unleashed the power of self-led employees understand the ultimate reward and satisfaction of managing these individuals.

Ideally, the SuperLeader comes to be surrounded by strong people—self-leaders in their own right—who pursue exceptional achievement because they love to. The SuperLeader's strength is greatly enhanced since it is drawn from the strength of many people who have been encouraged to grow, flourish, and become important contributors. The SuperLeader becomes "Super" through the talents and capabilities of others. As self-leadership is nurtured, the power for progress is unleashed.

SuperLeadership offers the most viable mechanism for establishing exceptional self-leading followers. True excellence can be achieved by facilitating the self-leadership system that operates within each person—by challenging each person to reach deep inside for the best each has to offer. Employee compliance is not enough. Leading others to lead themselves is the key to tapping the intelligence, the spirit, the creativity, the commitment, and most of all the tremendous unique potential of each individual.

To us, the message is clear: Excellence is achievable, but only if leaders are dedicated to tapping the vast potential within each individual. Most of all, this does *not* mean that more so-called charismatic or transformational leaders are needed to influence followers to comply with and carry out the vision of the leader. Rather, the vision itself needs to reflect and draw upon the vast resources contained within individual employees.

The currently popular notion that excellent leaders need to be visionary and charismatic may be a trap if taken too far. Wisdom on leadership for centuries has warned us about this potential trap. Remember what Abraham Lincoln said, "You cannot help men permanently by doing for them what they could and should do for themselves." Remember, also, the timeless words, "Give a man a fish and he will be fed for a day. Teach a man to fish and he will be fed for a lifetime."

It is time to transcend the notion of leaders as heroes and to focus instead on leaders as hero-makers. Is the spotlight on the leader, or on the achievements of the followers? To discover this new breed of leader, look *not* at the leader but at the followers. SuperLeaders have Super Followers that are dynamic self-leaders. The SuperLeader leads others to lead themselves. Perhaps this spirit was captured most succinctly by Lao-tzu, a sixth-century B.C. Chinese philosopher, when he wrote the following:

A leader is best
When people barely know he exists,
Not so good when people obey and acclaim him.
Worse when they despise him.
But of a good leader, who talks little,
When his work is done, his aim fulfilled,
They will say:
We did it ourselves.

Reflecting on the
SuperLeader of My Leadership

1. Has my leadership track record been one of a strong man, transactor, visionary hero, or SuperLeader?
2. Where did I learn my leadership style?
3. What are the unique challenges and risks associated with growing self-leaders in my organization?
4. Who is the best SuperLeader I have ever known personally?

Selected Bibliography

A more detailed description of the leadership approach addressed in this article is presented in the book *SuperLeadership: Leading Others to Lead Themselves* by Charles C. Manz and Henry P. Sims Jr. (NY: Prentice-Hall, 1989).

For an overview of self-leadership see Charles C. Manz's *Mastering Self-Leadership: Empowering Yourself for Personal Excellence,* Englewood Cliffs, NJ, Prentice-Hall, Summer 1991.

The book by Edward E. Lawler III, *High Involvement Management* (San Francisco: Jossey-Bass, 1986) provides a good overview of various approaches for facilitating increasing involvement of employees in organizations. Also, Richard Walton describes trends in "Control to Commitment in the Workplace," his article in *Harvard Business Review, 63,* 77–84.

For a good overview on the application of goal setting, see Gary Latham and Edwin Locke's "Goal Setting: A Motivational Technique That Works," *Organizational Dynamics,* Autumn 1979, pp. 68–80.

A study on the leadership of self-managing teams was presented in the article by Charles C. Manz and Henry P. Sims Jr., entitled "Leading Workers to Lead Themselves: The External Leadership of Self-Managing Work Teams," *Administrative Science Quarterly, 32,* 1987, pp. 106–129.

Also, the practical challenge for managers transitioning into the role of leading self-managed employees is addressed in the article by Charles C. Manz, David E. Keating, and Anne Donnellon entitled "Preparing for an Organizational Change to Employee Self-Management: The Managerial Transition" in *Organizational Dynamics,* Autumn 1990, pp. 15–26.

6

Ambition

Spiritual leadership blends natural and spiritual qualities. Yet even the natural qualities are supernatural gifts, since all good things come from God.

S PIRITUAL LEADERSHIP BY J. OSWALD Sanders is a small book that's had a huge impact. We consider it to be one of the all-time greatest works on faith and leadership—in fact, we've never heard a mediocre review from anyone we've talked to about it. People who have read the book have loved it, and what's more they've used it in their lives. Part of its strength is the instant applicability of the ideas. It's a paperback with a great shelf life.

Sanders, a longtime missionary and global communicator who spent much of his life teaching, training, and writing, covers a wide range of topics in his book. In the chapter we've picked out, "Natural and Spiritual Leadership," his thesis is simple: a man or woman of faith should demonstrate spiritual qualities when he or she is in a leadership position.

Does a spiritual leader look just like the other leader down the hall, except that he goes to church on Sunday? Not at all, Sanders says. Spiritual leadership is a radically different approach based on a difference in the origin of the leader's skills. Sanders contrasts two sets of leadership skills—one originating in ourselves, the other originating with God.

Spiritual leadership requires superior spiritual power, which can never be generated by the self. There is no such thing as a self-made spiritual leader. A true leader influences others spiritually only because the Spirit works in and through him to a greater degree than in those he leads.

That difference changes our ambition, approach, results, passion—everything we do! As you'll realize, when Sanders talks about spiritual leaders, he's not referring just to pastors or other vocational ministers. Anyone who is a man or woman of faith is a spiritual person, Sanders says; therefore every aspect of his or her leadership should have a spiritual component to it.

We trust that this chapter will cause you to stop and say, If I am a follower of Jesus, there ought to be a difference in my motivation and my methods of leadership because there's a difference in their origin. Is that true in my life?

Natural *and* Spiritual Leadership

• • •

J. Oswald Sanders

"When I came to you . . . my message and my preaching were not with wise and persuasive words, but with a demonstration of the Spirit's power." (1 Corinthians 2:1–4)

Leadership is influence, the ability of one person to influence others to follow his or her lead. Famous leaders have always known this. The great military leader Bernard Montgomery spoke of leadership in these terms: "Leadership is the capacity and will to rally men and women to a common purpose, and the character which inspires confidence."[1] An outstanding example of this statement was Sir Winston Churchill, leader of Britain during World War II.

Fleet Admiral Nimitz said: "Leadership may be defined as that quality that inspires sufficient confidence in subordinates as to be willing to accept his views and carry out his commands."

General Charles Gordon once asked Li Hung Chang, a leader in China, two questions: "What is leadership? And how is humanity divided?" Li Hung replied: "There are only three kinds of people—those who are immovable, those who are movable, and those who move them!"

John R. Mott, a world leader in student circles, believed that "a leader is a man who knows the road, who can keep ahead, and who pulls others after him."[2]

P. T. Chandapilla, an Indian student leader, defined Christian leadership as a vocation which blends both human and divine qualities in a harmony of ministry by God and His people for the blessing of others.[3]

President Harry S. Truman (1945–53) said cogently: "A leader is a person who has the ability to get others to do what they don't want to do, and like it."

Spiritual leadership blends natural and spiritual qualities. Yet even the natural qualities are supernatural gifts, since all good things come from God. Take personality, for instance. Montgomery said that "the degree of influence will depend on the personality, the 'incandescence' of which he is capable, the flame which burns within, the magnetism which will draw the hearts of others toward him."[4] Both natural and spiritual qualities reach their greatest effectiveness when employed in the service of God and for His glory.

Yet spiritual leadership transcends the power of personality and all other natural gifts. The personality of the spiritual leader influences others because it is irradiated, penetrated, and empowered by the Holy Spirit. As the leader gives control of his life to the Spirit, the Spirit's power flows through him to others.

Spiritual leadership requires superior spiritual power, which can never be generated by the self. There is no such thing as a self-made spiritual leader. A true leader influences others spiritually only because the Spirit works in and through him to a greater degree than in those he leads.

We can lead others only as far along the road as we ourselves have traveled. Merely pointing the way is not enough. If we are not walking, then no one can be following, and we are not leading anyone.

At a large meeting of mission leaders in China, the discussion turned to leadership and its qualifications. The debate was vigorous. But through it all, one person sat quietly listening. Then the chair asked if D. E. Hoste, general director of China Inland Mission, had an opinion. The auditorium became still.

With a twinkle in his eye, Hoste said in his high-pitched voice: "It occurs to me that perhaps the best test of whether one is qualified to lead, is to find out whether anyone is following."[5]

BORN *or* MADE?

Are leaders born or made? Surely, both. On the one hand, leadership is an "elusive and electric quality" that comes directly from God. On the other, leadership skills are distributed widely among every community and should be cultivated and developed. Often our skills lie dormant until a crisis arises.

Some people become leaders by luck and timing. A crisis comes, no one better qualified steps forward, and a leader is born. But closer investigation usually reveals that the selection was not accidental but was more the result of hidden training that made the person fit for leadership. Joseph is a perfect example. He became prime minister of Egypt through circumstances that most people would call "lucky stars." In fact his promotion was the outcome of thirteen years of rigorous, hidden training under the hand of God.

When we contrast natural and spiritual leadership, we see just how different they are:

Natural	*Spiritual*
Self-confident	Confident in God
Knows men	Also knows God
Makes own decisions	Seek God's will
Ambitious	Humble
Creates methods	Follows God's example
Enjoys command	Delights in obedience to God
Seeks personal reward	Loves God and others
Independent	Depends on God

People without natural leadership skills do not become great leaders at the moment of conversion. Yet a review of the history of the church reveals that the Holy Spirit sometimes releases gifts and qualities that were dormant beforehand. When that happens, a leader is born. A. W. Tozer wrote:

A true and safe leader is likely to be one who has no desire to lead, but is forced into a position by the inward pressure of the Holy Spirit and the press of [circumstances]. . . . There was hardly a great leader from Paul to the present day but was drafted by the Holy Spirit for the task, and commissioned by the Lord to fill a position he had little heart for. . . . The man who is ambitious to lead is disqualified as a leader. The true leader will have no desire to lord it over God's heritage, but will be humble, gentle, self-sacrificing and altogether ready to follow when the Spirit chooses another to lead.[6]

Sangster's biography includes a private manuscript written when the English preacher and scholar felt a growing conviction to take more of a leadership role in the Methodist church.

This is the will of God for me. I did not choose it. I sought to escape it. But it has come.

Something else has come, too. A sense of certainty that God does not want me only for a preacher. He wants me also for a leader—a leader in Methodism.

I feel a commissioning to work under God for the revival of this branch of His Church [Methodist]—careless of my own reputation; indifferent to the comments of older and jealous men.

I am thirty-six. If I am to serve God in this way, I must no longer shrink from the task—but *do* it.

I have examined my heart for ambition. I am certain it is not there. I hate the criticism I shall evoke and the painful chatter of people. Obscurity, quiet browsing among books, and the service of simple people is my taste—but by the will of God, this is my task, God help me.

Bewildered and unbelieving, I hear the voice of God say to me: "I want to sound the note through you." O God, did ever an apostle shrink from his task more? I dare not say "no" but, like Jonah, I would fain run away.[7]

Once Saint Francis of Assisi was confronted by a brother who asked him repeatedly, "Why you? Why you?"

Francis responded, in today's terms, "Why me *what?*"

"Why does everyone want to see you? Hear you? Obey you? You are not all so handsome, nor learned, nor from a noble family. Yet the world seems to want to follow you," the brother said.

Then Francis raised his eyes to heaven, knelt in praise to God, and turned to his interrogator:

You want to know? It is because the eyes of the Most High have willed it so. He continually watches the good and the wicked, and as His most holy eyes have not found among sinners any smaller man, nor any more insufficient and sinful, therefore He has chosen me to accomplish the marvelous work which God hath undertaken; He chose me because He could find none more worthless, and He wished to confound the nobility and grandeur, the strength, the beauty and the learning of this world.[8]

Montgomery outlined seven qualities necessary for a military leader, each appropriate to spiritual warfare: the leader must (1) avoid getting swamped in detail; (2) not be petty; (3) not be pompous; (4) know how to select people to fit the task; (5) trust others to do a job without the leader's meddling; (6) be capable of clear decisions; (7) inspire confidence.[9]

John Mott moved in student circles, and his tests covered different territory. One should inquire of a leader whether he or she (1) does little things well; (2) has learned to focus on priorities; (3) uses leisure well; (4) has intensity; (5) knows how to exploit momentum; (6) is growing; (7) overcomes discouragement and "impossible" situations; and (8) understands his or her weaknesses.[10]

A single life has immense possibilities for good or ill. We leave an indelible influence on people who come within our influence, even when we are not aware of it. Dr. John Geddie went to Aneityum in 1848 and worked there for twenty-four years. Written in his memory are these words:

When he landed, in 1848, there were no Christians.
When he left, in 1872, there were no heathen.[11]

When the burning zeal of the early church began to draw converts at an extraordinary rate, the Holy Spirit taught a wonderful lesson on leadership. The church had too few leaders to care for all the needs, especially among the poor and the widows. Another echelon of leaders was needed. "Brothers, choose seven men from among you who are known to be full of the Spirit and wisdom. We will turn this responsibility over to them" (Acts 6:3).

These new leaders were first and foremost to be full of the Spirit. Spirituality is not easy to define, but you can tell when it is present. It is the fragrance of the garden of the Lord, the power to change the atmosphere around you, the influence that makes Christ real to others.

If deacons are required to be full of the Spirit, should those who preach and teach the Word of God be any less? Spiritual goals can be achieved only by spiritual people who use spiritual methods. How our churches and mission agencies would change if leaders were Spirit-filled! The secular mind and heart, however gifted and personally charming, has no place in the leadership of the church.

John Mott captured well the heart of spiritual leadership:

> Leadership in the sense of rendering maximum service; leadership in the sense of the largest unselfishness; in the sense of full-hearted absorption in the greatest work of the world: building up the kingdom of our Lord Jesus Christ.[12]

Reflecting on my
Ambition in Regard to My Leadership

1. Have I tapped into the spiritual dimension of leadership, or am I "all-natural"?
2. What do I really think about the age-old question, Are leaders made or born?
3. How much ambition do I have to be a good leader? How much should a person have?
4. What makes someone ambitious for something?

Notes

1. Bernard L. Montgomery, *Memoirs of Field-Marshal Montgomery* (Cleveland: World, 1958), 70. Bernard Law Montgomery (1887–1976) made his mark in World War II as the first allied general to inflict a decisive defeat on the Axis, at El Alamein in Northern Africa, in October 1942. He was knighted that November.

Chester Nimitz (1885–1966), quoted in Sanders' text without citation, was commander of the Pacific Fleet and Pacific Ocean Areas during World War II.

Charles George Gordon (1833–1885), also quoted without citation, was an eccentric but effective British military commander in China during the 1860s (for which he was tagged "Chinese Gordon") and in Africa, where he died at Khartoum trying to withstand an overwhelming army led by the Mahdi, a mystic leader in Sudan.

2. Lettie B. Cowman, *Charles E. Cowman* (Los Angeles: Oriental Missionary Society, 1928), 251. John R. Mott (1865–1955) was a Methodist evangelist who served in the Student Volunteer Movement and the YMCA. His best known book is *Evangelizing the World in Our Generation* (1900), which was also the motto he was widely known for. He was a founder of the World Council of Churches.

3. P. T. Chandapilla was general secretary for the Union of Evangelical Students of India from 1956–71. His goal was to reach India's intellectuals with the gospel. Following Hudson Taylor, Chandapilla never asked for financial help. He worked closely with Inter-Varsity Fellowship and the International Fellowship of Evangelical Students.

4. Montgomery, p. 70.

5. Phyllis Thompson, *D. E. Hoste* (London: China Inland Mission, n.d.), 122.

6. A. W. Tozer, in *The Reaper*, February 1962, 459. Aiden Wilson Tozer (1897–1963) was a minister in the Christian and Missionary Alliance. Among his thirty books, the best known is *The Pursuit of God* (1948).

7. Paul E. Sangster, *Doctor Sangster* (London: Epworth, 1962), 109.

8. James Burns, *Revivals, Their Laws and Leaders* (London: Hodder & Stoughton, 1909), 95. The text in this quotation has been modernized.

9. Montgomery, p. 70.

10. B. Matthews, *John R. Mott* (London: S.C.M. Press, 1934), 346.

11. John Geddie (1815–72), born in Scotland, was called the father of foreign missions in the Presbyterian church in Canada. He went as a missionary to the New Hebrides (formerly called Aneityum) in 1848.

12. Matthews, p. 353.

Future Leader

Leaders take every opportunity to show others by their own example that they are deeply committed to the aspirations they espouse. Leading by example is how leaders make visions and values tangible. It is how they provide the *evidence* that they are personally committed.

READING SOMETHING WRITTEN BY James M. Kouzes and Barry Z. Posner is like eating a meal that's both delicious and healthy. You feast with relish, and when you're finished, you're well nourished without feeling stuffed or weighed down. This article is a perfect example. "Seven Lessons for Leading the Voyage to the Future" is like being served a perfectly balanced meal.

Kouzes and Posner have done a tremendous amount of research on what it takes to lead successfully; their principles are extracted from real people achieving real goals. They also consider their ideas in the context of a social environment that seems to be more and more cynical and less devoted to positive change. They know what today's leaders are up against and that it will take specific skills to transform the future. They know—because they have observed—that these qualities can be acquired; they must be acquired or society will not benefit from the many potential leaders who are out there. This article is filled with examples of people who decided that they could make a difference and took steps to do just that.

Those who are most successful at bringing out the best in others are the people who set achievable goals that stretch them, and who believe that they have the ability to develop the talents of others.

Although this article is a bit dated, we felt strongly that it had a place in this book for several reasons. First, although the examples took place between five and ten years ago, the principles are just as fresh and applicable today as they were when originally written. The writing is clear and forceful, and the ideas are practical in a variety of leadership situations. But also we want to expose you to this pair of authors so that you'll keep an eye out for them in the future. They've already made quite a contribution in analyzing, summarizing, and hypothesizing about leadership, and we don't think they're finished yet. We hope this is just the beginning of what we'll hear from Kouzes and Posner.

Seven Lessons *for* Leading *the* Voyage *to the* Future

· · ·

James M. Kouzes & Barry Z. Posner

The cynics are winning. People are fed up, angry, disgusted, and pessimistic about their future. Alienation is higher than it has been in a quarter-century. Loyalty to institutions—and institutions' loyalty to people—is sinking like a stone. No longer would we rather fight than switch; we just switch. Nearly half the population is cynical, and cynics don't participate in improving things. In such a climate, how can a leader possibly mobilize a seemingly unwilling constituency toward some unknown and even more uncertain future? Who would want to?

Perhaps it would be Charlie Mae Knight. When Knight was appointed the new superintendent for the Ravenswood School District in East Palo Alto, California, she was the twelfth superintendent in ten years. She encountered a district in which 50 percent of the schools were closed and 98 percent of the children were performing in the lowest percentile for academic achievement in California. The district had the state's lowest revenue rate. There were buckets in classrooms to catch the rain leaking through decrepit roofs, the stench from the restrooms was overwhelming, homeless organizations were operating out of the school sites, and pilfering was rampant. Gophers and rats had begun to take over the facilities. As if this weren't challenging enough, Knight had to wrestle with a lawsuit that had gone on for ten years, whose intent was to dissolve the district for its poor educational quality and force the children to transfer to schools outside of their community.

These challenges would discourage almost anyone. But not Knight. After assuming the post, she immediately enlisted support from Bay Area companies and community foundations to obtain the badly needed resources. The first project she undertook was refurbishing the Garden Oaks School. Volunteer engineers from nearby Raychem Corporation repaired the electrical wiring and phone systems. A volunteer rat patrol used pellet guns to eliminate the pesky rodents from the site. The community helped paint the building inside and out, and hardware stores donated supplies.

Before too long, local residents began calling to find out what color paint was used for the school so they could paint their houses in a matching shade. They went out and bought trees and sod and planted them in front of their homes. New leadership came forth from parents who began to demand more of a say. In response, an "Effort Hours" program for parents was set up so that they could volunteer time at the school. Teachers began to notice that something was happening, and they wanted to be part of it too. The district was on a roll.

Within two years of Knight's arrival, the children exceeded the goal of performing in the fifty-first percentile on academic achievement scores. (Today one of the district's schools has climbed to the sixty-eighth percentile, miles above the first percentile, where it started.) The district has one of the first schools in the state to use technology in every discipline, outdistancing every school in California technologically, and it has the first elementary school to join the Internet. The lawsuit has been dropped. Revenues are up from $1,900 per student to $3,500. And for the first time ever, East Palo Alto received the state's Distinguished School Award, based on its improved test scores and innovative programs.

If we are going to *have* a future—let alone thrive in one—we can learn a few things from the Charlie Mae Knights of the world. Here are seven lessons we've gained from her and thousands of other venturers about what it takes to clean up today's spirit-polluting cynicism and transform it into hope.

Lesson 1: Leaders Don't Wait

Like other leaders who achieve extraordinary results, Knight knew she had to produce some early victories. "It's hard to get anybody excited just about a vision. You must show something happening," she told us. "Winning at the beginning was so important because winning provided some indication of movement. I had to show some visible signs that change was taking place in order to keep up the momentum, and in order to restore confidence in the people that we *could* provide quality education."

This proactive leadership spirit is vividly illustrated in an early recruiting poster for Operation Raleigh, now called Youth Service International, with U.S. offices in Raleigh, North Carolina. At the top of the poster, printed in big, bold letters, are the words: "Venturers Wanted!" Below the headline is a photograph of a group of people neck deep in a swamp with broad smiles on their faces. The recruiting copy reads in part:

JOIN THE VOYAGE OF DISCOVERY

For 1500 young Americans between the ages of 17 and 24, it will be the adventure of a lifetime. Underwater archaeology on sunken ships, aerial walkways in tropical rainforests, medical relief for remote tribal villages—innovative, exciting, worthwhile projects. . . .

Science and service are the themes and leadership development is a primary goal. It is the pioneer spirit of Sir Walter Raleigh's day rekindled, and you are invited to apply.

Leadership opportunities are indeed adventures of a lifetime and require a pioneering spirit. Starting a new organization, turning around a losing operation, greatly improving the social condition, enhancing the quality of people's lives—these are all uplifting human endeavors. Waiting for permission to begin them is *not* characteristic of leaders. Acting with a sense of urgency *is*. If you're going to lead now or in the future, the first thing you've got to do is launch a voyage of discovery.

LESSON 2: CHARACTER COUNTS

For the last two decades we have asked people to tell us what they "look for and admire in a leader, in a person whose direction they would willingly follow." The qualities that were the consistent winners were "honest," "forward-looking," "inspiring," and "competent."

These characteristics comprise what communication experts refer to as "source credibility." In assessing the believability of sources of information—whether they are newscasters, salespeople, managers, physicians, politicians, or priests—those who rate more highly on these dimensions are considered to be more credible sources of information.

What we found in our investigation of admired leadership qualities is that, more than anything, we want leaders who are credible. We must be able to believe in them. We must believe that their word can be trusted, that they are personally excited and enthusiastic about the direction in which we are headed, and that they have the knowledge and skill to lead. We call it the *first law of leadership:* "If you don't believe in the messenger, you won't believe the message."

At the core of personal credibility are one's beliefs. (Credibility derives from the Latin word *credo,* meaning "I believe.") People expect their leaders to stand for something and to have the courage of their convictions. If leaders are not clear about what they believe in, they are much more likely to change their position with every fad or opinion poll. Therefore, the first milestone on the journey to leadership credibility is *clarity of personal values.*

LESSON 3: LEADERS HAVE THEIR HEAD *in the* CLOUDS *and* THEIR FEET *on the* GROUND

Not only do we demand that leaders be credible; we also demand that they be forward-looking: that they have a sense of direction and a vision for the future. This capacity to paint an uplifting and ennobling picture of the future is, in fact, what differentiates leaders from other credible sources.

Visions are about possibilities, about desired futures, and it is images of great potential that Nolan Dishongh most definitely wants to spark in his at-risk students. Many of the fourteen- to sixteen-year-olds in Dishongh's construction trades class at Alice Johnson Junior High School, twenty-five miles east of Houston, have well-earned reputations as troublemakers, as the students with short attention spans, low grades, and little interest in learning. Many are from broken or abusive homes; some are known gang members.

Dishongh sets the tone at the start of each school year by asking his students to lay their heads on their desks. Then, in a deep, soothing tone, he instructs them to think about their mother, to feel her loving them even before they were born, to think about her holding them closely as infants, feeding them, and singing to them. He asks them to try to remember how that felt, and he encourages them to think about how proud she was when they said their first word and took their first step. "See her smiling," he implores. "See her eyes shining as she claps her hands with joy and hugs you." Dishongh asks them to think about what they have done to repay their mother for all that she has done to raise them: cooking their food, washing their clothes. He says, "She *loves* you, no matter what, but what makes her happy is being proud of you."

Next, Dishongh tells the students to be very still and breathe deeply, saying, "Imagine now that you are dying. The next four or five breaths will be your last. As you call out her name with your last breath, are you calling out to a mother you have made proud by the things you did in your life, or to a mother who will always feel sorrow for the life you led? I believe that each and every one of you *wants* your mother to be proud of you. I know I do. And that's what we're doing here. It's not about grades. It's about your mother being proud."

At this point it is not unusual to see a few boys wipe tears from their eyes. Dishongh promises to start them on a journey of self-discovery, to help them find a sense of their own self-worth and their ability to change, a journey that will permanently affect their lives, not just a year at school. The youths quickly realize that this is not a normal classroom and Dishongh is not a "normal" teacher. He cares. He believes that they can be someone to be proud of—not at risk but full of possibilities.

LESSON 4: SHARED VALUES MAKE *a* DIFFERENCE

As important as it is for leaders to forthrightly articulate their vision and values, what they say must be consistent with the aspirations of their constituents. Constituents also have needs and interests, dreams and beliefs, of their own. If leaders advocate values that are not representative of the collective will, they will not be able to mobilize people to act as one. Leaders must be able to gain consensus on a common cause and a common set of principles. They must be able to build a community of shared values.

In our own research we have carefully examined the relationship between personal and organizational values. Our studies show that shared values:

- Foster strong feelings of personal effectiveness
- Promote high levels of loyalty to the organization
- Facilitate consensus about key organizational goals and the organization's stakeholders
- Encourage ethical behavior
- Promote strong norms about working hard and caring
- Reduce levels of job stress and tension
- Foster pride in the organization
- Facilitate understanding about job expectations
- Foster teamwork and esprit de corps

People tend to drift when they are unsure or confused about how they ought to be operating. The energy that goes into coping with, and repeatedly debating, incompatible values takes its toll on both personal effectiveness and organizational productivity. Consensus about long- and short-term values creates commitment to where the organization is going and how it's going to get there. Although leaders do not wait for anyone, if they don't build consensus on vision and values, they will be all alone!

LESSON 5: YOU CAN'T DO IT ALONE

Early in our research we asked Bill Flanagan, vice president of operations for Amdahl Corporation, to describe his personal best. After a few moments, Flanagan said that he couldn't do it. Startled, we asked him why. Flanagan replied, "Because it wasn't *my* personal best. It was *our* personal best. It wasn't *me*. It was *us*." Leadership is not a solo act. In the thousands of personal-best leadership cases we have studied, we have yet to encounter a single example of extraordinary achievement that occurred without the active involvement and support of many people. We don't expect to find any in the future, either.

Creating competition between group members is not the route to high performance; fostering collaboration is, particularly if the conditions are extremely challenging and urgent. Author and university lecturer Alfie Kohn, in *No Contest: The Case Against Competition* (1986), explains it this way: "The simplest way to understand why competition generally does not promote excellence is to realize that *trying to do well and trying to beat others are two different things*" (p. 55). One is about accomplishing the superior, the other about making another inferior. One is about achievement, the other about subordination. Rather than focusing on stomping the competition into the ground, true leaders focus on creating value for their customers, intelligence and skill in their students, wellness in their patients, and pride in their citizens. In a more complex, wired world, the winning strategies will always be based upon the "we," not "I," philosophy.

Lesson 6: *The* Legacy You Leave Is *the* Life You Lead

The first thing Les Cochran did after becoming president at Ohio's Youngstown State University (YSU) in July 1992 was to purchase an abandoned building on the edge of campus and spend his free weekends working with construction crews to transform it into a residence for his family. While it is not unusual for college presidents to live near their campus, Cochran's determination to do so attracted a great deal of attention and set the tone for his presidency.

To many, Cochran was literally putting his life on the line, for the once lovely neighborhoods surrounding YSU had surrendered to increasingly aggressive gangs and escalating drug-related crime following the collapse of Youngstown's steel-mill-dependent economy in the early 1980s. Cochran believed that the only way to reclaim YSU from the fear, hopelessness, apathy, and mistrust that paralyzed the campus and the surrounding community was to start the process by claiming as his home one of these decaying neighborhoods. His message was clear: "We are responsible, both individually and collectively, for the fate of this community." Thus, when he declared "Together we can make a difference" to be his philosophy of individual contribution to community involvement, people knew that he believed deeply in what he was saying. By buying and refurbishing a home in an area he was determined to reclaim for YSU, Cochran "walked the talk."

When asking others to change, as Cochran did, it is not enough for leaders to deliver a rousing speech. Even though compelling words are essential to uplift people's spirits, Cochran and other leaders know that constituents are moved by deeds. They expect leaders to show up, to pay attention, and to participate directly in the process of getting extraordinary things done. Leaders take every opportunity to show others by their own example that they are deeply committed to the aspirations they espouse. Leading by example is how leaders make visions and values tangible. It is how they provide the *evidence* that they are personally committed. That evidence is what people look for and admire in leaders, people whose direction they would willingly follow.

In our extensive research on credibility in leaders, we asked people to tell us how they know if someone is credible. The most frequent response was, "They do what they say they will do." Setting an example is essential to earning credibility. When it comes to deciding whether a leader is believable, people first listen to the words and then watch the actions. A judgment of "credible" is handed down when the two are consonant.

How you lead *your* life determines whether people want to put *their* life in your hands. If you dream of leaving a legacy, you'd better heed the golden rule of leadership: *Do what you say you will do.*

Lesson 7: Leadership Is Everyone's Business

Myth associates leadership with superior position. It assumes that leadership starts with a capital "L," and that when you are on top you are automatically a leader. But leadership is not a place; it is a process. It involves skills and abilities that are useful whether one is in the executive suite or on the front line, on Wall Street or Main Street.

The most pernicious myth of all is that leadership is reserved for only a very few of us. The myth is perpetuated daily whenever anyone asks, "Are leaders born or made?" Leadership is certainly not a gene, and it is most definitely not something mystical and ethereal that cannot be understood by ordinary people. It is not true that only a lucky few can ever decipher the leadership code. Our research has shown us that leadership is an observable, learnable set of practices. In over fifteen years of research we have been fortunate to hear and read the stories of over 2,500 ordinary people who have led others to get extraordinary things done. There are millions more. If we have learned one singular lesson about leadership from all of these cases, it is that leadership is everyone's business.

Just ask Melissa Poe of St. Henry's School in Nashville, Tennessee. On August 4, 1989, as a fourth-grader fearful of the continued destruction of the Earth's resources, Poe wrote a letter to President George Bush, asking for his assistance in her campaign to save the environment for the enjoyment of future generations.

After sending the letter, Poe worried that it would never be brought to the president's attention. After all, she was only a child. So, with the urgency of the issue pressing on her mind, she decided to get the president's attention by having her letter placed on a billboard. Through sheer diligence and hard work, the nine-year-old got her letter placed on one billboard free of charge in September 1989 and founded Kids for a Clean Environment (Kids F.A.C.E.), an organization whose goal is to develop programs to clean up the environment.

Almost immediately, Poe began receiving letters from children who were as concerned as she was about the environment and who wanted to help. When Poe finally received the disappointing form letter from the president, it didn't crush her dream. She no longer needed the help of someone famous to get her message across. Poe had found in herself the person she needed—that powerful someone who could inspire others to get involved and make her dream a reality.

Within nine months, more than 250 billboards across the country were displaying her letter free of charge, and membership in Kids F.A.C.E. had swelled. As the organization grew, Poe's first Kids F.A.C.E. project, a recycling program at her school, led to a manual full of ideas on how to clean up the environment. Poe's impatience and zest motivated her to do something—and her work has paid off. Today there are more than two hundred thousand members and two thousand chapters of Kids F.A.C.E. Poe is proof that you don't have to wait for someone else to lead, and you can lead without a title, a position, or a budget.

When leadership is viewed as a nonlearnable set of character traits or as equivalent to an exalted position, a self-fulfilling prophecy is created that dooms societies to having only a few good leaders. It is far healthier and more productive for us to start with the assumption that it is possible for everyone to lead. If we assume that leadership is learnable, we can discover how many good leaders there really are. Leadership may be exhibited on behalf of the school, the church, the community, the Boy Scouts or Girl Scouts, the union, or the family. Somewhere, sometime, the leader within each of us may get the call to step forward.

We should not mislead people into believing that they can attain unrealistic goals. Neither should we assume that only a few will ever attain excellence in leadership or any other human endeavor. Those who are most successful at bringing out the best in others are the people who set achievable goals that stretch them, and who believe that they have the ability to develop the talents of others.

From what we observed in our research, as more and more people answer the call, we will rejoice in the outcome. For we'd discovered, and rediscovered, that leadership is not the private reserve of a few charismatic men and women. It is a process that ordinary people use when they are bringing forth the best from themselves and others. We believe that whether you are in the private sector or the public sector, whether you are an employee or a volunteer, whether you are on the front line or in the senior echelon, whether you are a student or a parent, you are capable of developing yourself as a leader far more than tradition has ever assumed possible. When we liberate the leader in everyone, extraordinary things happen.

Reflecting on the
Future Leader element of My Leadership

1. How much of my leadership energy is focused on the Friday payroll as opposed to inventing the future? Should that energy be reallocated?

2. How does a leader stay in touch with the organization today but be years into the future at the same time?

3. How has the leadership landscape changed in the last five years?

4. What kind of leader profile will be most sought after ten years from now?

8

Charisma

The charismatic
leader may
become trapped
by the expectation
that the magic
often associated
with charisma
will continue
unabated.

FOR ALL THE TIMES WE READ OR
hear that leadership does not depend on personality, it's amazing how we refuse to let go of the
idea. More often than not, either we try to adopt a
personality that we think fits what a leader should
be or we look for a certain personality in the leaders
we choose. The label that usually gets attached to
this personality type is *charismatic*—a mystical,
magical quality that's supposed to invoke some
kind of fuzzy response in followers, which in turn
produces incredible results. Sound vague and eso-
teric? It is.

In "Beyond the Charismatic Leader: Leadership
and Organizational Change," David A. Nadler and
Michael L. Tushman strip the mysticism, magic,
and fuzziness from the term. They do a complete
vivisection of charisma by breaking it down into its
key components, describing the functions involved,
and discussing what results can be expected from
those actions.

Nadler and Tushman acknowledge that charisma
can play an important role in leadership, especially
during times of change. But they also explore the

It appears that the charismatic leader is a necessary component—but not a sufficient component—of the organizational leadership required for effective organizational re-organization. There is a need to move beyond the charismatic leader.

limitations and inadequacy of charisma and warn of the dangers inherent in relying on it alone—one of the most significant parts of this essay. They recommend instead an integrated approach that surrounds charismatic leadership with instrumental leadership, which creates mechanisms for achieving goals and ensures follow-through to see that those goals are accomplished.

These ideas are relevant for all types of leadership, whether it's the church pastor, the committee chair, the company president, or the core team leader. Nadler and Tushman provide us with a lucid, well-thought-out reminder that, for all its flash and dazzle, charisma alone just won't get the job done.

Beyond *the* Charismatic Leader

Leadership *and* Organizational Change

• • •

David A. Nadler & Michael L. Tushman

The CHARISMATIC LEADER

While the subject of leadership has received much attention over the years, the more specific issue of leadership during periods of change has only recently attracted serious attention.[1] What emerges from various discussions of leadership and organizational change is a picture of the special kind of leadership that appears to be critical during times of strategic organizational change. While various words have been used to portray this type of leadership, we prefer the label "charismatic" leader. It refers to a special quality that enables the leader to mobilize and sustain activity within an organization through specific personal actions combined with perceived personal characteristics.

The concept of the charismatic leader is not the popular version of the great speech maker or television personality. Rather, a model has emerged from recent work aimed at identifying the nature and determinants of a particular type of leadership that successfully brings about changes in an individual's values, goals, needs, or aspirations. Research on charismatic leadership has identified this type of leadership as observable, definable, and having clear behavioral characteristics.[2] We have attempted to develop a first cut description of the leader in terms of patterns of behavior that he/she seems to exhibit. The resulting approach is outlined in Figure 1, which lists three major types of behavior that characterize these leaders and some illustrative kinds of actions.

The first component of charismatic leadership is *envisioning.* This involves the creation of a picture of the future, or of a desired future state with which people can identify and which can generate excitement. By creating vision, the leader provides a vehicle for people to develop commitment, a common goal around which people can rally, and a way for people to feel successful. Envisioning is accomplished through a range of different actions. Clearly, the simplest form is through articulation of a compelling vision in clear and dramatic terms. The vision needs to be challenging, meaningful, and worthy of pursuit, but it also needs to be credible. People must believe that it is possible to succeed in the pursuit of the vision. Vision is also communicated in other ways, such as through expectations that the leader expresses and through the leader personally demonstrating behaviors and activities that symbolize and further that vision.

The second component is *energizing.* Here the role of the leader is the direct generation of energy—motivation to act—among members of the organization. How is this done? Different leaders engage in energizing in different ways, but some of the most common include demonstration of their own personal excitement and energy, combined with leveraging that excitement through direct personal contact with large numbers of people in the organization. They express confidence

---

FIGURE 1. *The Charismatic Leader.*

Envisioning
- articulating a compelling vision
- setting high expectations
- modeling consistent behaviors

Energizing	**Enabling**
• demonstrating personal excitement	• expressing personal support
• expressing personal confidence	• empathizing
• seeking, finding, and using success	• expressing confidence in people

in their own ability to succeed. They find, and use, successes to celebrate progress towards the vision.

The third component is *enabling*. The leader psychologically helps people act or perform in the face of challenging goals. Assuming that individuals are directed through a vision and motivated by the creation of energy, they then may need emotional assistance in accomplishing their tasks. This enabling is achieved in several ways. Charismatic leaders demonstrate empathy—the ability to listen, understand, and share the feelings of those in the organization. They express support for individuals. Perhaps most importantly, the charismatic leader tends to express his/her confidence in people's ability to perform effectively and to meet challenges. . . .

Assuming that leaders act in these ways, what functions are they performing that help bring about change? First, they provide a psychological focal point for the energies, hopes, and aspirations of people in the organization. Second, they serve as powerful role models whose behaviors, actions and personal energy demonstrate the desired behaviors expected throughout the firm. The behaviors of charismatic leaders provide a standard to which others can aspire. Through their personal effectiveness and attractiveness they build a very personal and intimate bond between themselves and the organization. Thus, they can become a source of sustained energy; a figure whose high standards others can identify with and emulate.

Limitations of the Charismatic Leader

Even if one were able to do all of the things involved in being a charismatic leader, it might still not be enough. In fact, our observations suggest that there are a number of inherent limitations to the effectiveness of charismatic leaders, many stemming from risks associated with leadership which revolves around a single individual. Some of the key potential problems are:

• *Unrealistic Expectations*—In creating a vision and getting people energized, the leader may create expectations that are unrealistic or unattainable. These can backfire if the leader cannot live up to the expectations that are created.

- *Dependency and Counterdependency*—A strong, visible, and energetic leader may spur different psychological responses. Some individuals may become overly dependent upon the leader, and in some cases whole organizations become dependent. Everyone else stops initiating actions and waits for the leader to provide direction; individuals may become passive or reactive. On the other extreme, others may be uncomfortable with strong personal presence and spend time and energy demonstrating how the leader is wrong—how the emperor has no clothes.

- *Reluctance to Disagree with the Leader*—The charismatic leader's approval or disapproval becomes an important commodity. In the presence of a strong leader, people may become hesitant to disagree or come into conflict with the leader. This may, in turn, lead to stifling conformity.

- *Need for Continuing Magic*—The charismatic leader may become trapped by the expectation that the magic often associated with charisma will continue unabated. This may cause the leader to act in ways that are not functional, or (if the magic is not produced) it may cause a crisis of leadership credibility.

- *Potential Feelings of Betrayal*—When and if things do not work out as the leader has envisioned, the potential exists for individuals to feel betrayed by their leader. They may become frustrated and angry, with some of that anger directed at the individual who created the expectations that have been betrayed.

- *Disenfranchisement of Next Levels of Management*—A consequence of the strong charismatic leader is that the next levels of management can easily become disenfranchised. They lose their ability to lead because no direction, vision, exhortation, reward, or punishment is meaningful unless it comes directly from the leader. The charismatic leader thus may end up underleveraging his or her management and/or creating passive/dependent direct reports.

- *Limitations of Range of the Individual Leader*—When the leadership process is built around an individual, management's ability to deal with various issues is limited by the time, energy, expertise, and interest of that individual. This is particularly problematic during periods of change when different types of issues demand different types of competencies (e.g., markets, technologies, products, finance) which a single individual may not possess. Different types of strategic changes make different managerial demands and call for different personal characteristics. There may be limits to the number of strategic changes that one individual can lead over the life of an organization.

In light of these risks, it appears that the charismatic leader is a necessary component—but not a sufficient component—of the organizational leadership required for effective organizational re-organization. There is a need to move beyond the charismatic leader.

INSTRUMENTAL LEADERSHIP

Effective leaders of change need to be more than just charismatic. Effective re-orientations seem to be characterized by the presence of another type of leadership behavior which focuses not on the excitement of individuals and changing their goals, needs or aspirations, but on making sure that individuals in the senior team and throughout the organization behave in ways needed for change to occur. An important leadership role is to build competent teams, clarify required behaviors, build in measurement, and administer rewards and punishments so that individuals perceive that behavior consistent with the change is central for them in achieving their own goals.[3] We will call this type of leadership *instrumental leadership,* since it focuses on the management of teams, structures, and managerial processes to create individual instrumentalities. The basis of this approach is in expectancy theories of motivation, which propose that individuals will perform those behaviors that they perceive as instrumental for acquiring valued outcomes.[4] Leadership, in this context, involves managing environments to create conditions that motivate desired behavior.[5]

In practice, instrumental leadership of change involves three elements of behavior (see Figure 2). The first is *structuring.* The leader invests time in building teams that have the required competence to execute and implement the re-orientation[6] and in creating structures that make it clear what types of behavior are required throughout the organization. This may involve setting goals, establishing standards, and defining roles and responsibilities. Re-orientations seem to require detailed planning about what people will need to do and how they will be required to act during different phases of the change. The second element of instrumental leadership is *controlling.* This involves the creation of systems and processes to measure, monitor, and assess both behavior and results and to administer corrective action.[7] The third element is *rewarding,* which includes the administration of both rewards and punishments contingent upon the degree to which behavior is consistent with the requirements of the change.

Instrumental leadership focuses on the challenge of shaping consistent behaviors in support of the re-orientation. The charismatic leader excites individuals, shapes their aspirations, and directs their energy. In practice, however, this is not enough to sustain patterns of desired behavior. Subordinates and colleagues may be committed to the vision, but over time other forces may influence their behavior, particularly when they are not in direct personal contact with the leader. This is particularly relevant during periods of change when the formal organization and the informal social system may lag behind the leader and communicate outdated messages or reward traditional behavior. Instrumental leadership is needed to ensure compliance over time consistent with the commitment generated by charismatic leadership. . . .

The Complementarity of Leadership Approaches

It appears that effective organizational re-orientation requires both charismatic and instrumental leadership. Charismatic leadership is needed to generate energy, create commitment, and direct individuals towards new objectives, values, or aspirations. Instrumental leadership is required to ensure that people really do act in a manner consistent with their new goals. Either one alone is insufficient for the achievement of change.

FIGURE 2.

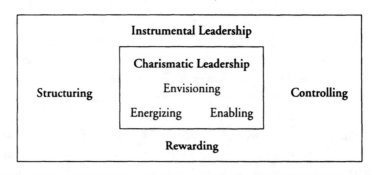

> ## Reflecting on the
> ## *Charisma* of My Leadership
>
> 1. In what ways has my charisma or personality helped me and
>   hindered me in my leadership posts?
> 2. Which of the seven limitations of the charismatic leader have
>   I experienced, if any?

References

1. J. M. Burns, *Leadership* (New York, NY: Harper & Row, 1978); W. Bennis and B. Nanus, *Leaders: The Strategies for Taking Charge* (New York, NY: Harper & Row, 1985); N. M. Tichy and D. Ulrich, "The Leadership Challenge: A Call for the Transformational Leader," *Sloan Management Review* (Fall 1984); N. M. Tichy and M. A. Devanna, *The Transformational Leader* (New York, NY: Wiley, 1986).

2. D. E. Berlew, "Leadership and Organizational Excitement," in D. A. Kolb, I. M. Rubin, and J. M. McIntyre, eds., *Organizational Psychology* (Englewood Cliffs, NJ: Prentice-Hall, 1974); R. J. House, "A 1976 Theory of Charismatic Leadership," in J. G. Hunt and L. L. Larson, eds., *Leadership: The Cutting Edge* (Carbondale, IL: Southern Illinois University Press, 1977); H. Levinson and S. Rosenthal, *CEO* (New York, NY: Basic Books, 1984); B. M. Bass, *Performance Beyond Expectations* (New York, NY: Free Press, 1985); R. House et al., "Personality and Charisma in the U.S. Presidency," Wharton Working Paper, 1989.

3. D. Hambrick, "The Top Management Team," *California Management Review* 30/1 (Fall 1987): 88–108; D. Ancona and D. Nadler, "Teamwork at the Top: Creating High Performing Executive Teams," *Sloan* Working Paper (1989).

4. V. H. Vroom, *Work and Motivation* (New York, NY: John Wiley & Sons, 1964); J. P. Campbell, M. D. Dunnette, E. E. Lawler, and K. Weick, *Managerial Behavior, Performances, and Effectiveness* (New York, NY: McGraw-Hill, 1970).

5. R. J. House, "Path-Goal Theory of Leader Effectiveness," *Administrative Science Quarterly*, 16 (1971): 321–338; G. R. Oldham, "The Motivational Strategies Used by Supervisors: Relationships to Effectiveness Indicators," *Organizational Behavior and Human Performance*, 15 (1976): 66–86.

6. See Hambrick, op. cit.

7. E. E. Lawler and J. G. Rhode, *Information and Control in Organizations* (Pacific Palisades, CA: Goodyear, 1976).

David A. Nadler is president of Delta Consulting Group and former professor at the Graduate School of Business, Columbia University. Michael L. Tushman is professor of management at Columbia University. He has lectured throughout Europe, Japan, and Brazil and has published several books and articles.

Followership

What distinguishes an effective from an ineffective follower is enthusiastic, intelligent, and self-reliant participation—without star billing—in the pursuit of an organizational goal.

A LEADER, BY DEFINITION, MUST have someone to lead, otherwise all the skills and vision in the world are useless. Followers are an essential part of the leadership formula, but they tend to get overlooked when the attention and glory rain down on the leader. Robert Kelley, in his essay "In Praise of Followers," has done a great service by inspecting followership just as closely as others have examined leadership.

His conclusions might surprise you. He asserts that effective followers require as many skills as leaders, skills that require cultivation and nourishment to flower into success. We might mistakenly think that the best followers are those that simply do what the leader says, no questions asked. Not true. The most effective followers are those that rank high on independent thinking and take an active approach to their work. They are actively engaged, questioning the leader when necessary, exercising control and independence and working without close supervision. These are the followers who are most likely to contribute successfully to the organization's goals. Kelley even cites examples of

Since each of us plays a follower's part at least from time to time, it is essential that we play it well, that we contribute our competence to the achievement of team goals, that we support the team leader with candor and self-control, that we do our best to appreciate and enjoy the role of quiet contribution to a larger, common cause.

teams without a leader that were able to operate more successfully than they had under a department head. In fact, effective followers look like leaders in training.

You might be wondering how a study of effective followership applies to you when you're trying to become a better leader. First of all, almost all leaders are also followers in certain situations, and many must switch roles several times a day. Second, effective followership doesn't just happen. It can be instilled in those you lead through training in self-management, commitment, and independent thinking. Cultivating good followers is just as essential to success as growing or choosing good leaders.

In Praise *of* Followers

• • •

Robert E. Kelley

We are convinced that corporations succeed or fail, compete or crumble, on the basis of how well they are led. So we study great leaders of the past and present and spend vast quantities of time and money looking for leaders to hire and trying to cultivate leadership in the employees we already have.

I have no argument with this enthusiasm. Leaders matter greatly. But in searching so zealously for better leaders we tend to lose sight of the people these leaders will lead. Without his armies, after all, Napoleon was just a man with grandiose ambitions. Organizations stand or fall partly on the basis of how well their leaders lead, but partly also on the basis of how well their followers follow.

In 1987, declining profitability and intensified competition for corporate clients forced a large commercial bank on the east coast to reorganize its operations and cut its work force. Its most seasoned managers had to spend most of their time in the field working with corporate customers. Time and energies were stretched so thin that one department head decided he had no choice but to delegate the responsibility for reorganization to his staff people, who had recently had training in self-management.

Despite grave doubts, the department head set them up as a unit without a leader, responsible to one another and to the bank as a whole for writing their own job descriptions, designing a training program determining criteria for performance evaluation, planning for operational needs, and helping to achieve overall organizational objectives.

They pulled it off. The bank's officers were delighted and frankly amazed that rank-and-file employees could assume so much responsibility so successfully. In fact, the department's capacity to control and direct itself virtually without leadership saved the organization months of turmoil, and as the bank struggled to remain a major player in its region, valuable management time was freed up to put out other fires.

What was it these singular employees did? Given a goal and parameters, they went where most departments could only have gone under the hands-on guidance of an effective leader. But these employees accepted the delegation of authority and went there alone. They thought for themselves, sharpened their skills, focused their efforts, put on a fine display of grit and spunk and self-control. They followed effectively.

To encourage this kind of effective following in other organizations, we need to understand the nature of the follower's role. To cultivate good followers, we need to understand the human qualities that allow effective followership to occur.

The ROLE *of* FOLLOWER

Bosses are not necessarily good leaders; subordinates are not necessarily effective followers. Many bosses couldn't lead a horse to water. Many subordinates couldn't follow a parade. Some people avoid either role. Others accept the role thrust upon them and perform it badly.

At different points in their careers, even at different times of the working day, most managers play both roles, though seldom equally well. After all, the leadership role has the glamour and attention. We take courses to learn it, and when we play it well we get applause and recognition. But the reality is that most of us are more often followers than leaders. Even when we have subordinates, we still have bosses. For every committee we chair, we sit as a member on several others.

So followership dominates our lives and organizations, but not our thinking, because our preoccupation with leadership keeps us from considering the nature and the importance of the follower.

What distinguishes an effective from an ineffective follower is enthusiastic, intelligent, and self-reliant participation—without star billing—in the pursuit of an organizational goal. Effective followers differ in their motivations for following and in their perceptions of the role. Some choose followership as their primary role at work and serve as team players who take satisfaction in helping to further a cause, an idea, a product, a service, or, more rarely, a person. Others are leaders in some situations but choose the follower role in a particular context. Both these groups view the role of follower as legitimate, inherently valuable, even virtuous.

Some potentially effective followers derive motivation from ambition. By proving themselves in the follower's role, they hope to win the confidence of peers and superiors and move up the corporate ladder. These people do not see followership as attractive in itself. All the same, they can become good followers if they accept the value of learning the role, studying leaders from a subordinates' perspective, and polishing the followership skills that will always stand them in good stead.

Understanding motivations and perceptions is not enough, however. Since followers with different motivations can perform equally well, I examined the behavior that leads to effective and less effective following among people committed to the organization and came up with two underlying behavioral dimensions that help to explain the difference.

One dimension measures to what degree followers exercise independent, critical thinking. The other ranks them on a passive/active scale. The resulting diagram identifies five followership patterns. (See Figure 1.)

FIGURE 1. *Five Followership Patterns.*

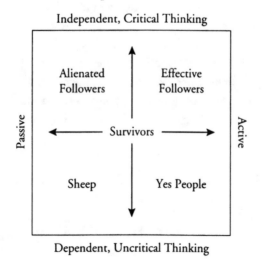

Independent, Critical Thinking

Alienated
Followers

Effective
Followers

Passive ←——— Survivors ———→ Active

Sheep

Yes People

Dependent, Uncritical Thinking

Sheep are passive and uncritical, lacking in initiative and sense of responsibility. They perform the tasks given them and stop. Yes people are a livelier but equally unenterprising group. Dependent on a leader for inspiration, they can be aggressively deferential, even servile. Bosses weak in judgment and self-confidence tend to like them and to form alliances with them that can stultify the organization.

Alienated Followers are critical and independent in their thinking but passive in carrying out their role. Somehow, sometime, something turned them off. Often cynical, they tend to sink gradually into disgruntled acquiescence, seldom openly opposing a leader's efforts. In the very center of the diagram we have Survivors, who perpetually sample the wind and live by the slogan "better safe than sorry." They are adept at surviving change.

In the upper right-hand corner, finally, we have Effective Followers, who think for themselves and carry out their duties and assignments with energy and assertiveness. Because they are risk takers, self-starters, and independent problem solvers, they get consistently high ratings from peers and many superiors. Followership of this kind can be a positive and acceptable choice for parts or all of our lives—a source of pride and fulfillment.

Effective followers are well-balanced and responsible adults who can succeed without strong leadership. Many followers believe they offer as much value to the organization as leaders do, especially in project or task-force situations. In an organization of effective followers, a leader tends to be more an overseer of change and progress than a hero. As organizational structures flatten, the quality of those who follow will become more and more important. As Chester I. Barnard wrote 50 years ago in *The Functions of the Executive,* "The decision as to whether an order has authority or not lies with the person to whom it is addressed, and does not reside in 'persons of authority' or those who issue orders."

The QUALITIES *of* FOLLOWERS

Effective followers share a number of essential qualities:

1. They manage themselves well.

2. They are committed to the organization and to a purpose, principle, or person outside themselves.

3. They build their competence and focus their efforts for maximum impact.

4. They are courageous, honest, and credible.

Self-Management

Paradoxically, the key to being an effective follower is the ability to think for oneself—to exercise control and independence and to work without close supervision. Good followers are people to whom a leader can safely delegate responsibility, people who anticipate needs at their own level of competence and authority.

Another aspect of this paradox is that effective followers see themselves—except in terms of line responsibility—as the equals of the leaders they follow. They are more apt to openly and unapologetically disagree with leadership and less likely to be intimidated by hierarchy and organization structure. At the same time, they can see that the people they follow are, in turn, following the lead of others, and they try to appreciate the goals and needs of the team and the organization. Ineffective followers, on the other hand, buy into the hierarchy and, seeing themselves as subservient, vacillate between despair over their seeming powerlessness and attempts to manipulate leaders for their own purposes. Either their fear of powerlessness becomes a self-fulfilling prophecy—for themselves and often for their work units as well—or their resentment leads them to undermine the team's goals.

Self-managed followers give their organizations a significant cost advantage because they eliminate much of the need for elaborate supervisory control systems that, in any case, often lower morale. In 1985, a large midwestern bank redesigned its personnel selection system to attract self-managed workers. Those conducting interviews began to look for particular types of experience and capacities—initiative, teamwork, independent thinking of all kinds—and the bank revamped its orientation program to emphasize self-management. At the executive level, role playing was introduced into the interview process: how you disagree with your boss, how you prioritize your in-basket after a vacation. In the three years since, employee turnover has dropped dramatically, the need for supervisors has decreased, and administrative costs have gone down.

Of course not all leaders and managers like having self-managing subordinates. Some would rather have sheep or yes people. The best that good followers can do in this situation is to protect themselves with a little career self-management—that is, to stay attractive in the marketplace. The qualities that make a good follower are too much in demand to go begging for long.

Commitment

Effective followers are committed to something—a cause, a product, an organization, an idea—in addition to the care of their own lives and careers. Some leaders misinterpret this commitment. Seeing their authority acknowledged, they mistake loyalty to a goal for loyalty to themselves. But the fact is that many effective followers see leaders merely as coadventurers on a worthy crusade, and if they suspect their leader of flagging commitment or conflicting motives they may just withdraw their support, either by changing jobs or by contriving to change leaders.

The opportunities and the dangers posed by this kind of commitment are not hard to see. On the one hand, commitment is contagious. Most people like working with colleagues whose hearts are in their work. Morale stays high. Workers who begin to wander from their purpose are jostled back into line. Projects stay on track and on time. In addition, an appreciation of commitment and the way it works can give managers an extra tool with which to understand and channel the energies and loyalties of their subordinates.

On the other hand, followers who are strongly committed to goals not consistent with the goals of their companies can produce destructive results. Leaders having such followers can even lose control of their organizations.

A scientist at a computer company cared deeply about making computer technology available to the masses, and her work was outstanding. Since her goal was in line with the company's goals, she had few problems with top management. Yet she saw her department leaders essentially as facilitators of her dream, and when managers worked at cross-purposes to that vision, she exercised all of her considerable political skills to their detriment. Her immediate supervisors saw her as a thorn in the side, but she was quite effective in furthering her cause because she saw eye to eye with company leaders. But what if her vision and the company's vision had differed?

Effective followers temper their loyalties to satisfy organizational needs—or they find new organizations. Effective leaders know how to channel the energies of strong commitment in ways that will satisfy corporate goals as well as a follower's personal needs.

Competence and Focus

On the grounds that committed incompetence is still incompetence, effective followers master skills that will be useful to their organizations. They generally hold higher performance standards than the work environment requires, and continuing education is second nature to them, a staple in their professional development.

Less effective followers expect training and development to come to them. The only education they acquire is force-fed. If not sent to a seminar, they don't go. Their competence deteriorates unless some leader gives them parental care and attention.

Good followers take on extra work gladly, but first they do a superb job on their core responsibilities. They are good judges of their own strengths and weaknesses, and they contribute well to teams. Asked to perform in areas where they are poorly qualified, they speak up. Like athletes stretching their capacities, they don't mind chancing failure if they know they can succeed, but they are careful to spare the company wasted energy, lost time, and poor performance by accepting challenges that coworkers are better prepared to meet. Good followers see coworkers as colleagues rather than competitors.

At the same time, effective followers often search for overlooked problems. A woman on a new product development team discovered that no one was responsible for coordinating engineering, marketing, and manufacturing. She worked out an interdepartmental review schedule that identified the people who should be involved at each stage of development. Instead of burdening her boss with yet another problem, this woman took the initiative to present the issue along with a solution.

Another woman I interviewed described her efforts to fill a dangerous void in the company she cared about. Young managerial talent in this manufacturing corporation had traditionally made careers in production. Convinced that foreign competition would alter the shape of the industry, she realized that marketing was a neglected area. She took classes, attended seminars, and read widely. More important, she visited customers to get feedback about her company's and competitors' products, and she soon knew more about the product's customer appeal and market position than any of her peers. The extra competence did wonders for her own career, but it also helped her company weather a storm it had not seen coming.

Courage

Effective followers are credible, honest, and courageous. They establish themselves as independent, critical thinkers whose knowledge and judgment can be trusted. They give credit where credit is due, admitting mistakes and sharing successes. They form their own views and ethical standards and stand up for what they believe in.

Insightful, candid, and fearless, they can keep leaders and colleagues honest and informed. The other side of the coin of course is that they can also cause great trouble for a leader with questionable ethics.

CULTIVATING EFFECTIVE FOLLOWERS

You may have noticed by now that the qualities that make effective followers are, confusingly enough, pretty much the same qualities found in some effective leaders. This is no mere coincidence, of course. But the confusion underscores an important point. If a person has initiative, self-control, commitment, talent, honesty, credibility, and courage, we say, "Here is a leader!" By definition, a follower cannot exhibit the qualities of leadership. It violates our stereotype.

But our stereotype is ungenerous and wrong. Followership is not a person but a role, and what distinguishes followers from leaders is not intelligence or character but the role they play. As I pointed out at the beginning of this article, effective followers and effective leaders are often the same people playing different parts at different hours of the day.

In many companies, the leadership track is the only road to career success. In almost all companies, leadership is taught and encouraged while followership is not. Yet effective followership is a prerequisite for organizational success. Your organization can take four steps to cultivate effective followers in your work force.

1. Redefining Followership and Leadership

Our stereotyped but unarticulated definitions of leadership and followership shape our expectations when we occupy either position. If a leader is defined as responsible for motivating followers, he or she will likely act toward followers as if they needed motivation. If we agree that a leader's job is to transform followers, then it must be a follower's job to provide the clay. If followers fail to need transformation, the leader looks ineffective. The way we define the roles clearly influences the outcome of the interaction.

Instead of seeing the leadership role as superior to and more active than the role of the follower, we can think of them as equal but different activities. The operative definitions are roughly these: people who are effective in the leader role have the vision to set corporate goals and strategies, the interpersonal skills to achieve consensus, the verbal capacity to communicate enthusiasm to large and diverse groups of individuals, the organizational talent to coordinate disparate efforts, and, above all, the desire to lead.

People who are effective in the follower role have the vision to see both the forest and the trees, the social capacity to work well with others, the strength of character to flourish without heroic status, the moral and psychological balance to pursue personal and corporate goals at no cost to either, and, above all, the desire to participate in a team effort for the accomplishment of some greater common purpose.

This view of leadership and followership can be conveyed to employees directly and indirectly—in training and by example. The qualities that make good followers and the value the company places on effective followership can be articulated in explicit follower training. Perhaps the best way to convey this message, however, is by example. Since each of us plays a follower's part at least from time to time, it is essential that we play it well, that we contribute our competence to the achievement of team goals, that we support the team leader with candor and self-control, that we do our best to appreciate and enjoy the role of quiet contribution to a larger, common cause.

2. Honing Followership Skills

Most organizations assume that leadership has to be taught but that everyone knows how to follow. This assumption is based on three faulty premises: (1) that leaders are more important than followers, (2) that following is simply doing what you are told to do, and (3) that followers inevitably draw their energy and aims, even their talent, from the leader. A program of follower training can correct this misapprehension by focusing on topics like:

Improving independent, critical thinking.

Self-management.

Disagreeing agreeably.

Building credibility.

Aligning personal and organizational goals and commitments.

Acting responsibly toward the organization, the leader, coworkers, and oneself.

Similarities and differences between leadership and followership roles.

Moving between the two roles with ease.

3. Performance Evaluation and Feedback

Most performance evaluations include a section on leadership skills. Followership evaluation would include items like the ones I have discussed. Instead of rating employees on leadership qualities such as self-management, independent thinking, originality, courage, competence, and credibility, we can rate them on these same qualities in both the leadership and followership roles and then evaluate each individual's ability to shift easily from the one role to the other. A variety of performance perspectives will help most people understand better how well they play their various organizational roles.

Moreover, evaluations can come from peers, subordinates, and self as well as from supervisors. The process is simple enough: peers and subordinates who come into regular or significant contact with another employee fill in brief, periodic questionnaires where they rate the individual on followership qualities. Findings are then summarized and given to the employee being rated.

4. Organizational Structures That Encourage Followership

Unless the value of good following is somehow built into the fabric of the organization, it is likely to remain a pleasant conceit to which everyone pays occasional lip service but no dues. Here are four good ways to incorporate the concept into your corporate culture:

In leaderless groups, all members assume equal responsibility for achieving goals. These are usually small task forces of people who can work together under their own supervision. However hard it is to imagine a group with more than one leader, groups with none at all can be highly productive if their members have the qualities of effective followers.

Groups with temporary and rotating leadership are another possibility. Again, such groups are probably best kept small and the rotation fairly frequent, although the notion might certainly be extended to include the administration of a small department for, say, six-month terms. Some of these temporary leaders will be less effective than others, of course, and some may be weak indeed, which is why critics maintain that this structure is inefficient. Why not let the best leader lead? Why suffer through the tenure of less effective leaders? There are two reasons. First, experience of the leadership role is essential to the education of effective followers. Second, followers learn that they must compensate for ineffective leadership by exercising their skill as good followers. Rotating leader or not, they are bound to be faced with ineffective leadership more than once in their careers.

Delegation to the lowest level is a third technique for cultivating good followers. Nordstrom's, the Seattle-based department store chain, gives each sales clerk responsibility for servicing and satisfying the customer, including the authority to make refunds without supervisory approval. This kind of delegation makes even people at the lowest level responsible for their own decisions and for thinking independently about their work.

Finally, companies can use rewards to underline the importance of good followership. This is not as easy as it sounds. Managers dependent on yes people and sheep for ego gratification will not leap at the idea of extra rewards for the people who make them most uncomfortable. In my research, I have found that effective followers get mixed treatment. About half the time, their contributions lead to substantial rewards. The other half of the time they are punished by their superiors for exercising judgment, taking risks, and failing to conform. Many managers insist that they want independent subordinates who can think for themselves. In practice, followers who challenge their bosses run the risk of getting fired.

In today's flatter, leaner organization, companies will not succeed without the kind of people who take pride and satisfaction in the role of supporting player, doing the less glorious work without fanfare. Organizations that want the benefits of effective followers must find ways of rewarding them, ways of bringing them into full partnership in the enterprise. Think of the thousands of companies that achieve adequate performance and lackluster profits with employees they treat like second-class citizens. Then imagine for a moment the power of an organization blessed with fully engaged, fully energized, fully appreciated followers.

Reflecting on My *Followership*

1. Am I a good follower?
2. Do I really believe that being a good follower impacts my leadership? How?
3. Do I build healthy followers?
4. At what time in my life did I most enjoy following? What characteristics did the leader in front of me demonstrate?
5. Are following and leading more about personality or about discipline and decisions?

Robert E. Kelley is a professor at the Graduate School of Industrial Administration at Carnegie Mellon University and president of Consultants to Executives and Organizations, Ltd. His most recent book is *The Power of Followership*.

Servant-Leadership

I believe that serving and competing are antithetical; the stronger the urge to serve, the less the interest in competing.

ROBERT GREENLEAF'S LEGACY AS a writer and thinker is still growing more than a decade after his death. Although he didn't invent the idea of servant-leadership (it originated with the early figures of the Old Testament), he coined the term in a contemporary institutional context and was a trailblazer in articulating what a servant-leader looks like, giving form to the vision in a variety of life arenas.

Originally Greenleaf was director of management research at AT&T, and he later taught at both MIT and Harvard. He was an exceptionally broad thinker, and over the years he approached the topic of servant-leadership from a variety of perspectives, including those of government, entrepreneurship, social change, small business enterprise, the world of corporate conglomerates, even America's relationship with and responsibility to the rest of the world. But Greenleaf's observations weren't merely theory; they were thoroughly grounded in his experience in the business community. He attached his ideas firmly to the real world and strongly believed

The prospect for the servant idea rests almost entirely, I believe, on some among us *investing the energy and taking the risks to inspire with a vision.*

that servant-leadership could transform reality and make the world a better place for its inhabitants.

Today The Greenleaf Center for Servant-Leadership carries on his work. Instead of becoming stale and dated, the materials Greenleaf originated grow more and more relevant. The essay we've selected, "Servant: Retrospect and Prospect" from *The Power of Servant-Leadership,* is a thesis work in which he looks backward and forward at the topics that form his core thinking. Significantly for people of faith, Greenleaf's deep grounding in a Judeo-Christian heritage informs his commentary on the subject, and this background comes through without caution or apology. His ideas are clearly rooted in ethical and theological soil. We think you'll agree that Greenleaf's theories must be a significant part of the foundation of a larger construct of leadership.

Servant: Retrospect *and* Prospect

• • •

Robert K. Greenleaf

The major focus of my adult life may best be described as a student of organization, how things get done—particularly in large institutions. Fortuitous advice from a wise college professor helped shape this interest and led me, upon graduation, to find my way into the largest business organization in the world, American Telephone and Telegraph Company. Early on, I became a student of the history of what seemed to be an extraordinary institution. I managed to carve out a career in which I could be both involved and within watching distance of its top structure, and yet maintain sufficient detachment so that I could be reflective about what was going on. My tenure embraced the expansion of the 1920s, the Depression, World War II, and the growth years of the 1950s and 1960s. I never carried heavy executive responsibility and was spared the debilitating effects of such a role which seem almost inevitable, given conventional organizational structures.

In the latter part of my career, I held the position of Director of Management Research. With the help of a professional staff, and within a broad charter, I could both study and advise regarding the management and leadership of this huge institution—over 1 million employees—immersed as it is in sophisticated technology, elaborate human organization, and regulated public service. I was concerned with its values, with its history and myth, and, intimately, with its top leadership. I learned the hard way about the profound influence that history, and the myths of institutions that have a considerable history, have on values, goals, and leadership. And I was painfully aware of the cost in these terms of any insensitivity to history and myth—especially among the top officers. In any institutional setting, one really cannot understand one's involvement in it *now* without a clear sense of the course of events that form that institution's past, out of which grows the mythology that surrounds the record of those events. History and myth, in my view, need each other in order to illuminate the present.

This experience at AT&T gave me a good perspective and the impetus, in my retirement years that began in 1964, to venture into close working relationships with a wide range of institutions: universities (especially in the turbulent 1960s), foundations (as trustee, consultant, and staff member), churches (local, regional, and national), and related church institutions, professional associations, healthcare, and businesses—in the United States, in Europe, and in the third world.

This post-retirement experience, following 38 years with AT&T, has been enriching and stimulating; but one facet of it, in particular, prompted me to begin to write and to pull together a thread of thinking that has emerged around the *servant* theme.

The servant theme evolved out of close association with several colleges and universities during their disturbed period in the 1960s. This was a searing experience, to be intimately involved with students, faculty, administrators, and trustees at a time when some of these venerable institutions literally crumbled—when the hoops came off the barrel.

My first servant essay, "The Servant as Leader," was prompted by my concern for student attitudes which then—and now, although the manifestations are different—seemed low in hope. One cannot be hopeful, it seems to me, unless one accepts and believes that one can live productively in the world as it is—striving, violent, unjust, as well as beautiful, caring, and supportive. I hold that hope, thus defined, is absolutely essential to both sanity and wholeness of life.

Partly in search for a structural basis for hope, partly out of awareness that our vast complex of institutions—particularly colleges and universities in the late sixties—seemed so fragile and inadequate, two further essays were written: "The Institution as Servant" and "Trustees as Servants." The three essays were then collected in a book with some related writings and published in 1977 under the title *Servant Leadership*. Another projected essay, "The Servant as a Person," turned out to be a book and was published in 1979 with the title *Teacher as Servant: A Parable* [published by The Greenleaf Center].

Out of the struggle to write these things, while contending with the modest ferment they stirred, came the belief that, as a world society, we have not yet come to grips with the *institutional revolution* that came hard on the heels of the industrial revolution, and that we confront a worldwide crisis of institutional leadership. How can we ordinary mortals lead governments, businesses, churches, hospitals, schools, philanthropies, communities—yes, even families—to become more serving in this turbulent world? And what does it mean to serve? I prefer not to define *serve* explicitly at this time. Rather, I would let the meaning it has for me evolve as one reads through this essay.

How can an institution become more serving? I see no other way than that the people who inhabit it serve better and work together toward synergy—the whole becoming greater than the sum of its parts.

I believe that the transforming movement that raises the serving quality of any institution, large or small, begins with the initiative of one individual person—no matter how large the institution or how substantial the movement. If one accepts, as I do, the principle of synergy, one has difficulty with the idea that *only* small is beautiful. The potential for beauty (largely unrealized to be sure) is much greater in large institutions—because of the phenomenon of synergy. Because we are now dominated by large institutions, how to make *big* also *beautiful* is a major challenge for us.

How to achieve *community* under the shelter of bigness may be the essence of this challenge because so much of caring depends upon knowing and interacting with persons in the intimacy of propinquity. The stimulus and support that some individuals need to be open to inspiration and imaginative insight often come from the nurture of groups. There may not be a "group mind" (inspiration and imaginative insight may be gifts only to individuals), but there is clearly a climate favorable to creativity by individuals that the group, as community, can provide. Achieving many small-scale communities, under the shelter that is best given by bigness, may be the secret of synergy in large institutions.

The IDEA of SERVANT

The idea of "servant" is deep in our Judeo-Christian heritage. The concordance to the Standard Revised Version of the Bible lists over 1300 references to *servant* (including serve and service). Yet, after all of these millennia, there is ample evidence that ours is a low-caring society when judged by what is reasonable and possible with the resources at hand. There are many notable servants among us, but they sometimes seem to be losing ground to the neutral or nonserving people. It is argued that the outlook for our civilization at this moment is not promising, probably because not enough of us care enough for our fellow humans.

I am personally hopeful for the future because knowledge is available to do two things that we are not now doing, things that are well within our means to do and that would give caring people great joy to do, things that would infuse more of the servant quality into our society. (1) We know how to mature the servant motive as a durable thing in many who arrive in their teens with servanthood latent in them—and this, I believe, is quite a large number. This is what my book *Teacher as Servant* is about. (2) We know how to transform institutions so that they will be substantially more serving to all who are touched by them. A chapter in *Teacher as Servant* deals with such a transformation. But formidable obstacles stand in the way of using this knowledge, obstacles that I will call "mind-sets."

The PROBLEM *of* MIND-SETS

Mind-sets that seem to restrain otherwise good, able people from using the two bits of knowledge mentioned above are often tough and unyielding. Whether obstacles like these can be sufficiently reduced before the deterioration of this civilization has become irreversible is open to question. For the older ones among us who are "in charge," nothing short of a "peak" experience, like religious conversion or psychoanalysis or an overpowering new vision, seems to have much chance of converting a confirmed nonservant into an affirmative servant. But for some, those few older ones who have a glimmer of the servant disposition *now*, it is worth their making the effort to try to stem the tide of deterioration. Life can be more whole for those who try, regardless of the outcome.

Civilizations have risen and fallen before. If ours does not make it, perhaps when the archeologists of some future civilization dig around among the remains of this one they may find traces of the effort to build a more caring society, bits of experience that may give useful cues to future people. It is a reasonable prospect that, in the civilization that succeeds ours—whether it evolves from ours in a constructive way or whether it is reconstructed from the ruins after long dark ages—those future people will be faced with the same two problems that confront us now: (1) *how to produce as many servants as they can from those who, at maturity, have the potential for it;* and (2) *how to elicit optimal service from such group endeavors (institutions) as emerge.* And, unless some unforeseeable transmutations in human nature occur along the way, those future people may be impeded by the same unwillingness to use what they know that marks our times. Knowledge may be power, but not without the willingness, and the release from inhibiting mind-sets, to use that knowledge.

Over a century ago, when the then-stagnant Danish culture was reconstructed as a result of the work of the Folk High School, the motto of that effort was *The Spirit is Power.* A chapter in the essay "The Servant as Leader" tells the story of a remarkable social transformation that followed when the spirit of the Danish young people was aroused so that they sought to find a way out of their dilemma, a stagnant culture, by building a new social order.

Worth noting about this 19th-century Danish experience is that Bishop Grundtvig, the prophetic visionary who gave leadership to the Folk High School movement, did not offer a model for others to follow, nor did he himself found or direct such a school. He gave the vision, the dream, and he passionately and persuasively advocated that dream for over 50 years of his long life. The indigenous leaders among the peasants of Denmark responded to that vision and built the schools—with no model to guide them. *They knew how to do it!* Grundtvig gave the prophetic vision that inspired them to act on what they knew.

VISION *for* OUR TIMES: WHERE IS IT?

"Where there is no vision, the people perish." This language (Proverbs 29:18) from the King James Version of the Bible stays with me even though modern translators make something else of that passage.

What Grundtvig gave to the indigenous leaders of the common people of Denmark in the 19th century was a compelling vision that they should do something that they knew how to do: *they could raise the spirit of young people so that they would build a new society—and they did.* Without that vision, 19th-century Denmark was on the way to perishing.

Our restless young people in the 1960s wanted to build a new society too. But their elders who could have helped prepare them for that task just "spun their wheels." As a consequence of this neglect, a few of those young people simply settled for tearing up the place. And, in the absence of new visionary leadership to inspire effort to prepare our young people to build constructively, some of them may tear up the place again! Do not be surprised if they do just that. The provocation is ample. We simply are not giving the maturing help to young people that is well within our means to do. Instead, we are acting on the principle that knowledge, not the spirit, is power. Knowledge is but a tool. The spirit is of the essence.

Perhaps the older people who could help them do not do what they know how to do because, as in the 1960s, they are not inspired by a vision that lifts their sights to act on what they know. No such vision is being given in our times. And the paralysis of action that restrains us in preparing young people to live productively in the 21st century is still with us. We may be courting disaster by our neglect.

This is an interesting thesis (as said earlier): (1) We know how to increase the proportion of young people who, at maturity, are disposed to be servants; and (2) we know how to transform contemporary institutions so that they will be substantially more serving to all who are touched by them. What is needed, this thesis holds, is a vision that will lift the sights of those who know and release their will to act constructively. This vision might be prompted by conscience and self-generated out of a conscious search, or it may be without known cause, or it might be forcefully communicated by a strong leader-type person (as Grundtvig did in 19th-century Denmark).

This leader might present a vision that has a benign result, as Grundtvig did; or he or she might be a leader like Adolph Hitler, who brought a major disaster; or the vision might be given by an Elvis Presley who can release the inhibiting constraints and incite a frenzy of action that has no seeming value-laden consequence, good or bad.

The late Rabbi Abraham Joshua Heschel had given a lecture on the Old Testament Prophets to an undergraduate audience. In the question period a student asked, "Rabbi Heschel, you spoke of false prophets and true prophets. How does one tell the difference?"

The good rabbi drew himself into the stern stance of the prophet of old and answered in measured tones, "There—is—no—way!" and looked intently at his questioner for an embarrassing moment. Then his face broke into a gentle smile, and he said, "My friend, if there were a 'way,' if we had a gauge that we could slip over the head of the prophet and say with certainty that he is or is not a true prophet, there would be no human dilemma and life would have no meaning." Then, returning to his stern Old Testament stance he said emphatically, "But it is terribly important that we know the difference."

Thus, one who is inspired by a vision must know the difference between an action that points toward a benign result, or simply aimless activity. I believe it is possible to prepare most of the emerging adults to know the difference. This is the first step in increasing the proportion of young people who are disposed to be servants. My book, *Teacher as Servant*, describes how a teacher on his own and without the support of either colleagues or university, can prepare young people to know the difference. I will comment later on one other opportunity within colleges and universities. Neither approach costs any money!

What Do We Know—*or* Don't Want *to* Know?

I have said that (1) we know how to increase the proportion of young people who, at maturity, are disposed to be servants, and (2) we know how to transform institutions so that they will be substantially more serving to all who are touched by them. But it is not knowledge that is codified and systematized and bearing the appropriate establishment imprimatur. It is knowledge like that which the leaders among the Danish peasants had when they were inspired to build schools which would kindle the spirit of their young people. They had always known how to do that, but until Bishop Grundtvig gave them the vision, they were unable, or lacked the will, to act on what they knew.

There is nothing mystical about the available knowledge to do the two things (as suggested above) that need to be done in our times to raise the servant quality of our society. To my knowledge, clear and complete models do not exist, but there are fragments of experience here and there that can readily be assembled to give a workable basis for moving to solidify that experience—*to know!* Let me give examples from four widely differing contemporary institutions in which, it seems to me, able, honest, people lack the vision to act on what they know—or could easily know—*and seem not to want to know!* They seem to have mind-sets that block them.

Business

A certain important industrial field is occupied by half a dozen large companies and many small and medium sized ones. It is a field that is subject to quite wide cyclical economic fluctuations and in which disruptions by labor disputes are common. One of the larger companies (not the largest) stands in conspicuous contrast to the other large ones on three counts: no matter what happens to the economic fortunes of the others, this firm, up to now, has always made money; they have never had a strike or work stoppage; their product is generally recognized as superior. (What makes their product superior will be commented on later.)

Let us call this company X. A close observer of this industry recently asked the head of one of the other large companies in this field this simple question: "What do you folks learn from company X?" The response was a hand gesture of dismissal and the brusque comment, "I don't want to talk about it!"

One can speculate about why, in a highly competitive field, the head of one large company would brush off a suggestion that he might learn something from a more successful competitor. But what distinguishes company X from its competitors is not the dimensions that usually separate companies, such as superior technology, more astute marketing strategy, better financial base, etc. Company X is not too different from its competitors in dimensions like these. What separates company X from the rest is unconventional thinking about its "dream"—what this business wants to be, how its priorities are set, and how it organizes to serve. It has a radically different philosophy and self-image. According to the conventional business wisdom, company X ought not to succeed at all. Conspicuously less successful competitors seem to say, "The ideas that company X holds *ought* not to work, therefore we will learn nothing from them." They "don't want to talk about it."

University

In the field of higher education, there is another consequence of a lack of vision that cannot be as clearly identified as in the above business example. For many years, I have tried to stir an interest in universities in making a more determined effort to develop the servant-leadership potential that exists among their students. When new money is produced to support such an effort, a pass will be made at doing it. But when the money stops, the effort stops. It does not take root. Here and there the occasional professor, on his own, without the support of his university, and sometimes with the opposition of his colleagues, has taken an interest in this aspect of student growth—with conspicuous success.

In contrast, a student with athletic potential will find elaborate coaching resources available to develop this talent—even in the poorest and feeblest of institutions. But the young potential servant-leader will find that the position of the best and strongest university is that the development of leadership potential is something that just happens, and nothing explicit is to be done about it in the crucial undergraduate years. I wrote an article about this in an educational journal stating that the only way I see for work in the undergraduate years to help alleviate the leadership crisis we seem now to be in is to find and encourage the rare professor who will take it on—unrecognized and uncompensated, and perhaps denigrated by his colleagues. A university president responded to my article with this concurring comment:

> I am coming more and more to agree with your opinion that it is almost impossible to mount anything like an organized program in developing leadership in our university students. Reluctantly, I am reaching your conclusion that the best and only hope of success will be an effort on the part of a few dedicated individuals who will take that cross upon themselves. If this is truly the case, then we need to try to discover who and where they are and give them all the assistance we can.

When John W. Gardner wrote his sharp criticism of universities for administering what he called the *antileadership vaccine* (his parting message when he left the presidency of Carnegie Corporation for a career in politics in 1964), the response from academe seemed to be, "We don't want to talk about it!"

Health Profession

In the medical profession, there is a widely held position against accepting nutrition as an important factor in health. The average doctor knows that the human body is a chemical-psychic organism. But in treating illness or in advice regarding health building, there is not much concern for nutrition.

The Hill Foundation in St. Paul, Minnesota, which has a long record of generous giving to medical education, recently made a grant to establish a program in nutrition in a *new* medical school. The foundation's annual report for 1973 commented on this grant as follows:

It is a true paradox: Americans are often overweight and undernourished. We are wasteful of our food assets and unwise in our dietary patterns; meanwhile, much of the rest of the world struggles to assure its people an adequate food supply. There is an immediate need for more basic research in nutrition; more communication on ways to plan and control food production, processing, presentation and preparation; and for more public education on sound nutritional practices. But the fact is that there are too few well-trained people to perform this task. . . .

An important aspect of the nutrition problem is related to the medical school curriculum. Few medical schools have major departments devoted to the field of nutrition research and education. Generally the young doctor gets a briefing on aspects of nutrition as they relate to specific diseases such as diabetes, allergies or coronary problems. Most of the emphasis, however, is on the remedial care of patients, with little attention devoted to the maintenance of health or the prevention of illness. . . . The same weaknesses exist in the training of such paramedical personnel as nurses and dietitians. . . . The Foundation believes Mayo Medical School ideally is suited to develop and implement a broad nutrition education program *because it is a new institution* (italics ours), and hence is still flexible in its approach to medical training.

What this says to me is that the mind-set among doctors on nutrition is such that only a new medical school will offer a chance to use fully the available nutritional knowledge as an important factor in health building. The medical establishment would seem to say, as the head of the business said when asked what he learned from his more successful but unconventional competitor, "We don't want to talk about it!"

Church Leader

My interpretation of a bit of 19th-century history is that when Karl Marx sat in the British Museum composing the doctrines that would shape so much of the 20th-century world, he was filling a void that was left by the failure of the churches of his day to deal adequately with the consequences of the industrial revolution. If the 19th-century churches (or church leaders) had taken the trouble to suggest a design for the new society that the industrial revolution made imperative, and if they had advocated it persuasively as a new vision, Marx might still have written his tracts; but they would not have found the field relatively unoccupied.

Recently, I met with a group of church leaders, professionals, who were convened for three days on the subject of "The Churchman as Leader." I listened for a day as they discussed their leadership opportunities and problems as they saw them. Then, in commenting on what I had heard, I noted three words that are sometimes used interchangeably but have quite different connotations: *manage* (from *manus*—hand) suggesting control; *administer* (from *administrare*—to serve) suggesting to care for; and *lead*, of uncertain origin but commonly used to mean "going out ahead to show the way." Manage and administer, along with the ceremonial aspects of the office, are the *maintenance* functions—they help keep the institution running smoothly—*as it is*. Important as maintenance is in the current performance of any institution, it does not assure adaptation to serve a changing society. That assurance can come only from *leading*—venturing creatively. Having made this distinction in the meaning of terms as they are commonly used, I commented that, as I observed their discussion, these church-men were talking mostly about *maintenance,* not *leading.*

In most institutions, churches included, managing and adminis-tering, the maintenance functions, are delegated and resources are allo-cated in order that those to whom these functions are assigned can carry on. Those who manage and administer (maintain) may also *lead—go out ahead to show the way.* But leadership is not delegated; it is assumed. If there are sanctions to compel or induce compliance, the process would not qualify as leadership. The only test of leadership is that somebody follows—*voluntarily.*

At this point, I was asked by the church leaders, "If you do not see us as *leading,* in our terms, what could persons in positions like ours do in order to lead?"

I repeated my credo, as stated in the beginning of this essay [I believe that caring for persons, the more able and the less able serving each other, is what makes a good society. Most caring was once per-son to person. Now much of it is mediated through institutions—often large, powerful, impersonal; not always competent; sometimes corrupt], which concludes with ". . . If a better society is to be built, one more just and caring and providing opportunity for people to grow, the most open course, the most effective and economical way, while supportive of the social order, is to raise the performance as ser-vant of as many institutions as possible by new voluntary regenerative forces initiated within them by committed individuals—*servants.*" Then I said:

"What church leaders can do to really *lead* in our times is to use their influence to bring into being a contemporary *theology of institu-tions* that will underwrite the commitment of church members within our many institutions and support them as they become new regen-erative forces: to the end that their particular institution, in which they have some power of influence, will become more serving—and con-tinue to grow in its capacity to serve.

"The leadership of the 19th-century churches did not accept the challenge to suggest a new design for postindustrial revolution society, and they left a void to be filled by a concerned and articulate atheist. The leaders of late-20th-century churches are not accepting the chal-lenge of an institution-bound society (which Marx did not provide for in his doctrines, and, as a consequence, Marxist societies today have the same problem in getting their institutions to serve as we have). The opportunity that church leaders have today is to take the initiative to see that an adequate theology of institutions evolves so the churches have a firm basis for preparing their members to become regenerative servants in the institutions with which they are involved. *Leadership is initiating—going out ahead to show the way.*"

There was not much response to this suggestion in the meeting of church leaders. When we concluded, I noted this paucity of response and said that I would write to them about it when I got home. I later sent to those present a memorandum entitled "The Need for a Theology of Institutions," in which I suggested a detailed procedure that a church leader might follow in producing this new theology. Only 2 of the 16 present at the conference acknowledged the receipt of the memo, and they were noncommittal. A supplementary memorandum six months later got the same response.

I would conclude that these church leaders—all responsible, able, good people—took the same position as the head of the business did when asked what he learned from his much more successful (if unconventional) competitor: "We don't want to talk about it!"

When 19th-century church leaders were confronted with the radical impact of the industrial revolution, if some audacious consultant had suggested that a new theology was needed to deal with this problem, the response of church leaders of that day might have been the same—"we don't want to talk about it."

My reflection on these last ten years leads me to conclude that *vision,* without which we perish, is required to open us to willingness to use what we know and to work to extract hard reality from a dream. In the absence of a powerful liberating vision, church leaders, like others in responsible roles, "don't want to talk about it." Why, over such a long span of history, has the production of vision been so difficult to do? Why are these liberating visions so rare?

WHY ARE LIBERATING VISIONS SO RARE?

It seems to me important to accept that the mind-sets that are so frustrating to all reformers, those who are urging others to use what they know, actually serve a useful purpose. What if every person and every institution was "open" in the sense of being free of all inhibiting mind-sets that block action on what we know? Every question and every situation would be faced as if nothing like it had happened before. This would be a reformer's dream; but the world would be in chaos. Few of us can survive without a good deal of dogma that prompts reflexive actions. We would not be able to act quickly in emergencies, and moral choices that require prompt action would paralyze us. Most of us get along as well as we do by a good deal of "what if" anticipatory thinking that pre-sets responses to common situations. If we were all completely "open," much of our traditional wisdom might be lost, as might "manners" that enable us to interact spontaneously in appropriate ways with fellow humans.

Liberating visions are rare because ours is partly a traditional society—but only partly. It is also an evolving society about which Cardinal Newman is quoted as saying, "To live is to change; to live well is to have changed often." The mixture of *traditional* and *changing* is an important aspect of the human dilemma.

Therefore, in answer to the question, "Why are liberating visions so rare?" one must say that they are rare because a stable society requires that *a powerful liberating vision must be difficult to deliver,* and that the test for the benign character of such a vision shall be rigorous. Yet to have none, or not enough such visions, is to seal our fate. We cannot run back to be a wholly traditional society, comforting as it may be to contemplate it. There must be change—sometimes great change.

Moods and spirit of people vary. There are moments when people are more open to charismatic vision than others. Some times seem "plastic"; others seem "hard." We but dimly understand the forces that open and close people to liberating visions.

The word *prudence* comes to mind. We should try to change with a minimum of threat of damage to stability—as embodied in the four kinds of mind-sets I have described. If stability is significantly lowered or lost, no matter how noble the end sought, the cost in human suffering may be inordinate. When an imprudent effort toward change, one in which the liberating vision is not sufficiently compelling and benign in intent, may make it more difficult for a later prudent effort to succeed, reformers take note: in the end, most people choose *order*—even if it is delivered to them by brutal nonservants. The ultimate choice of order is one of the most predictable mind-sets because it is a first condition of a civilized society.

If the writer in Proverbs 29:18 is correctly quoted in saying "Where there is no vision, the people perish," there is remarkable consistency between the common dilemmas in ancient times and in ours. The four examples of firm mind-sets in the fields of business, education, health, and church suggest that there has been failure to give sufficiently powerful liberating visions. This kind of deprivation has been the common lot of humankind from the earliest times. And because of that, the threat of perishing is always with us.

Summoning *and* Articulating *a* Vision

So far I have given only half an answer to the question, Why are liberating visions so rare?—because it is so difficult to give them. The other half is: because so few of those who have the gift for summoning a vision, and the power to articulate it persuasively, have either the urge or the courage or the will to try! And it takes all three. We in America may be in a transition period between an era of "growth" and one of "restraint" and liberating visions may have a hollow sound. This is discouraging to visionaries!

One of the requirements of a caring, serving society, in both favorable and discouraging times, is that it provides in its structures a place for visionaries and surrounds those in the place with the expectation that they will produce those liberating visions of which they are capable. A new view of a structure of the institutions that serve us may be in order—a view that embraces both internal structure as well as the relationship between institutions and how they influence one another.

When "The Servant as Leader" was published in 1970, I had this to say about prophetic vision:

I now embrace the theory of prophecy, which holds that prophetic voices of great clarity, and with a quality of insight equal to that of any age, are speaking cogently all of the time. Men and women of a stature equal to the greatest of the past are with us now addressing the problems of the day and pointing to a better way and to a personeity better able to live fully and serenely in these times.

The variable that marks some periods as barren and some as rich in prophetic vision may be in the interest, the level of seeking, and the responsiveness of the *hearers*. The variable may not be in the presence or absence or the relative quality and force of prophetic voices. The prophet grows in stature as people respond to his message. If his or her early attempts are ignored or spurned, the talent may wither away.

It is *seekers*, then, who make the prophet; and the initiative of any of us in searching for and responding to the voice of a contemporary prophet may mark the turning point in her or his growth and service.

I came by this point of view from reading the history of the Religious Society of Friends (Quakers), and I concluded that George Fox, the powerful 17th-century voice in England that gave this Society its remarkable vision, probably would not have been heard had there not been in existence in England for 100 years prior a group known as *seekers*. This was a small band of people whose common bond was that they were *listening* for prophetic vision. They were held together by a religious concern, but they knew that it lacked articulation in a contemporary formulation that would make of them a vital social and religious force in their day. And as they heard and responded to George Fox, they became for a short time a great movement that had a remarkable impact on English institutions, notably a new business ethic and a pervasive social concern that influenced the western world and carried forward to 18th-century America, where it made of the Quakers the first religious group to formally condemn slavery and forbid slaveholding among its members—100 years before the Civil War.

But this movement very quickly crystallized into a church, as too many of its members ceased to be seekers. Instead of *seeing*, being open to new prophecy, they "*had it*," tested and tried—what churches have always done. What they had was, and remains, good. But the Quakers were no longer on the growing edge.

The servant-leader may be not so much the prophetic visionary (that is a rare gift) as the convener, sustainer, discerning guide for seekers who wish to remain open to prophetic visions.

SERVANT LEADERSHIP—*by* PERSUASION

In my personal credo stated earlier I said, "If a better society is to be built, one more just and more caring and providing opportunity for people to grow, the most effective and economical way, while supportive of the social order, is to raise the performance as servant of as many institutions as possible by new voluntary regenerative forces initiated within them by committed individuals—*servants.*"

So far I have not found it helpful to define *servant* and *serving* in other terms than the consequences of the serving on the one being served or on others who may be affected by the action. In *Teacher as Servant,* I describe a semifictional servant in some detail.

In "The Servant as Leader," the definition was: "Do those being served grow as persons: do they, while being served, become healthier, wiser, freer, more autonomous, more likely themselves to become servants? *And* what is the effect on the least privileged in society; will she or he benefit, or, at least, not be further deprived?" I would now add one further stipulation: "No one will knowingly be hurt by the action, *directly or indirectly.*"

Thus the servant would reject the "utilitarian" position, which would accept a very large gain in, say, justice at the cost of a small but real hurt to some. The servant would reject the nonviolent tactic for societal change, however noble the intent, if, as a consequence, some who are disposed to violence are likely to resort to it, or some may be threatened or coerced. (I would fault Mohandas Gandhi on these grounds. Great leader and tremendous person that he was, I do not find his tactic an appropriate model for the servant. John Woolman, as described in "The Servant as Leader" is, for me, such a model.)

The servant would reject the rapid accomplishment of any desirable social goal by coercion in favor of the slower process of persuasion—even if no identifiable person was hurt by the coercion.

To some determined reformers, such a set of beliefs would lead to paralysis of action. The servant (in my view) is generally a "gradualist." And, while granting that, in an imperfect world, because we have not yet learned how to do better, coercion by governments and some other institutions will be needed to restrain some destructive actions and to provide some services best rendered authoritatively, the servant will stand as the advocate of persuasion in human affairs to the largest extent possible.

This view is supported by a belief about the nature of humankind, a belief that leads to a view of persuasion as the critical skill of servant leadership. Such a leader is one who ventures and takes the risks of going out ahead to show the way and whom others follow, *voluntarily, because they are persuaded that the leader's path is the right one—for them,* probably better than they could devise for themselves.

One is persuaded, I believe, on arrival at a feeling of rightness about a belief or action through one's own intuitive sense—checked, perhaps, by others' intuitive judgment, but, in the end, one relies on one's own intuitive sense. One takes that intuitive step, from the closest approximation to certainty one can reach by conscious logic (sometimes not very close), to that state in which one may say with conviction, "This is where I stand!" The act of persuasion will help order the logic and favor the intuitive step. And this takes time! The one being persuaded must take that intuitive step alone, untrammeled by coercion or manipulative stratagems. Both leader and follower respect the integrity and allow the autonomy of the other; and each encourages the other to find her or his own intuitive confirmation of the rightness of the belief or action.

To the servant (as I view that person), *persuasion,* thus defined, stands in sharp contrast to *coercion* (the use, or threat of use, of covert or overt sanctions or penalties, the exploitation of weaknesses or sentiments, or any application of pressure). Persuasion also stands in sharp contrast to *manipulation* (guiding people into beliefs or actions that they do not fully understand).

If one accepts such definitions, has the servant become limited to a passive role and yielded the carrying of the tougher burdens to those with fewer scruples? No, I do not believe so; not if the preparation of servants can begin when they are young. There are some old and valuable burden carriers around who are much too coercive and manipulative; and they might lose their usefulness if they attempted too radical change. It may be better to tolerate their ways as long as they are useful so long as they do not hurt others.

I realize that in adding to the definition of servant the admonition, "no one will knowingly be hurt," some people who might otherwise think of themselves as servants (as I have defined it) will reject that identification. The problem is that some do not believe they can carry the leadership roles they now have without causing some hurt, or that necessary social changes can be made without some being hurt.

In an imperfect world, some will continue to be hurt, as they always have been. I know that, in the course of my life, I have caused some hurt. But, as my concern for servanthood has evolved, the scars from these incidents are more prominent in my memory and self-questioning is sharper: Could I have been more aware, more patient, more gentle, more forgiving, more skillful? The intent of the servant, as I see that person now, is that, as a result of any action she or he initiates, *no one will knowingly be hurt.* And if someone *is* hurt, there is a scar that henceforth will endure to be reckoned with. Hurting people, only a few, is not accepted as a legitimate cost of doing business.

I find eleemosynary institutions most at fault on this issue—particularly with their employed staffs. There seems to be the assumption that since the cause being served is noble, what happens to the people who render the service is not a particular concern.

I once sat with the governing board of a large church as they discussed the many ramifications of their affairs. In listening to their discussions I was appalled at some of the attitudes they held and the cavalier actions they took regarding their employed staff. When it was appropriate for me to comment, I noted my observation on their attitudes and actions and I said: "I have spent my life in a business and had responsibility, directly or indirectly, for the careers of many people. If I had held attitudes like those you have revealed and had your record of hiring and firing people, at some point I would have been taken aside and told, 'Greenleaf, you may be good for something, but we will not let you manage people. We can't afford this!' With the predominantly economic motive, most businesses I know about take greater care with their people than you do. This may have been part of what Emerson had in mind when he said (in *Works and Days*), 'The greatest meliorative force in the world is selfish huckstering trade!'"

It all reminds me of that powerful line with which Shakespeare opens his 94th sonnet:

They that have power to hurt and will do none.

(Not very little, but none.) This is the sonnet that concludes with those caustic lines:

> For sweetest things turn sourest by their deeds;
> Lilies that fester smell far worse than weeds.

The intervening eleven lines will bear close scrutiny.

The firm aim of the servant is that *no one* will be hurt.

Preparation of a servant, particularly for the exacting role of servant-leader, should start not later than secondary school (before if possible) because, I believe, the servant needs to learn to stand against the culture on two critical issues: *power* and *competition*.

Power

I have no definite view of power to offer: only some fragmentary thoughts. I grant that, in an imperfect world, some raw use of power will always be with us. But as ours has become a huge, complex, institution-bound society, power seems more of an issue than it was in simpler times when it was easier to identify where coercive pressures came from. Also, within the past 200 years, the damage to power wielders has been clearly signaled—beginning with William Pitt's statement in the House of Commons in 1770, "Unlimited power is apt to corrupt the minds of those who possess it"; and then, in the late 19th century, Lord Acton's more quoted line, "Power tends to corrupt and absolute power corrupts absolutely." It is interesting to note that Lord Acton, a Catholic layman, made this statement in heated opposition to the assumption of Papal infallibility in 1870. And what is the corruption that both Pitt and Acton might have had in mind? I believe it is *arrogance,* and all of the disabilities that follow in the wake of arrogance.

In "The Servant as Leader," I tell of John Woolman, the 18th-century American Quaker who persuaded slaveholding Quakers, one by one, to free their slaves. Half his persuasive argument was concern for the slave, the other half was concern for the damage done to the slaveholder and his family. John Woolman also used the word *corruption* in referring to the legacy of the slaveholder to his heirs.

Along the way, in a conversation I had with the chief executive of a large business concerning the incentives that make his job attractive, he listed as first "The opportunity to wield power!" This came before monetary reward, prestige, service, and creative accomplishment—all of which, together, he said, would not compensate for carrying such a heavy burden.

A few years ago, a friend called to tell me that he had just been made head of a philanthropic foundation—his first work of this kind. My immediate response, drawing on my own considerable experience with foundations, was, "The first thing that will happen to you is that you will no longer know who your friends are." This is a serious disability.

I will never forget my first venture as a foundation representative when I made a tour of a dozen universities on a new grant program. My wife met me at the airport when I returned and asked how it went.

"I have no idea," was my reply.

"I have never experienced anything like this before. In most of my work life, I have had to do battle for my ideas every inch of the way, and nothing I have tried to do has been a pushover. But here, in these conversations with high-ranking officers of prestigious universities, every word I uttered was received as a pearl of wisdom." *This was a corrupting experience.*

I am aware that some foundation representatives seem to rise above this corrupting influence; but I hold that the power of the almoner is near the absolute; and it is corrupting, as I am sure all power is. If it were not so clear in my own experience, I would not be so sure of it.

Somehow, the young potential servant should be helped to an awareness of power and its consequences on both the wielder and the object. In my essay *Trustees as Servants,* I contend that "No one, *absolutely no one,* is to be entrusted with the operational use of power without the close oversight of fully functioning trustees." I would now generalize further and say that young potential servant-leaders should be advised to shun any power-wielding role which is not shared with able colleagues who are equals. (See *The Institution as Servant* for an elaboration of this thesis.) If a young potential servant-leader can accept that the first protection against the corruption of power is never to undertake a power-wielding role alone; if this can be established when one is young, a lifestyle may be built on this principle that will be easy and natural. It is not easy and natural for one who is deeply entrenched as a lone wielder of power to contemplate carrying a major responsible role without a firm grip on power—in one's own hands, *alone.* One who is firmly established as a chief executive officer (a lone power wielder) will almost universally say, "It won't work, one person *must* hold the ultimate power." But if enough of today's able young-sters catch the vision of servant-leadership and incorporate it into their lifestyles early, the day may come, when these people are in their prime years, that they will label, categorically, the current commonly accepted power striving of some successful people as *pathological*—because it makes for a sick society. Those who embrace the spirit of servant-leadership early in their lives are likely to take a similar view of competition—and come to see it as an aberration, not a normal human trait. And when enough able people take that view, it will make a different world. But that will take some time.

COMPETITION

It is difficult to know whether humankind's seemingly "normal" com-petitive urges are innate—the nature of the human animal—or whether they are acquired. It is difficult to know because the culture is so thoroughly competitive, and imposes its shaping imprint from infancy onward, that one cannot sort out what *homo sapiens* would be like if raised in a noncompetitive culture.

Recently I was on a panel in a conference in a medical school that was discussing the subject of "the ethics of the drug industry." In preparation for the conference, someone had made a video recording of drug ads on TV over a period of weeks; and we sat for 20 minutes watching these, one after another.

It is bad enough to have to look at these zany ads when they appear once in a while as the price of watching commercial TV. But to sit through 20 minutes of nothing else—well, it was nauseating, an affront to taste, intellect, and integrity; and the conference erupted in indigna-tion—"Something ought to be done about this!" After listening for a minute or two to this heated reaction I interjected with, "You shouldn't be so upset by these ads. As a nation, we have made a clear social pol-icy, backed by tough laws with criminal sanctions, that an industry like this will be *forced* to serve by requiring dog-eat-dog competition as a rule of doing business. When you decide to *force* service this way (and you really don't influence much but price), then you should not be surprised if you get a result like we have just witnessed."

The conference erupted again, "What would *you* do, repeal the antitrust laws?" And I answered, "I don't know what I would do. I have only one point: if you decree (and you have so decreed) that dog-eat-dog competition is to be the regulator, then do not be surprised if you get this kind of result. Anyway, what is so sacred about the antitrust laws? They were not brought down off the mountain chiseled in stone. They are crude man-made devices to deal with a clear social problem: how to elicit the best service we can get from a business. But there are several unhealthy by-products, one of which you have just seen." This promoted considerable discussion, without conclusion. And there is not likely to be a better answer to the question: How can we elicit optimal service from people and institutions, as long as competition is uncritically accepted as *good* and is deeply imbedded in the culture? In the preparation of young potential servants to be servant-leaders, the issue of competition must be critically examined and alternatives sought.

This is a curious bit of history of usage of the word *compete.* Modern usage puts it as "To strive or contend with another," while the Latin origin of the word is *competere*—to seek or strive together. The clear implications of the origin of this word is that competition is a cooperative rather than a contending relationship.

This reference may not help us to resolve our own personal dilemmas as we find ourselves in a struggle to beat out somebody else, in a society that supports that struggle with both moral and legal sanctions. (Recently I attended a conference on the subject of "The Judeo-Christian Ethic and the Modern Business Corporation." There were about 25 theologians of the major faiths present. In the papers and the discussions there was frequent reference to "unfair" competition, but I do not recall a single question by a theologian about competition per se.)

My position is: if we are to move toward a more caring, serving society than we now have, competition must be muted, if not eliminated. If theologians will not lead in this move (and I sense no initiative from that quarter), practicing servants will, and theologians will rationalize the result after the fact. The servant will be noncompetitive; but what can be the servant's affirmative position?

I believe that serving and competing are antithetical; the stronger the urge to serve, the less the interest in competing. (Read Petr Kropotkin's classic *Mutual Aid* for perspective on this issue.) The servant is importantly concerned with the consequences of his or her actions: those being served, *while being served* become healthier, wiser, freer, more autonomous, more likely themselves to become servants. *And,* what is the effect on the least privileged in society; will they benefit, or, at least, not be further deprived? *And,* no one will knowingly be hurt by the action?—the servant is strong *without* competing. But, unfortunately, we have decreed that ours shall be a competitive society. How does a servant function in such a society?

Servant-Leader: Strong *or* Weak?

The power-hungry person, who relishes competition and is good at it (meaning: usually wins) will probably judge the servant-leader, as I have described that person, to be weak or naïve or both. But let us look past the individual to the institution in which he or she serves: what (or who) makes that institution strong?

The strongest, most productive institution over a long period of time is one in which, other things being equal, there is the largest amount of voluntary action in support of the goals of the institution. The people who staff the institution do the "right" things at the right time—things that optimize total effectiveness—because the goals are clear and comprehensive and they understand what ought to be done. They believe they are the right things to do, and they take the necessary actions without being instructed. No institution ever achieves this perfectly. But I submit that, other things being equal, the institution that achieves the most of this kind of voluntary action will be judged *strong,* stronger than comparable institutions that have fewer of these voluntary actions.

Earlier, in the discussion of mind-sets, I gave the example of the more successful business in a highly competitive field that stands above its competitors in profitability, in the quality of the product it delivers, and in the absence of labor conflict that plagues all of the others. The principal difference is that this unusual company has more voluntary effort; its people do more, voluntarily, than other companies' people do for them. And it is not accidental. The man who built this business, dead for some years, put the people who worked for him *first*. As a consequence, his employees delivered all that people can deliver—and the business came to lead its field. It is a "people" business. There are other companies in other fields that have taken this view and, when other things are equal, they are all strong when compared with competitors who do not take this view of people.

From my own experience with businesses, I would say that even when "people first" is not the policy of the top executives, *"strong"* subordinate executives may take the "people first" position and add strength to the business. In AT&T, when we occasionally conducted attitude surveys, we noted what we called the "umbrella" effect. A strong subordinate manager would produce positive attitudes among his or her subordinates when the stance of higher level managers caused the prevailing attitudes in other parts of the company to be more negative. I believe that able subordinate managers who are servants can build strength in the people they lead even when the policy that is projected on them from above works to destroy it. But such subordinate managers must be really strong in terms of toughness, conviction, and tenacity.

Further, when there is a sticky organizational problem in a business, an astute power-wielding executive sometimes tries to find a person who is accepted as servant who will get into the situation and correct it—with persuasion. *And for purely practical reasons*: it comes out better than if somebody swings on it in a coercive or manipulative way!

Both the words *servant* and *persuasion* are "soft" words to some people. They do not connote the tough attitudes that are thought to be needed to hold this world together and get its work done.

In 1970, when I chose to advocate, in writing, the servant-leader concept, both words *serve* and *lead* were in a shadow. *Lead* seems to have recovered some stature, but *serve* is still questioned by many thoughtful people. I chose to stay with *serve, lead,* and *persuade* because I see, through the meaning they have for me, a path to restoring much of the dignity that has been lost through the depersonalization that industrialization has brought to us. And dignity adds strength both to individuals and to the institutions of which they are a part—strength to serve.

PROSPECTS *for the* SERVANT IDEA—
SOME SPECULATIONS

In much of what I have written on the servant theme, including most of this essay, I have dealt with issues of leadership and institution building. After ten years of circulation of these writings and considerable interaction about them with people who have their hands on the levers of power and influence, I am not persuaded that much movement toward our society becoming more caring is likely to be initiated by those who are now established as leaders. Mind-sets like the four discussed earlier are much too prevalent and entrenched, and we seem not to have the resources to generate, or the openness to receive, liberating visions. Whatever older people can do to make ours a more serving, caring society should be encouraged; but I do not expect much from my contemporaries.

We (some of us) do know how to prepare and inspire young people to press the limits of the reasonable and possible, with some of them becoming skilled builders of more serving institutions. The overarching vision that will inspire and energize mentors of the young is my prime concern. These mentors are strong, able people who believe that well-prepared young people, in whom servant-leadership is an integral part of their lifestyles, are likely to bring to reality some of what we oldsters can only dream about.

My hope for the future, and I do have hope, is that some (perhaps many) young people whose lifestyles may yet be shaped by conscious choices may be helped to more serving roles than most of their elders occupy today. What I have written is not likely to give this help directly to young people. But it may be useful to those who have the gifts and the will and the courage to be mentors of the young. And I believe that the psychic rewards to these mentors can be very great. What could bring more satisfaction to oldsters than helping some of the young to become servant-leaders?

In *Teacher as Servant*, I described in detail how a university teacher could, without the support of university or colleagues, encourage, in a decisive way, the growth as servant of a large number of students. I hazarded a guess that, if there were a way to alert them to the opportunity, perhaps as many as one in a thousand of the 500,000 or so university and college faculty in the United States might take the initiative to give this precious help to students. And I reasoned that the 500, if they worked at it over a career, could favor the time of the next generation becoming a golden age of leadership in our country. It can be done without adding to college and university budgets. It would require no changes in the curriculum, no administrative or faculty actions, no trustee initiatives. All that is needed is a handful, really, of determined and perceptive faculty members who, deep down inside, are true servants and who, without extra compensation and recognition—perhaps in the face of some opposition—will *lead* in this most fundamental way. They will go out ahead to show, by their example, how one may be a servant in what appears to be a cold, low-caring, highly competitive, violence-prone society. These servant teachers may be a saving remnant, in the biblical sense. And saving remnants are usually not empowered, approved, or well-financed.

I would now amend the language of this assertion in just one particular way. In place of "alert them (the one in a thousand teachers) to the opportunity" I would substitute "inspire them with a vision of the opportunity."

One who might respond to this suggestion is the president, especially in a small college; but it also might be a large university. The president might personally offer to lead a noncredit seminar for elected student leaders. The agenda of the seminar might be discussions with invited resource people and sharing between the president and these student leaders on matters of mutual concern in their current leadership roles. In my conversations with student leaders, I have found them concerned with some of the same issues that are on the minds of presidents—matters of the spirit. Presidents might find in these seminars a helpful close contact with students, and students would have the opportunity to learn about leadership from each other and from the president—experientially. The president may learn something about leadership, too—a new perspective on that job.

The prospect for the servant idea rests almost entirely, I believe, on some among us *investing the energy and taking the risks to inspire with a vision*. In our large and complex society, a single compelling prophetic voice may not, as Grundtvig did in 19th-century Denmark, move those few who will educate and inspire enough young people to rebuild the entire culture. In our times, the orchestration of many prophetic visionaries may be required. But I believe that the ultimate effect will be the same: *teachers* (individuals, not institutions) will be inspired to raise the society-building consciousness of the young. And *teachers* may be anybody who can reach young people who have the potential to be servants and prepare them to be servant leaders. These teachers may be members of school faculties, presidents of colleges and universities, those working with young people in churches. Some may be parents, others may be either professionals or volunteers working with youth groups. But whoever and wherever they are, these teachers will catch the vision and *do what they know how to do.* First, they will reinforce or build hope. Young people will be helped to accept the world, and to believe that they can learn to live productively in it *as it is*—striving, violent, unjust, as well as beautiful, caring, and supportive. They will be helped to believe that they can cope, and that, if they work at it over a lifetime, they may leave a little corner of the world a bit better than they found it. Then these teachers will nourish the embryo spark of servant in as many as possible and help prepare those who are able—*to lead!*

Reflecting on Myself as a *Servant-Leader*

1. How would I rate my comprehension of the servant-leader concept?
   - I totally get it and apply it.
   - I totally get it but am still struggling with application.
   - I kind of get it, I'm kind of doing it . . . I think . . . maybe.
   - I'm not sure exactly what it means, much less using it (or maybe I am but am not aware of it).

2. In what ways did Jesus pioneer the concept of servant-leadership?

3. In which environments is it easier to lead as a servant and in which is it more difficult?

4. What are the most common misconceptions about servant-leadership?

Tasks

> To have "a sense
> of where the
> whole enterprise
> is going and
> must go" is, I am
> inclined to say,
> the very core
> and essence of
> leadership.

L EADERSHIP IS HARD WORK. WE
sometimes tend to get caught up in the glamour, prestige, and power of being the one in charge. But if we strip away all those trappings (much of which is illusion, anyway), we find underneath the essentials, the nuts-and-bolts everyday work that leaders do day in and day out. We find the tasks of leadership.

The primary definition of the word *task*, according to *Webster's*, is "a usually assigned piece of work often to be finished within a certain time." It comes from the Latin word *tasca*, which in the Middle Ages was a tax or service imposed by the lord of a feudal estate. Synonyms are *duty, job, chore*, and *assignment*. In our discussion, tasks are the actions required by the very position of leadership, the duties that a leader must perform in order to accomplish the overall goals of the organization.

John W. Gardner, a giant in the field of leadership study who has served presidents, worked in academia, and consulted in American business, identifies in this selection from *On Leadership* nine tasks that form the core of a leader's activities. They

It would be easy to imagine that the tasks described are items to be handled separately, like nine items on a shopping list, each from a separate store. But the effective leader is always doing several tasks simultaneously.

help us answer the question, "What does a leader do every day?" Whether written or unwritten, these tasks form the job description for leaders of every variety. Not only does Gardner approach this topic with dead-on accuracy and practicality; he's also a gifted writer who has the ability to treat words as a valuable commodity in the communication process.

The Tasks *of* Leadership

• • •

John W. Gardner

Examination of the tasks performed by leaders takes us to the heart of some of the most interesting questions concerning leadership. It also helps to distinguish among the many kinds of leaders. Leaders differ strikingly in how well they perform various functions.

The following nine tasks seem to me to be the most significant functions of leadership, but I encourage readers to add to the list or to describe the tasks in other ways. Leadership activities implicit in all of the tasks (e.g., communicating, relating effectively with people) are not dealt with separately.

ENVISIONING GOALS

The two tasks at the heart of the popular notion of leadership are goal setting and motivating. As a high school senior put it, "Leaders point us in the right direction and tell us to get moving." Although we take a more complicated view of the tasks of leadership, it is appropriate that we begin with the envisioning of goals. Albert Einstein said, "Perfection of means and confusion of ends seems to characterize our age."

Leaders perform the function of goal setting in diverse ways. Some assert a vision of what the group (organization, community, nation) can be at its best. Others point us toward solutions to our problems. Still others, presiding over internally divided groups, are able to define overarching goals that unify constituencies and focus energies. In today's complex world, the setting of goals may have to be preceded by extensive research and problem solving.

Obviously, a constituency is not a blank slate for the leader to write on. Any collection of people sufficiently related to be called a community has many shared goals, some explicit, some unexpressed (perhaps even unconscious), as tangible as better prices for their crops, as intangible as a better future for their children. In a democracy, the leader takes such shared goals into account.

The relative roles of leaders and followers in determining goals varies from group to group. The teacher of first-grade children and the sergeant training recruits do not do extensive consulting as to goals; congressional candidates do a great deal. In the case of many leaders, goals are handed to them by higher authority. The factory manager and the combat commander may be superb leaders, but many of their goals are set at higher levels.

In short, goals emerge from many sources. The culture itself specifies certain goals; constituents have their concerns; higher authority makes its wishes known. Out of the welter, leaders take some goals as given, and making their own contribution, select and formulate a set of objectives. It may sound as though leaders have only marginal freedom, but in fact there is usually considerable opportunity, even for lower-level leaders, to put their personal emphasis and interpretation on the setting of goals.

There is inevitable tension between long- and short-term goals. On the one hand, constituents are not entirely comfortable with the jerkiness of short-term goal seeking, and they value the sense of stability that comes with a vision of far horizons. On the other hand, long-term goals may require them to defer immediate gratification on at least some fronts. Leaders often fear that when citizens enter the voting booth, they will remember the deferral of gratification more vividly than they remember the reason for it.

Before the Civil War, Elizabeth Cady Stanton saw virtually the whole agenda for women's rights as it was to emerge over the succeeding century. Many of her contemporaries in the movement were not at all prepared for such an inclusive vision and urged her to play it down.

Another visionary far ahead of his time was the South American liberator, Simon Bolívar. He launched his fight in that part of Gran Colombia which is now Venezuela, but in his mind was a vision not only of independence for all of Spain's possessions in the New World, but also a peaceful alliance of the new states in some form of league or confederation. Although he was tragically ahead of his time, the dream never died and has influenced generations of Latin American leaders striving toward unity.

AFFIRMING VALUES

A great civilization is a drama lived in the minds of a people. It is a shared vision; it is shared norms, expectations, and purposes. When one thinks of the world's great civilizations, the most vivid images that crowd in on us are apt to be of the physical monuments left behind—the Pyramids, the Parthenon, the Mayan temples. But in truth, all the physical splendor was the merest by-product. The civilizations themselves, from beginning to end, existed in the minds of men and women.

If we look at ordinary human communities, we see the same reality: A community lives in the minds of its members—in shared assumptions, beliefs, customs, ideas that give meaning, ideas that motivate. And among the ideas are norms or values. In any healthy, reasonably coherent community, people come to have shared views concerning right and wrong, better and worse—in personal conduct, in governing, in art, whatever. They define for their time and place what things are legal or illegal, virtuous or vicious, good taste or bad. They have little or no impulse to be neutral about such matters. Every society is, as Philip Rieff puts it, "a system of moralizing demands."[1]

Values are embodied in the society's religious beliefs and its secular philosophy. Over the past century, many intellectuals have looked down on the celebration of our values as an unsophisticated and often hypocritical activity. But every healthy society celebrates its values. They are expressed in art, in song, in ritual. They are stated explicitly in historical documents, in ceremonial speeches, in textbooks. They are reflected in stories told around the campfire, in the legends kept alive by old folks, in the fables told to children.

In a pluralistic community there are, within the broad consensus that enables the community to function, many and vigorous conflicts over specific values.

The Regeneration of Values

One of the milder pleasures of maturity is bemoaning the decay of once strongly held values. *Values always decay over time. Societies that keep their values alive do so not by escaping the processes of decay but by powerful processes of regeneration.* There must be perpetual rebuilding. Each generation must rediscover the living elements in its own tradition and adapt them to present realities. To assist in that rediscovery is one of the tasks of leadership.

The leaders whom we admire the most help to revitalize our shared beliefs and values. They have always spent a portion of their time teaching the value framework.

Sometimes the leader's affirmation of values challenges entrenched hypocrisy or conflicts with the values held by a segment of the constituency. Elizabeth Cady Stanton, speaking for now-accepted values, was regarded as a thoroughgoing radical in her day.[2] Jesus not only comforted the afflicted but afflicted the comfortable.

MOTIVATING

Leaders do not create motivation out of thin air. They unlock or channel existing motives. Any group has a great tangle of motives. Effective leaders tap those that serve the purposes of collective action in pursuit of shared goals. They accomplish the alignment of individual and group goals. They deal with the circumstances that often lead group members to withhold their best efforts. They call for the kind of effort and restraint, drive and discipline that make for great performance. They create a climate in which there is pride in making significant contributions to shared goals.

Note that in the tasks of leadership, the transactions between leaders and constituents go beyond the rational level to the nonrational and unconscious levels of human functioning. Young potential leaders who have been schooled to believe that all elements of a problem are rational and technical, reducible to words and numbers, are ill-equipped to move into an area where intuiting and empathy are powerful aids to problem solving.

MANAGING

Most managers exhibit some leadership skills, and most leaders on occasion find themselves managing. Leadership and management are not the same thing, but they overlap. It makes sense to include managing in the list of tasks leaders perform.

In the paragraphs that follow I focus on those aspects of leadership that one might describe as managing without slipping into a conventional description of managing as such. And I try to find terminology and phrasing broad enough to cover the diverse contexts in which leadership occurs in corporations, unions, municipalities, political movements, and so on.

1. *Planning and Priority Setting.* Assuming that broad goals have been set, someone has to plan, fix priorities, choose means, and formulate policy. These are functions often performed by leaders. When Lyndon B. Johnson said, early in his presidency, that education was the nation's number one priority, he galvanized the nation's education leaders and released constructive energies far beyond any governmental action that had yet been taken. It was a major factor in leading me to accept a post in his Cabinet.

2. *Organizing and Institution Building.* We have all seen leaders enjoy their brilliant moment and then disappear without a trace because they had no gift for building their purposes into institutions. In the ranks of leaders, Alfred Sloan was at the other extreme. Though he sold a lot of automobiles, he was not primarily a salesman; he was an institution builder. His understanding of organization was intuitive and profound.

Someone has to design the structures and processes through which substantial endeavors get accomplished over time. Ideally, leaders should not regard themselves as indispensable but should enable the group to carry on. Institutions are a means to that end. Jean Monnet said, "Nothing is possible without individuals; nothing is lasting without institutions."[3]

3. *Keeping the System Functioning.* Presiding over the arrangements through which individual energies are coordinated to achieve shared goals sounds like a quintessential management task. But it is clear that most leaders find themselves occasionally performing one or another of the essential chores; mobilizing and allocating resources; staffing and ensuring the continuing vitality of the team; creating and maintaining appropriate procedures; directing, delegating and coordinating; providing a system of incentives; reporting, evaluating and holding accountable.

4. *Agenda Setting and Decision Making.* The goals may be clear and the organization well set up and smoothly operating, but there remain

agenda-setting and decision-making functions that must be dealt with. The announcement of goals without a proposed program for meeting them is a familiar enough political phenomenon—but not one that builds credibility. There are leaders who can motivate and inspire but who cannot visualize a path to the goal in practical, feasible steps. Leaders who lack that skill must bring onto their team people who have it.

One of the purest examples of the leader as agenda setter was Florence Nightingale.[4] Her public image was and is that of the lady of mercy, but under her gentle manner, she was a rugged spirit, a fighter, a tough-minded system changer. She never made public appearances or speeches, and except for her two years in the Crimea, held no public position. Her strength was that she was a formidable authority on the evils to be remedied, she knew what to do about them, and she used public opinion to goad top officials to adopt her agenda.

5. *Exercising Political Judgment.* In our pluralistic society, persons directing substantial enterprises find that they are presiding over many constituencies within their organizations and contending with many outside. Each has its needs and claims. One of the tasks of the leader/ manager is to make the political judgments necessary to prevent secondary conflicts of purpose from blocking progress toward primary goals. Sometimes the literature on administration and management treats politics as an alien and disruptive force. But Aaron Wildavsky, in his brilliant book, *The Nursing Father: Moses as a Political Leader,* makes the point that leaders are inevitably political.[5]

Achieving Workable Unity

A pluralistic society is, by definition, one that accepts many different elements, each with its own purposes. Collisions are inevitable and often healthy—as in commercial competition, in civil suits, and in efforts to redress grievances through the political process. Conflict is necessary in the case of oppressed groups that must fight for the justice that is due them. All our elective officials know the intense conflict of the political campaign. Indeed, one could argue that willingness to engage in battle when necessary is a sine qua non of leadership.

But most leaders most of the time are striving to diminish conflict rather than increase it. Some measure of cohesion and mutual tolerance is an absolute requirement of social functioning.

Sometimes the problem is not outright conflict but an unwilling-ness to cooperate. One of the gravest problems George Washington faced as a general was that the former colonies, though they had no doubt they were all on the same side, were not always sure they wanted to cooperate. As late as 1818, John Randolph declared, "When I speak of my country, I mean the Commonwealth of Virginia."[6]

The unifying function of leaders is well illustrated in the actions of George Bush after winning the presidential election of 1988. He promptly met with his defeated opponent, Michael Dukakis; with his chief rival for the nomination, Senator Robert Dole; and with Jesse Jackson and Coretta Scott King, both of whom had opposed his elec-tion. He asked Jack Kemp, another of his rivals for the nomination, to be Secretary of Housing and Urban Development, and Senator Doles' wife, Elizabeth Hanford Dole, to be Secretary of Labor.

Leaders in this country today must cope with the fragmentation of the society into groups that have great difficulty in understanding one another or agreeing on common goals. It is a fragmentation rooted in the pluralism of our society, in the obsessive specialization of mod-ern life, and in the skill with which groups organize to advance their concerns.

Under the circumstances, all our leaders must spend part of their time dealing with polarization and building community. There is a false notion that this is a more bland, less rigorous task than leader-ship of one of the combative segments. In fact, the leader willing to combat polarization is the braver person, and is generally under fire from both sides. I would suggest that Jean Monnet, the father of the European Common Market, is a useful model for future leaders. When there were conflicting purposes Monnet saw the possibility of shared goals, and he knew how to move his contemporaries toward those shared goals.

Trust

Much depends on the general level of trust in the organization or society. The infinitely varied and complex doings of the society—any society—would come to a halt if people did not trust other peo-ple most of the time—trust them to observe custom, follow the rules, and behave with some predictability. Countless circumstances operate to diminish that trust, but one may be sure that if the society is functioning at all, *some* degree of trust survives.

Leaders can do much to preserve the necessary level of trust. And the first requirement is that they have the capacity to inspire trust in themselves. In sixteenth-century Italy, where relations among the warring kingdoms were an unending alley fight, Machiavelli's chilling advice to the Prince—"It is necessary . . . to be a feigner and a dissembler," or, as another translator renders the same passage, "You must be a great liar and hypocrite"—may have been warranted.[7] And, under conditions of iron rule, Hitler and Stalin were able to live by betrayals. But in our society, leaders must work to raise the level of trust.

EXPLAINING

Explaining sounds too pedestrian to be on a list of leadership tasks, but every leader recognizes it. People want to know what the problem is, why they are being asked to do certain things, why they face so many frustrations. Thurman Arnold said, "Unhappy is a people that has run out of words to describe what is happening to them."[8] Leaders find the words.

To be heard above the hubbub in the public forum today, explaining generally requires more than clarity and eloquence. It requires effective access to the media of communication or to those segments of the population that keep ideas in circulation—editors, writers, intellectuals, association leaders, advocacy groups, chief executive officers, and the like.

The task of explaining is so important that some who do it exceptionally well play a leadership role even though they are not leaders in the conventional sense. When the American colonies were struggling for independence, Thomas Paine was a memorable explainer. In the powerful environmentalist surge of the 1960s and 70s, no activist leader had as pervasive an influence on the movement as did Rachel Carson, whose book *Silent Spring* burst on the scene in 1963.[9] Betty Friedan's *The Feminine Mystique* played a similar role for the women's movement.[10]

Leaders teach. Lincoln, in his second inaugural address, provided an extraordinary example of the leader as teacher. Teaching and leading are distinguishable occupations, but every great leader is clearly teaching—and every great teacher is leading.

SERVING *as a* SYMBOL

Leaders are inevitably symbols. Workers singled out to be supervisors discover that they are set apart from their old comrades in subtle ways. They try to keep the old camaraderie but things have changed. They are now symbols of management. Sergeants symbolize the chain of command. Parish religious leaders symbolize their churches.

In a group threatened with internal strife, the leader may be a crucial symbol of unity. In a minority group's struggle to find its place, combative leaders—troublesome to others—may be to their own people the perfect symbol of their anger and their struggle.

The top leader of a community or nation symbolizes the group's collective identity and continuity. For this reason, the death of a president produces a special reaction of grief and loss. Americans who were beyond childhood when John F. Kennedy was assassinated remember, despite the passage of decades, precisely where they were and what they were doing when the news reached them. Even for many who did not admire him, the news had the impact of a blow to the solar plexus. And those old enough to remember Franklin D. Roosevelt's death recognize the reaction.

For late eighteenth-century Americans, George Washington was the symbol of all that they had been through together. Thomas Jefferson became such a powerful symbol of our democratic aspirations that for generations politicians fought over his memory. Those who favored Hamiltonian views sought bitterly and unsuccessfully to shatter the Jefferson image. As Merrill Peterson has cogently argued, the man himself lost reality and the symbol took over.[11] In the dark days of the Great Depression, the American impulse to face events in a positive spirit found its symbol in the ebullient Franklin D. Roosevelt.

Outside the political area, Albert Schweitzer, the gifted theologian and musician who in 1913 gave up a comfortable and respected life in this native Germany to spend the remainder of his years presiding over a medical mission in Equatorial Africa, stands as the pristine example of leader as symbol.

Some individuals newly risen to leadership have a hard time adjusting to the reality that they are symbols. I recall a visit with a young college president who had just come into the job fresh from a professorship, with no prior administrative experience. He confided that he was deeply irked by an incident the preceding day. In his first speech before faculty, students, trustees and alumni he had simply been himself—a man of independent mind full of lively personal opinions—and many of his listeners were nonplussed and irritated. They were not interested in a display of idiosyncratic views. They had expected him to speak as their new leader, their symbol of institutional continuity, their ceremonial collective voice. I told him gently that they had expected him to be their spokesman and symbol, and this simply angered him further. "I'll resign," he said, "if I can't be myself!" Over time, he learned that leaders can rarely afford the luxury of speaking for themselves alone.

Most leaders become quite aware of the symbolic aspects of their roles and make effective use of them. One of the twentieth-century leaders who did so most skillfully was Gandhi.[12] In the issues he chose to do battle on, in the way he conducted his campaigns, in the jail terms and the fasting, in his manner of dress, he symbolized his people, their desperate need, and their struggle against oppression.

Needless to say leaders do not always function as benign symbols. In the Iran-Contra affair of 1986–87 it became apparent that men bound by their oath of office were lying to the public, lying to the Congress of the United States, and lying to one another. To some Americans they became symbols of all the falsehoods and betrayals committed by a distant and distrusted government.

Representing *the* Group

In quieter times (we love to imagine that there were quieter times) leaders could perhaps concentrate on their own followers. Today, representing the group in its dealings with others is a substantial leadership task.

It is a truism that all of the human systems (organizations, groups, communities) that make up the society and the world are increasingly interdependent. Virtually all leaders at every level must carry on dealings with systems external to the one in which they themselves are involved—tasks of representing and negotiating, of defending institutional integrity, of public relations. As one moves higher in the ranks of leadership, such chores increase.

It goes without saying that people who have spent their careers in the world of the specialist or within the boundaries of a narrow community (their firm, their profession) are often ill-equipped for such leadership tasks. The young potential leader must learn early to cross boundaries and to know many worlds. The attributes that enable leaders to teach and lead their own constituencies may be wholly ineffective in external dealings. Military leaders who are revered by their troops may be clumsy with civilians. The business leader who is effective within the business culture may be lost in dealing with politicians. A distinctive characteristic of the ablest leaders is that they do not shrink from external representation. They see the long-term needs and goals of their constituency in the broadest context, and they act accordingly. The most capable mayors think not just of that city but of the metropolitan area and the region. Able business leaders are alert to the political climate and to world economic trends.

The most remarkable modern example of a leader carrying out the representative function is Charles DeGaulle. DeGaulle has his detractors, but none can fail to marvel at his performance in successfully representing the once and future France-as-a-great-power at a time when the nation itself was a defeated, demoralized, enemy-occupied land. By his own commanding presence, he kept France's place at the table through the dark days. Years later Jean Monnet wrote:

> It took great strength of character for him, a traditional soldier, to cross the great dividing line of disobedience to orders from above. He was the only man of his rank with the courage to do so; and in the painful isolation felt by those Frenchmen who had decided to continue the Allied struggle, DeGaulle's rare example was a source of great moral strength.[13]

RENEWING

Leaders need not be renewers. They can lead people down old paths, using old slogans, toward old objectives. Sometimes that is appropriate. But the world changes with disconcerting swiftness. Too often the old paths are blocked and the old solutions no longer solve anything. DeGaulle, writing of France's appalling unpreparedness for World War II, said:

> The Army became stuck in a set of ideas which had had their heyday before the end of the First World War. It was all the more inclined that way because its leaders were growing old at their posts, wedded to errors that had once constituted their glory.[14]

Leaders must foster the process of renewal.

So much for the tasks of leadership. The individual with a gift for building a leadership team may successfully delegate one or another of those tasks to other members of the team. One function that cannot be delegated is that of serving as symbol. That the leader is a symbol is a fact, not a matter of choice. The task is to take appropriate account of that reality and to use it well in the service of the group's goals.

Another function that cannot be delegated entirely is the envisioning of goals. Unless the leader has a sense of where the whole enterprise is going and must go, it is not possible to delegate (or carry out personally) the other functions. To have "a sense of where the whole enterprise is going and must go" is, I am inclined to say, the very core and essence of the best leadership.

In a discussion of the tasks of leadership, a colleague of mine said, "I do not see 'enabling' or 'empowering' on the list. Aren't those the central tasks of leadership?" For those unfamiliar with contemporary discussions of leadership, I should explain that reference to *enabling* or *empowering* has become the preferred method of condensing into a single word the widely held conviction that the purpose of leaders is not to dominate nor diminish followers but to strengthen and help them to develop.

But enabling and empowering are not separable tasks. They require a variety of actions on the parts of leaders. For example:

- Sharing information and making it possible for followers to obtain appropriate kinds of education
- Sharing power by devolving initiative and responsibility

- Building the confidence of followers so that they can achieve their own goals through their own efforts
- Removing barriers to the release of individual energy and talent
- Seeking, finding, and husbanding the various kinds of resources that followers need
- Resolving the conflicts that paralyze group action
- Providing organizational arrangements appropriate to group effort

Any attempt to describe a social process as complex as leadership inevitably makes it seem more orderly than it is. Leadership is not tidy. Decisions are made and then revised or reversed. Misunderstandings are frequent, inconsistency inevitable. Achieving a goal may simply make the next goal more urgent: inside every solution are the seeds of new problems. And as Donald Michael has pointed out, most of the time most things are out of hand.[15] No leader enjoys that reality, but every leader knows it.

It would be easy to imagine that the tasks described are items to be handled separately, like nine items on a shopping list, each from a separate store. But the effective leader is always doing several tasks simultaneously. The best antidote to the shopping list conception is to look at the setting in which all the tasks are mingled—the complex interplay between leaders and those "led."

Reflecting on the *Tasks* of My Leadership

1. Am I a good motivator? Would those with whom I work most closely agree or disagree?
2. What is the difference between intrinsic and extrinsic motivation, and how does a leader practice both?
3. Do all managers lead, and do all leaders manage? In what ways?

Notes

1. Philip Rieff, *The Triumph of the Therapeutic* (New York: Harper and Row, 1966).

2. Elisabeth Griffith, *In Her Own Right: The Life of Elizabeth Cady Stanton* (New York: Oxford University Press, 1984).

3. Jean Monnet, *Memoirs,* trans. Richard Mayne (New York: Doubleday Publishing, 1978).

4. Elspeth Huxley, *Florence Nightingale* (New York: G. P. Putnam's Sons, 1975).

5. Aaron Wildavsky, *The Nursing Father: Moses as a Political Leader* (Tuscaloosa: University of Alabama Press, 1984).

6. William Cabell Bruce, *John Randolph of Roanoke* (New York: Putnam, 1922).

7. Niccolò Machiavelli, *The Prince* (New York: New American Library, 1952), p. 93.

8. Thurman Arnold, *The Folklore of Capitalism* (New Haven: Yale University Press, 1937).

9. Rachel Carson, *Silent Spring* (New York: Houghton Mifflin, 1963).

10. Betty Friedan, *The Feminine Mystique* (New York: Dell, 1963).

11. Merrill D. Peterson, *The Jefferson Image in the American Mind* (New York: Oxford University Press, 1960).

12. Erik Erikson, *Gandhi's Truth* (New York: W. W. Norton, 1969); Mohandas D. Gandhi, *An Autobiography* (Boston Beacon Press, 1957).

13. Monnet, *Memoirs,* p. 147.

14. Charles DeGaulle, *The War Memoirs, 1940–1946* (New York: Simon & Schuster, 1964), I:7.

15. Donald M. Michael, "Competence and Compassion in an Age of Uncertainty," *World Future Society Bulletin,* January–February 1983.

Flexibility

"I have always
felt that managers
who restricted
themselves to
either extreme
were only 'half
a manager.' . . .
A whole manager
is flexible and is
able to use four
different leader-
ship styles."

Y
OU PROBABLY NEED NO INTRODUCTION
to Ken Blanchard, CEO of The Blanchard
Companies. From *The One Minute Manager* and
his other best-selling books to his academic contributions and commitment, Blanchard has made a
name for himself as one of the most effective com-
municators of simple, practical business truth.
When people read Blanchard or hear him speak,
they say "Got it" and know immediately what to
do. Part of his effectiveness is the no-nonsense
applicability of his ideas; part of it is his engaging,
creative style of presentation. If you haven't read
any of his books already, you'll notice in this selection that he uses dialogue between fictional characters to make his points, a technique that draws
readers into the conversation.

The chapter we've selected, from *Leadership
and the One Minute Manager,* is essentially a synop-
sis of the idea around which he's built many books:
the four leadership styles. In contrast to what some
experts say, Blanchard asserts that there is no one
single leadership style that is right all the time. The
best leaders, he says, combine different amounts of

"A *directing* leadership style is better with *enthusiastic beginners* whereas *coaching* is the right style for *disillusioned learners.*"
"Experienced people like to be listened to and supported."

authoritarianism and cheerleading in their approach to each person and situation; it is this combination that results in the four categories: directing, coaching, supporting, and delegating. The degree to which a leader can show flexibility in adopting these behaviors will in large part determine how effective he or she is.

But even beyond Blanchard's considerable contribution to the world of business literature, we also wanted to include him in this compilation because he is a great example of what we advocate. In recent years he has become deliberate and intentional about blending faith and leadership and helping people understand how they can do that as well. We've gotten the sense that he's on a spiritual pilgrimage and is inviting others to join him in that journey.

Leadership Style Flexibility

• • •

Ken Blanchard, Patricia Zigarmi, & Drea Zigarmi

"A situational leader . . ." That phrase kept going through the entrepreneur's mind as she headed back to the One Minute Manager's office. When she arrived, Mrs. Johnson ushered her in to see the One Minute Manager.

"Well, how did I do?" asked the One Minute Manager.

"Just fine," said the entrepreneur. "Your philosophy of Different Strokes for Different Folks is alive and well. And what's more, your folks don't seem to mind being treated differently. How can I become a situational leader?"

"You need to learn three skills," said the One Minute Manager.

"I knew you would have it down to some simple formula," the entrepreneur teased.

"I'm not sure it's so simple," chuckled the One Minute Manager, "but there are three skills involved. You have to learn how to diagnose the needs of the people you work with. You have to learn to use a variety of leadership styles flexibly. And you have to learn how to come to some agreements with them about the leadership style they need from you. In other words, the three skills are: *flexibility, diagnosis,* and *partnering.*"

"Sounds fascinating," said the entrepreneur. "Where do I start?"

"We usually start by teaching people about flexibility," said the One Minute Manager. "That's why I sent you to talk to some of my people—to find out about the different leadership styles I use with them."

"I thought I had a handle on your styles until I talked to DaLapa," said the entrepreneur.

"What do you mean?" asked the One Minute Manager.

"I thought you were either autocratic or democratic," said the entrepreneur, "but that didn't fit with DaLapa."

"That always surprises people," said the One Minute Manager. "For a long time people thought there were only two leadership styles—autocratic and democratic. In fact, people used to shout at each other from these two extremes, insisting that one style was better than the other. Democratic managers were accused of being too soft and easy, while their autocratic counterparts were often called too tough and domineering. But I have always felt that managers who restricted themselves to either extreme were only 'half a manager.'"

"What makes someone a whole manager?" asked the entrepreneur.

"A whole manager is flexible and is able to use four different leadership styles," said the One Minute Manager as he showed the entrepreneur a sheet of paper.

THE FOUR BASIC
LEADERSHIP STYLES ARE:

Style 1: DIRECTING

THE LEADER PROVIDES SPECIFIC DIRECTION AND CLOSELY
MONITORS TASK ACCOMPLISHMENT.

Style 2: COACHING

THE LEADER CONTINUES TO DIRECT AND CLOSELY MONITOR
TASK ACCOMPLISHMENT, BUT ALSO EXPLAINS DECISIONS,
SOLICITS SUGGESTIONS, AND SUPPORTS PROGRESS.

Style 3: SUPPORTING

THE LEADER FACILITATES AND SUPPORTS PEOPLE'S EFFORTS
TOWARD TASK ACCOMPLISHMENT AND SHARES RESPONSI-
BILITY FOR DECISION-MAKING WITH THEM.

Style 4: DELEGATING

THE LEADER TURNS OVER RESPONSIBILITY FOR DECISION-
MAKING AND PROBLEM-SOLVING TO PEOPLE.

As the entrepreneur studied the information on the sheet of paper, the One Minute Manager began to explain it.

"These four styles consist of different combinations of two basic leadership behaviors that a manager can use when trying to influence someone else: *Directive Behavior* and *Supportive Behavior.* Four words can be used to define Directive Behavior: STRUCTURE, ORGANIZE, TEACH, and SUPERVISE. Different words are used to describe Supportive Behavior: PRAISE, LISTEN, ASK, EXPLAIN, and FACILITATE."

"Directive behavior seems to be related to autocratic leadership," said the entrepreneur.

"Precisely," said the One Minute Manager. "It's largely one-way communication. You tell the person what, when, where, and how to do something and then you closely monitor the person on the problem or task."

"That sounds exactly like the way you are managing McKenzie," said the entrepreneur. "You're using a Style 1."

"You're right," said the One Minute Manager. "We refer to Style 1 as *directing* because when you use that style you are high on directive behavior but low on supportive behavior. You tell the person what the goal is and what a good job looks like, but you also lay out a step-by-step plan about how the task is to be accomplished. You solve the problem. You make the decisions; the person carries out your ideas."

"But that's not the style you've been using with Murrow. You've been more supportive, more democratic."

"You've got it," said the One Minute Manager. "That's why we call Style 3, which is high on supportive behavior but low on directive behavior, *supporting.* You support your people's efforts, listen to their suggestions, and facilitate their interactions with others. And to build up their confidence and motivation, you encourage and praise. Rarely do Style 3 managers talk about how they would go about solving a particular problem or accomplishing a particular task. They help their people reach their own solutions by asking questions that expand their thinking and encourage risk-taking."

"But isn't it inconsistent to treat McKenzie one way and Murrow another, not to mention DaLapa?" asked the young woman.

"I believe in being consistent, but I think I have a different definition of consistency. It sounds as if your definition is 'treating everybody the same way.' My definition is 'using the same leadership style in similar situations.'"

"But isn't it unfair to treat people differently?" asked the entrepreneur.

The One Minute Manager pointed to a plaque on the wall.

There Is Nothing

So Unequal

As The Equal Treatment

Of

Unequals

"You must be a fan of Emerson," said the young woman. "He said, 'A foolish consistency is the hobgoblin of little minds.'"

The One Minute Manager smiled. "That's always been one of my favorite sayings."

"Just to clarify in my mind the four styles you described, could you give me an example of each?" asked the entrepreneur.

"Sure," said the One Minute Manager. "Suppose there was some noise in the outside office that was bothering us. If I said to you, 'Please go out now and tell Mrs. Johnson to get those people to move their conversation down the hall and when you've done that report back to me,' what leadership style would that be?"

"A *directing style*," said the entrepreneur. "How would you deal with the noise if you wanted to use a *supporting style?*"

"I'd say something like 'There's noise in the outside office that's bothering us—what do you think we could do about it?'"

"I see," said the entrepreneur. "What about Style 2?"

"*Coaching* combines both direction and support," said the One Minute Manager. "If I wanted to use a coaching style in handling the noise I would say, 'There's a lot of noise in the outside office that's bothering us. I think you should go outside and ask Mrs. Johnson to tell those people to move their conversation down the hall. Do you have any questions or suggestions?'"

"So with a *coaching* style," said the entrepreneur, "you begin to engage in two-way communication by asking for suggestions. Does the manager end up making the final decision?"

"Absolutely," said the One Minute Manager, "but you get input from others. You also provide a lot of support because some of the ideas they suggest are good and as a manager you always want to reinforce initiative and risk-taking. That's where the listening and encouraging comes in. You're trying to teach your people how to evaluate their own work."

"So Style 2 means you consult with the subordinate. What if you were using Style 4—*delegating*?" asked the entrepreneur. "I would imagine you would just say, 'That noise outside is bothering us. Would you please take care of it?'"

"That would be perfect for a *delegating* style," said the One Minute Manager. "In Style 4 you are turning over responsibility for day-to-day decision-making and problem-solving to the person doing the task. So you can see that with the same problem and the same task—to do something about the noise—you can use any of the four leadership styles."

"Of the four leadership styles," asked the entrepreneur, "isn't there a 'best' leadership style? I hear a lot about how important it is to use a participative management style."

"Many people believe that," said the One Minute Manager. "But that's where the word 'situational' comes into play. A participative-supporting style may be a better approach in some situations, but not in others."

"I can't imagine when an autocratic-directing style would be appropriate," said the entrepreneur.

"There are several situations," said the One Minute Manager. "Suppose you were at a meeting and the room burst into flames. Would you ask everyone to break into small groups to discuss what was the best way out of the room and then have each group report back so that the whole group could agree on the best course of action?"

"Absolutely not," laughed the entrepreneur. "I'd say, 'There's the door; everyone follow me.'"

"So a *directing* style is appropriate when a decision has to be made quickly and the stakes are high," said the One Minute Manager.

"I'll buy that example," said the entrepreneur. "In what other situations would a *directing* style be appropriate?"

"Suppose you hire someone who has little experience but, you think, real potential for learning a certain job," said the One Minute Manager. "Does it make sense to ask that person what, when, where, and how to do things?"

"Not unless you're interested in pooling ignorance," said the entrepreneur. "I understand what you're getting at now. *Directing* is also appropriate for inexperienced people who you think have the potential to be self-directive."

"Definitely," said the One Minute Manager. "*Directing* might also be appropriate for someone who has some skills but doesn't know the company—its priorities, policies, or ways of doing business."

"Don't people often resent direction and close supervision?" wondered the entrepreneur.

"Usually not in the beginning," said the One Minute Manager. "When they are first learning a task, most people are enthusiastic beginners. They're ready for any help you can give them. After all, they want to perform well."

"Do you really think people want to perform well?" the entrepreneur asked. "I've observed a lot of people in organizations who appear to be trading time on the job to satisfy needs elsewhere. They seem to be working just for the money. They don't care whether the organization accomplishes its goals or not."

"You are right," said the One Minute Manager. "There are people—too many I'm sad to say—who don't seem to care and are just putting in time for a check at the end of the week. But if you could go back and observe them when they were first starting a new job, I doubt if you would see that lack of commitment. I think people lose their commitment only after they realize that good performance doesn't make a difference."

"What do you mean?" asked the entrepreneur.

"I mean," said the One Minute Manager, "that good performance often goes unrecognized. When people do something good, their managers don't say anything. When they make a mistake, they hear about it right away."

"The old 'leave alone-zap' leadership style I've heard people say you talk about all the time," smiled the entrepreneur.

"I now call it 'seagull management,'" said the One Minute Manager. "Seagull managers fly in, make a lot of noise, dump on everyone, and then fly out."

The entrepreneur and the One Minute Manager had a good laugh because they both knew how true that was.

"So I think it's how inexperienced people are managed that causes them to lose their commitment," said the One Minute Manager. "Once you've lost commitment, providing direction is not enough; you also have to provide support and encouragement."

"Now you're talking about a *coaching* style, aren't you?" suggested the entrepreneur.

"Yes," said the One Minute Manager. "A *coaching* style works best when disillusionment sets in."

"Disillusionment?" echoed the entrepreneur.

"Haven't you noticed," said the One Minute Manager, "that as people begin to work on a task, they often find it harder to master than they thought it was going to be, so they lose interest. Or maybe the drop in commitment comes because they don't think the rewards are going to be worth all the effort. Or maybe they aren't getting the direction they need—in fact, they're continually getting zapped. Or progress is so slow or nonexistent that they lose confidence in their ability to learn to do the task well. When this disillusionment happens, when the initial excitement wears off, the best style is a *coaching* style, which is high on direction and support."

"You want to continue to direct because they still need to build skills?" the entrepreneur asked.

"Yes," said the One Minute Manager. "But you also want to listen to their concerns, provide perspective, and praise progress. And you want to involve them in decision-making as much as you can because that's how you'll build back their commitment."

"You make it sound as if everyone gets disillusioned at some point when they're learning a new task or taking over a new project," the entrepreneur added.

"Some people more than others," said the One Minute Manager. "It depends on how much praise the manager provides and how available the manager is. But I'm getting ahead of myself."

"Interesting," said the entrepreneur. "So a *directing* leadership style is better with *enthusiastic beginners* whereas *coaching* is the right style for *disillusioned learners.*"

"Right," said the One Minute Manager. "What kind of people do you think dislike *directing* or *coaching*?"

"Experienced people," said the entrepreneur. "They would probably like a more participative management style."

"You've got it," said the One Minute Manager. "Experienced people like to be listened to and supported. I think you talked to Cindy Murrow. She responds well to a *supporting* style because even though she's experienced and competent she's sometimes a *reluctant or cautious contributor.* When I ask her to take on a project, she has a lot of ideas, but she'll often want to test her ideas out with me first. She wants to be involved in decision-making, but she sometimes doesn't have as much faith in her ideas as I do. She needs recognition, which a *supporting* style provides. And yet a *supporting* style is not a universally good style."

"For example?" asked the entrepreneur.

"We had a classic example with a close friend of ours," said the One Minute Manager. "His marriage was in trouble—he and his wife were putting each other down all the time. Finally we persuaded them to go for marriage counseling and then we sat back figuring we'd done what we could."

"Hadn't you?" asked the entrepreneur.

"No," continued the One Minute Manager. "We didn't ask them what kind of counselor they were going to. They went to a supportive, nondirective counselor."

"Well, what happened?" the entrepreneur wanted to know.

"They paid the counselor one hundred dollars an hour," said the One Minute Manager, "while they screamed and yelled at each other. During those discussions the counselor would do nothing but rub his beard and say, 'Hmmm, I sense some anger here.' They had three sessions with him and split up."

"What you're suggesting is that they needed a good directive counselor," said the entrepreneur, "one who would tell them exactly what they needed to do to start to turn their marriage around. But I'll bet the counselor they went to was effective with other couples."

"Right," said the One Minute Manager. "Their counselor was very effective with couples who had problems they could solve themselves, with couples who needed someone who could listen and support them while they problem-solved. It sounds as if you're convinced now that there is no one best leadership style."

"You're getting to me," the entrepreneur said, smiling. "But what about *delegating*? How does it fit in?"

"*Delegating* is appropriate for people who are *self-reliant achievers*—people who are competent and committed. Therefore they don't need much direction, and they are also able to provide their own support," said the One Minute Manager.

"You mean they praise themselves?" asked the entrepreneur.

"In many cases they do," said the One Minute Manager. "When you go to see them, they often take you on 'praising tours'—pointing out all the things they and their people have done right. Top performers don't need much supervision or praise as long as they know how well they are doing. I heard a cute story the other day that emphasizes the importance of delegating."

"What story is that?" asked the entrepreneur.

"I thought you would never ask," laughed the One Minute Manager.

"One day a little girl asked her father, 'Daddy, why does Mommy bring so much work home at night?'

"'Because she doesn't have time to finish it at work,' answered the father.

"'Then why don't they put her in a slower group?' asked the little girl."

"That's a great story," laughed the entrepreneur. "If the little girl had known about Situational Leadership, she could have asked why Mommy didn't delegate more.

"I think I'm convinced now that there's no best way to influence others," said the entrepreneur, "yet I need some more information to help me decide when to use which leadership style in what situation. You gave me some good thoughts but I'm afraid your examples depend upon my ability to determine whether my people have all the skills and experience they need to do the job they're assigned and my sense of whether they want to or believe they can do it."

"That skill of diagnosing a situation before you act is the key to being a situational leader," agreed the One Minute Manager. "And yet most managers aren't willing to stop for a minute to try to decide what needs to be done before they act. They just keep driving themselves and others." As he pointed to a plaque on the wall, the One Minute Manager said, "That's why I keep that reminder." It read:

When I
Slow Down

I Go
Faster

"So I should think before I act," said the entrepreneur.

"That's what diagnosing is all about," said the One Minute Manager. "Why don't you go and talk to Alice Marshall, one of my other key people, about developing your diagnostic skills."

"That would be great," said the entrepreneur. "But let me review my notes with you just to make sure I understand all about flexibility."

"Good idea," said the One Minute Manager as the entrepreneur showed him her notes.

LEADERSHIP STYLE is how you behave when you are trying to influence the performance of someone else. Leadership Style is a combination of directive and supportive behaviors.

DIRECTIVE BEHAVIOR

Involves: clearly telling people what to do, how to do it, when to do it, and then closely monitoring their performance.

SUPPORTIVE BEHAVIOR

Involves: listening to people, providing support and encouragement for their efforts, and then facilitating their involvement in problem solving and decision-making.

There are four leadership styles: *Directing, Coaching, Supporting,* and *Delegating* BUT . . . THERE IS NO ONE BEST LEADERSHIP STYLE.

As the One Minute Manager read the entrepreneur's notes he smiled. "You're ready for Alice, but before I call her, let me give you this summary of the four basic leadership styles."

While the entrepreneur studied the chart, the One Minute Manager called Marshall.

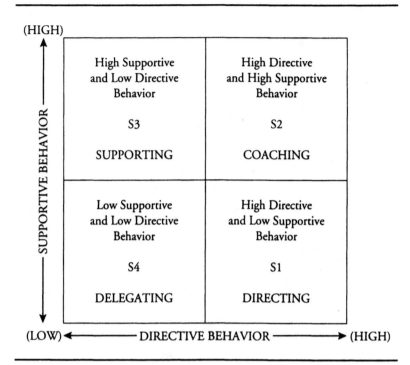

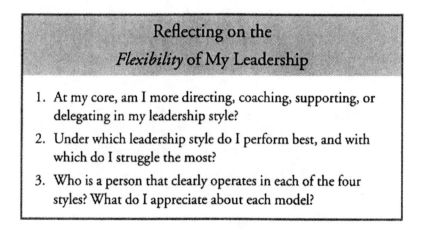

Reflecting on the
Flexibility of My Leadership

1. At my core, am I more directing, coaching, supporting, or delegating in my leadership style?

2. Under which leadership style do I perform best, and with which do I struggle the most?

3. Who is a person that clearly operates in each of the four styles? What do I appreciate about each model?

I3

Selection

One can not
transform a world
except as individ-
uals in the world
are transformed,
and individuals
cannot be
changed except as
they are molded
in the hands of
the Master.

A LEADER'S BASIC TOOL IS PEOPLE,
and nowhere in history is this principle more
clearly illustrated than in the account of Jesus'
selection of the twelve disciples. These men, a
rather ragtag lot by the standards of the day, went
on to bring the gospel message to the world and to
establish the church that God would use to build
his kingdom. No matter what a person's spiritual
outlook is, there is no denying that Jesus' model of
choosing and training leaders to carry on his work
after he was gone was radically effective.

Whereas many people have examined Jesus'
work through a soft, inspirational lens, Robert
Coleman, author of the forty-year-old classic *The
Master Plan of Evangelism,* from which this chapter
is taken, actually analyzes with precision and in
detail the steps that Jesus took to recruit, train,
empower, and release his followers. In this chapter,
Coleman describes Jesus' task—to communicate
a message of forgiveness and redemption. Jesus
picked *people* as his method of accomplishing that
task. He deposited his message into the mind,
hearts, and hands of his disciples, letting them

His concern was not with programs to reach the multitudes, but with men whom the multitudes would follow.

become propagators of the message. Coleman tells us about the kind of people Jesus recruited and how he recruited them.

Although the book's title indicates that the central message is about evangelism (which is a church term), we believe that this model of selection has an important place in a discussion of leadership as well. In a sense, Jesus and his disciples can be viewed as an executive and an executive leadership team. Any leader trying to wield a positive influence on a community or organization can look at Christ's life and gain tremendous insight into what it means to recruit effective followers who will in turn become leaders. Coleman gives us a window, a frame, through which to see the ultimate servant-leader carrying out the most important mission in the history of humankind.

Selection

• • •

Robert E. Coleman

MEN WERE HIS METHOD

It all started by Jesus calling a few men to follow Him. This revealed immediately the direction His evangelistic strategy would take. His concern was not with programs to reach the multitudes, but with men whom the multitudes would follow. Remarkable as it may seem, Jesus started to gather these men before He ever organized an evangelistic campaign or even preached a sermon in public. Men were to be his method of winning the world to God.

The initial objective of Jesus' plan was to enlist men who could bear witness to His life and carry on His work after He returned to the Father. John and Andrew were the first to be invited as Jesus left the scene of the great revival of the Baptist at Bethany beyond the Jordan (John 1:35–40). Andrew in turn brought his brother Peter (John 1:41, 42). The next day Jesus found Philip on His way to Galilee, and Philip found Nathaniel (John 1:43–51). There is no evidence of haste in the selection of these disciples; just determination. James, the brother of John, is not mentioned as one of the group until the four fishermen are recalled several months later by the Sea of Galilee (Mark 1:19, Matt. 4:21). Shortly afterward Matthew is bidden to follow the Master as Jesus passed through Capernaum (Mark 2:13, 14; Matt. 9:9; Luke 5:27, 28). The particulars surrounding the call of the other disciples are not recorded in the Gospels, but it is believed that they all occurred in the first year of the Lord's ministry.[1]

As one might expect, these early efforts at soul winning had little or no immediate effect upon the religious life of his day, but that did not matter greatly. For as it turned out these few early converts of the

Lord were destined to become the leaders of His church that was to go with the Gospel to the whole world, and from the standpoint of His ultimate purpose, the significance of their lives would be felt throughout eternity. That's the only thing that counts.

MEN WILLING *to* LEARN

What is more revealing about these men is that at first they do not impress us as being key men. None of them occupied prominent places in the Synagogue, nor did any of them belong to the Levitical priesthood. For the most part they were common laboring men, probably having no professional training beyond the rudiments of knowledge necessary for their vocation. Perhaps a few of them came from families of some considerable means, such as the sons of Zebedee, but none of them could have been considered wealthy. They had no academic degrees in the arts and philosophies of their day. Like their Master, their formal education likely consisted only of the Synagogue schools. Most of them were raised in the poor section of the country around Galilee. Apparently the only one of the twelve who came from the more refined region of Judea was Judas Iscariot. By any standard of sophisticated culture then and now they would surely be considered as a rather ragged aggregation of souls. One might wonder how Jesus could ever use them. They were impulsive, temperamental, easily offended, and had all the prejudices of their environment. In short, these men selected by the Lord to be His assistants represented an average cross section of the lot of society in their day.[2] Not the kind of group one would expect to win the world for Christ.

Yet Jesus saw in these simple men the potential of leadership for the Kingdom. They were indeed "unlearned and ignorant" according to the world's standard (Acts 4:13), but they were teachable. Though often mistaken in their judgments and slow to comprehend spiritual things, they were honest men, willing to confess their need. Their mannerisms may have been awkward and their abilities limited, but with the exception of the traitor, their hearts were big. What is perhaps most significant about them was their sincere yearning for God and the realities of His life. The superficiality of the religious life about them had not obsessed their hope for the Messiah (John 1:41, 45, 49; 6:69). They were fed up with the hypocrisy of the ruling aristocracy.

Some of them had already joined the revival movement of John the Baptist (John 1:35). These men were looking for someone to lead them in the way of salvation. Such men, pliable in the hands of the Master, could be molded into a new image—Jesus can use anyone who wants to be used.

CONCENTRATED UPON *a* FEW

In noting this fact, however, one does not want to miss the practical truth of how Jesus did it. Here is the wisdom of His method, and in observing it, we return again to the fundamental principle of concentration upon those He intended to use. One can not transform a world except as individuals in the world are transformed, and individuals cannot be changed except as they are molded in the hands of the Master. The necessity is apparent not only to select a few laymen, but to keep the group small enough to be able to work effectively with them.

Hence, as the company of followers around Jesus increased, it became necessary by the middle of His second year of ministry to narrow the select company to a more manageable number. Accordingly Jesus "called His disciples, and He chose from them twelve, whom also He named apostles" (Luke 6:13–17; cf., Mark 3:13–19). Regardless of the symbolical meaning one prefers to put upon the number twelve,[3] it is clear that Jesus intended these men to have unique privileges and responsibilities in the Kingdom work.

This does not mean that Jesus' decision to have twelve apostles excluded others from following Him, for as we know, many more were numbered among His associates, and some of these became very effective workers in the Church. The seventy (Luke 10:1); Mark and Luke, the Gospel revelators; James, His own brother (1 Cor. 15:7; Gal. 2:9, 12; cf., John 2:12 and 7:2–10), are notable examples of this. Nevertheless, we must acknowledge that there was a rapidly diminishing priority given to those outside the twelve.

The same rule could be applied in reverse, for within the select apostolic group Peter, James and John seemed to enjoy a more special relationship to the Master than did the other nine. Only these privileged few are invited into the sick room of Jairus' daughter (Mark 5:37; Luke 8:51); they alone go up with the Master and behold His glory on the Mount of Transfiguration (Mark 9:2; Matt. 17:1; Luke 9:28); and amid the olive trees of Gethsemane casting their ominous shadows in the light of the full Passover moon, these members of the inner circle waited nearest to their Lord while He prayed (Mark 14:33; Matt. 26:37). So noticeable is the preference given to these three that had it not been for the incarnation of selflessness in the Person of Christ, it could well have precipitated feelings of resentment on the part of the other apostles. The fact that there is no record of the disciples complaining about the pre-eminence of the three, though they did murmur about other things, is proof that where preference is shown in the right spirit and for the right reason offence need not arise.[4]

The PRINCIPLE OBSERVED

All of this certainly impresses one with the deliberate way that Jesus proportioned His life to those He wanted to train. It also graphically illustrates a fundamental principle of teaching: that other things being equal, the more concentrated the size of the group being taught, the greater the opportunity for effective instruction.[5]

Jesus devoted most of His remaining life on earth to these few disciples. He literally staked His whole ministry upon them. The world could be indifferent toward him and still not defeat His strategy. It even caused Him no great concern when His followers on the fringes of things gave up their allegiance when confronted with the true meaning of the Kingdom (John 6:66). But He could not bear to have His close disciples miss His purpose. They had to understand the truth and be sanctified by it (John 17:17), else all would be lost. Thus He prayed "not for the world," but for the few God gave Him "out of the world" (John 17:6, 9).[6] Everything depended upon their faithfulness if the world would believe on Him "through their word" (John 17:20).

NOT NEGLECTING *the* MASSES

It would be wrong, however, to assume on the basis of what has here been emphasized that Jesus neglected the masses. Such was not the case. Jesus did all that any man could be asked to do and more to reach the multitudes. The first thing He did when He started his ministry was to identify Himself boldly with the great mass revival movement of His day through baptism at the hands of John (Mark 1:9–11;

Matt. 3:13–17; Luke 3:21, 22), and He later went out of His way to praise this work of the great prophet (Matt. 11:7–15; Luke 7:24–28). He Himself continuously preached to the crowds that followed His miracle-working ministry. He taught them. He fed them when they were hungry. He healed their sick and cast out demons among them. He blessed their children. Sometimes the whole day would be spent ministering to their needs, even to the extent that he had "no leisure so much as to eat" (Mark 6:31). In every way possible Jesus manifested to the masses of humanity a genuine concern. These were the people that He came to save—He loved them, wept over them, and finally died to save them from their sin. No one could think that Jesus shirked mass evangelism.

Multitudes Aroused

In fact, the ability of Jesus to impress the multitudes created a serious problem in His ministry. He was so successful in expressing to them His compassion and power that they once wanted "to take Him by force, to make Him King" (John 6:15). One report by the followers of John the Baptist said that "all men" were clamoring for His attention (John 3:26). Even the Pharisees admitted among themselves that the world had gone after Him (John 12:19), and bitter as the admission must have been, the chief priests concurred in this opinion (John 11:47, 48). However one looks at it, the Gospel record certainly does not indicate that Jesus lacked any popular following among the masses, despite their hesitating loyalty, and this condition lasted right on down to the end. Indeed, it was the fear of this friendly mass feeling for Jesus that prompted His accusers to capture Him in the absence of the people (Mark 12:12; Matt. 21:26; Luke 20:19).

Had Jesus given any encouragement to this popular sentiment among the masses, He easily could have had all the Kingdoms of men at His feet. All He had to do was to satisfy the temporal appetites and curiosities of the people by His supernatural power. Such was the temptation presented by Satan in the wilderness when Jesus was urged to turn stones into bread and to cast himself down from a pinnacle of the temple that God might bear him up (Matt. 4:1–7; Luke 4:1–4, 9–13). These spectacular things would surely have excited the applause of the crowd. Satan was not offering Jesus anything when he promised Him all the Kingdoms of the world if the Master would only worship him (Matt. 4:8–10). The arch deceiver of men knew full well that Jesus automatically would have this if He just turned His concentration from the things that mattered in the eternal Kingdom.[7]

But Jesus would not play to the galleries. Quite the contrary. Repeatedly He took special pains to allay the superficial popular support of the multitudes which had been occasioned by His extraordinary power (e.g., John 2:23–3:3; 6:26, 27). Frequently He would even ask those who were the recipients of His healing to say nothing about it in order to prevent mass demonstrations by the easily aroused multitudes.[8] Likewise, with the disciples following His transfiguration on the Mount "He charged them that they should tell no man what things they had seen" until after His resurrection (Mark 9:9; Matt. 17:9). On other occasions when applauded by the crowd, Jesus would slip away with His disciples and go elsewhere to continue His ministry.[9]

His practice in this respect sometimes rather annoyed His followers who did not understand His strategy. Even his own brothers and sisters, who yet did not believe on Him, urged Him to abandon this policy and make an open show of Himself to the world, but He refused to take their advice (John 7:2–9).

Few Seemed *to* Understand

In view of this policy, it is not surprising to note that few people were actually converted during the ministry of Christ, that is, in any clear cut way. Of course, many of the multitudes believed in Christ in the sense that His divine ministry was acceptable,[10] but comparatively few seemed to have grasped the meaning of the Gospel. Perhaps His total number of devoted followers at the end of His earthly ministry numbered little more than the 500 brethren to whom Jesus appeared after the resurrection (1 Cor. 15:6), and only about 120 tarried in Jerusalem to receive the baptism of the Holy Spirit (Acts 1:15). Though this number is not small considering that His active ministry extended only over a period of three years, yet if at this point one were to measure the effectiveness of His evangelism by the number of His converts, Jesus doubtless would not be considered among the most productive mass evangelists of the church.

HIS STRATEGY

Why? Why did Jesus deliberately concentrate His life upon comparatively so few people? Had he not come to save the world? With the glowing announcement of John the Baptist ringing in the ears of multitudes, the Master easily could have had an immediate following of thousands if He wanted them. Why did He not then capitalize upon His opportunities to enlist a might army of believers to take the world by storm? Surely the Son of God could have adopted a more enticing program of mass recruitment. Is it not rather disappointing that one with all the powers of the universe at His command would live and die to save the world, yet in the end have only a few ragged disciples to show for His labors?

The answer to this question focuses at once the real purpose of His plan for evangelism. Jesus was not trying to impress the crowd, but to usher in a Kingdom. This meant that He needed men who could lead the multitudes. What good would it have been for His ultimate objective to arouse the masses to follow Him if these people had no subsequent supervision nor instruction in the Way? It had been demonstrated on numerous occasions that the crowd was an easy prey to false gods when left without proper care. The masses were like helpless sheep wandering aimlessly without a shepherd (Mark 6:34; Matt. 9:36; 14:14). They were willing to follow almost anyone that came along with some promise for their welfare, be it friend or foe. That was the tragedy of the hour—the noble aspirations of the people were easily excited by Jesus, but just as quickly thwarted by the deceitful religious authorities who controlled them. The spiritually blind leaders of Israel (John 8:44; 9:39–41; 12:40; cf., Matt. 23:1–39), though comparatively few in number,[11] completely dominated the affairs of the people. For this reason, unless Jesus' converts were given competent men of God to lead them on and protect them in the truth they would soon fall into confusion and despair and the last state would be worse than the first. Thus, before the world could ever be permanently helped men would have to be raised up who could lead the multitudes in the things of God.

Jesus was a realist. He fully realized the fickleness of depraved human nature as well as the Satanic forces of this world amassed against humanity, and in this knowledge He based his evangelism on a plan that would meet the need. The multitudes of discordant and bewildered souls were potentially ready to follow Him, but Jesus individually could not possibly give them the personal care they needed. His only hope was to get men imbued with His life who would do it for Him. Hence, He concentrated himself upon those who were to be the beginning of this leadership. Though He did what He could to help the multitudes, He had to devote Himself primarily to a few men, rather than the masses, in order that the masses could at last be saved. This was the genius of His strategy.

The PRINCIPLE APPLIED TODAY

Yet, strangely enough, it is scarcely comprehended in practice today. Most of the evangelistic efforts of the church begin with the multitudes under the assumption that the church is qualified to conserve what good is done. The result is our spectacular emphasis upon numbers of converts, candidates for baptism, and more members for the church, with little or no genuine concern manifested toward the establishment of these souls in the love and power of God, let alone the preservation and continuation of the work.

Surely if the pattern of Jesus at this point means anything at all it teaches that the first duty of a pastor as well as the first concern of an evangelist is to see to it that a foundation is laid in the beginning upon which can be built an effective and continuing evangelistic ministry to the multitudes. This will require more concentration of time and talents upon fewer men in the church while not neglecting the passion for the world. It will mean raising up trained leadership "for the work of ministering" with the pastor (Ephesians 4:12).[12] A few people so dedicated in time will shake the world for God. Victory is never won by the multitudes.

Some might object to this principle when practiced by the Christian worker on the ground that favoritism is shown toward a select group in the church. But be that as it may, it is still the way that Jesus concentrated His life, and it is necessary if any permanent leadership is to be trained. Where it is practiced out of a genuine love for the whole church, and due concern is manifested toward the needs of the people, objections can at least be reconciled to the mission being accomplished. However, the ultimate goal must be clear to the worker, and there can be no hint of selfish partiality displayed in his relationships to all. Everything that is done with the few is for the salvation of the multitudes.

A MODERN DEMONSTRATION

This principle of selectivity and concentration is engraved in the universe, and will bring results no matter who practices it, whether the church believes it or not. It is surely not without significance that the Communists, always alert to what works, adopted in a large measure this method of the Lord as their own. Using it to their own devious end they have multiplied from a handful of zealots seventy-five years ago to a vast conspiracy of followers that enslave nearly half the peoples of the world. They have proved in our day what Jesus demonstrated so clearly in His day that the multitudes can be won easily if they are just given leaders to follow. Is not the spread of this vicious Communistic philosophy, in some measure, a judgment upon the church, not only upon our flabby commitment to evangelism, but also upon the superficial way that we have tried to go about it?

TIME *for* ACTION

It is time that the church realistically face the situation. Our days of trifling are running out. The evangelistic program of the Church has bogged down on nearly every front. What is worse, the great missionary thrust of the Gospel into new frontiers has largely lost its power. In most lands the enfeebled church is not even keeping up with the exploding population. All the while the Satanic forces of this world are becoming more relentless and brazen in their attack. It is ironic when one stops to think about it. In an age when facilities for rapid communication of the Gospel are available to the Church as never before, we are actually accomplishing less in winning the world for God than before the invention of the horseless carriage.

Yet in appraising the tragic condition of affairs today, we must not become frantic in trying to reverse the trend overnight. Perhaps that has been our problem. In our concern to stem the tide, we have launched one crash program after another to reach the multitudes with the saving Word of God. But what we have failed to comprehend in our frustration is that the real problem is not with the masses—what they believe, how they are governed, whether they are fed a wholesome diet or not. All these things considered so vital are ultimately manipulated by others, and for this reason, before we can resolve the exploitation of the people we must get to those whom the people follow.

This, of course, puts a priority on winning and training those already in responsible positions of leadership. But if we can't begin at the top, then let us begin where we are and train a few of the lowly to become the great. And let us remember, too, that one does not have to have the prestige of the world in order to be greatly used in the Kingdom of God. Anyone who is willing to follow Christ can become a mighty influence upon the world providing, of course, this person has the proper training himself.

Here is where we must begin just like Jesus. It will be slow, tedious, painful and probably unnoticed by men at first, but the end result will be glorious, even if we don't live to see it. Seen this way, though, it becomes a big decision in the ministry. One must decide where he wants his ministry to count—in the momentary applause of popular recognition or in the reproduction of his life in a few chosen men who will carry on his work after he has gone. Really it is a question of which generation we are living for.

But we must go on. It is necessary now to see how Jesus trained His men to carry on His work. The whole pattern is part of the same method, and we can not separate one phase from the other without destroying its effectiveness.

Reflecting on My *Selection* as a Leader

1. Am I good at selecting people?

2. What criteria do I use to identify and recruit someone to my team?

3. How has the multiplication principle been applied and proven in my business world? My family world? My church world?

4. What is the best plan to handle a "bad draft choice" that doesn't appear to be one until after the fact?

Notes

1. One qualification of an apostle mentioned in Acts 1:21, 22 was that he should have been with Jesus, "beginning from the baptism of John, unto the day that he was received up." Although this does not tell us from what point in John's baptismal work we are to reckon (certainly not at the beginning or from the Lord's own baptism), it does argue for an early association of all the apostles with Jesus, perhaps dating from the time of John the Baptist's imprisonment. See Samuel J. Andrews, *The Life of Our Lord*. Grand Rapids, MI: Zondervan, 1954 (reprint of 1891 ed.), p. 268; cf., Alfred Edersheim, *The Life and Times of Jesus the Messiah*. Vol. 1. New York: E. R. Herrick & Co., 1886, 521.

2. Many authors have sought to give us a picture of the twelve apostles. Among those which treat them all, the following provide popular reading: George Matheson, *The Representative Men of the New Testament* (New York: Eaton & Mains, 1905); Edward Augustus George, *The Twelve* (New York: Fleming H. Revell, 1916); W. Mackintosh Mackay, *The Men Whom Jesus Made* (New York: George H. Doran Co., 1924); J.W.G. Ward, *The Master and the Twelve* (New York: George H. Doran Co., 1924); Charles R. Brown, *The Twelve* (New York: Harper, 1926); Francis Witherspoon, *The Glorious Company* (New York: Harcourt, Brace and Co., 1928); Asbury Smith, *The Twelve Christ Chose* (New York: Harper, 1958); William Barclay, *The Master's Men* (London: SCM Press, 1959); William Sanford LaSor, *Great Personalities of the New Testament* (Westwood, N.J.: Fleming H. Revell, 1961).

3. Various opinions have been advanced as to why arbitrarily twelve disciples were designated apostles, for He could have selected more or gotten along with less, but probably the most plausible theory is that the number suggests a spiritual relationship of the apostolic company with the Messianic Kingdom of God. As Edwin Schell put it: "Twelve is the number of the spiritual Israel. Whether observed in the twelve patriarchs, in the twelve tribes, or in the twelve foundations of the twelve gates of the heavenly Jerusalem, the number twelve everywhere symbolizes the indwelling of God in the human family—the interpretation of the world by divinity," Edwin Schell, *Traits of the Twelve*. Cincinnati: Jennings and Graham, 1911, p. 26; cf., A. B. Bruce, *The Training of the Twelve*. 3rd ed. New York: Richard R. Smith, Inc., 1930, p. 32. It is altogether possible that the Apostles saw in the number a more literal meaning, and built up around it at first delusive hopes of the restoration of Israel in a political sense. They certainly were aware of their own place within the twelve, and were careful to fill up the vacancy created at the loss of Judas (Acts 1:15–26; cf., Matt. 19:28). One thing is certain, however, the number served to impress upon those chosen their importance in the future work of the Kingdom.

4. Henry Latham suggests that the selection of these three served to impress upon the whole company the need for "self abnegation." In his analysis it actually was intended to show the apostles that "Christ gave what charge He would to whom He would; that in God's service it is honor enough to be employed at all; and that no man is to be discouraged because he sees allotted to another what appears to be a higher sphere of work than his own." Henry Latham, *Pastor Pastorum*. Cambridge: Deighton Bell and Co., 1910, p. 325.

5. The principle of concentration exemplified in the ministry of Jesus was not new with Him. It had always been God's strategy from the beginning. The Old Testament records how God selected a comparatively small nation of Israel through which to effect His redemptive purpose for mankind. Even within the nation, the leadership

was concentrated usually within family lines, especially the Davidic branch of the tribe of Judah.

6. The High Priestly Prayer of Christ in the 17th chapter of John is especially meaningful in this connection. Of the 26 verses in the prayer, 14 relate immediately to the twelve disciples (John 17:6–19).

7. This is not intended to suggest that this was all that was involved in the temptation, but only to emphasize that the temptation appealed to the strategy of Jesus for world evangelism as well as to the spiritual purpose of His mission. Another interpretation of this temptation experience from the standpoint of evangelistic method, somewhat similar, is given by Colin W. Williams in his book, *Where In The World?* (New York: Nat'l Council of Churches of Christ), pp. 24–27.

8. Instances of this are the case of the cleansed leper (Mark 1:44, 45; Matt. 8:4; Luke 5:14–16); those freed from unclean spirits by the Sea of Galilee (Mark 3:11, 12); Jarius after seeing his daughter raised from the dead (Mark 5:42, 43; Luke 8:55, 56); the two blind men restored to sight (Matt. 9:30); and with the blind man in Bethsaida (Mark 8:25, 26).

9. Some examples of this are in John 1:29–43; 6:14, 15; Mark 4:35, 36; 6:1, 45, 46; 7:24–8:30; Matt. 8:18, 23; 14:22, 23; 15:21, 39; 16:4; Luke 5:16; 8:22; and others.

10. Examples of this are John 2:23–25; 6:30–60; 7:31–44; 11:45, 46; 12:11; 17–19; Luke 14:25–35; 19:36–38; Matt. 21:8–11; 14–17; Mark 11:8–11.

11. The Pharisees and Sadducees were the principle leaders of Israel, outside of the ruling Roman forces, and the whole religious, social, educational, and to a limited degree, political life of the approximately 2,000,000 people in Palestine was moulded by their action. Yet the number of persons belonging to the Pharisaic guild, composed mostly of rabbis and well-to-do lay folk, according to the estimate of Josephus (*Ant.,* XVII, 2, 4), did not exceed 6,000; while the total number of Sadducees, made up mostly of the chief priests and Sanhedrin families in Jerusalem, probably did not amount to more than a few hundred. See Anthony C. Deane, *The World Christ Knew* (London: Guild Books, 1944), pp. 57, 60; Alfred Edersheim, *The Life and Times of Jesus the Messiah.* Vol. 1. New York: E. R. Herrick & Co., 1886, p. 311. When it is considered that this small privileged group of less than 7,000 people, representing about one-third of one percent of the population of Israel, guided the spiritual destiny of a nation, it is not difficult to see why Jesus spoke so much about them, while also teaching His disciples the strategic need for better leadership.

12. This idea is brought out clearly in the translation of Ephesians 4:11 and 12 in the *New English Bible,* which reads: "And these were his gifts: some to be apostles, some prophets, some evangelists, some pastors and teachers, to equip God's people for work in His service, to the building up of the body of Christ." Other modern versions bring out the same essential meaning, including the Weymouth, Phillips, Wuest, Berkeley, Williams and the Amplified New Testament. The three clauses in verse 12 are made successively dependent upon the other, with the last being the climax. According to this interpretation, Christ gave a special gift to some officials in the Church for the purpose of perfecting the saints to do the service they have each to perform in the one great goal of building up Christ's body. The ministry of the Church is seen as a work involving all members of the body (compare I Cor. 12:18 and II Cor. 9:8). Luther brings out the same thing in his commentary on "Ephesians," as also does Weiss, Meier, DeWitte, and Salmond. For a good exposition of this verse from this point of view, see the volume on Ephesians in *The Expositor's Greek Testament* (Grand Rapids: Wm. B. Eerdmans Pub-

lishing Co.), pp. 330–331. Other views are ably presented by Abbott in "Ephesians and Colossians," *International Critical Commentary* (Edinborough: T. T. Clark, 1897), pp. 119, 120; and Lange, "Galatians—Colossians," *Commentary on the Holy Scriptures* (Grand Rapids: Zondervan), pp. 150–151. A practical treatment of this overall idea may be found in Gaines S. Dobbins' book, *A Ministering Church* (Nashville: Broadman Press, 1960), Ch. II, "A Church Needs Many Ministers," pp. 15–29; and from still a different angle in Watchman Nee, *The Normal Christian Church Life* (Washington, D.C.: International Students Press, 1962).

Integrity

> Image is what
> people think we
> are. Integrity is
> what we really are.

WHAT DOES THE WORD *INTEGRITY* mean to you? Faithfulness to a spouse? Honesty in business? Keeping one's word to others? Each of these is one aspect of integrity, but the word itself encompasses much more than any single pattern of behavior. Integrity, as John Maxwell explains, is a state of being whole, complete, and sound. The integrity of a building's foundation refers to its ability to support the structure completely—at the corners, along the sides, and in the middle. If one section is made of inferior materials or is damaged, the integrity of the foundation is compromised, and the building will eventually collapse.

Likewise, to live our lives with integrity means there is consistency between what we believe, what we say, and what we do. If someone were to scrape off the surface of the image we present to the world and examine what's underneath, would they be surprised to find that our exterior is merely a thin layer of cosmetic art disguising something completely different? Or would the inside match the outside?

These are the questions Maxwell explores in "The Most Important Ingredient of Leadership:

The only way to keep the goodwill and high esteem of the people you work with is to deserve it. No one can fool all of the people all of the time. Each of us, eventually, is recognized for exactly what we are—not what we try to appear to be.

Integrity." He goes beyond many of our superficial assumptions about what it means to live a life of integrity and challenges us to examine our own beliefs, words, and actions to see if they match up. He applies this discussion specifically in the context of leadership because a leader without integrity is a hollow shell without the confidence or trust of followers.

Maxwell is a popular speaker and writer on leadership—not because he says what he thinks people want to hear but because he addresses the tough issues surrounding success in character as well as success in the organization.

The Most Important Ingredient *of* Leadership: *Integrity*

...

John C. Maxwell

The dictionary defines *integrity* as "the state of being complete, unified." When I have integrity, my words and my deeds match up. I am who I am, no matter where I am or who I am with.

Sadly integrity is a vanishing commodity today. Personal standards are crumbling in a world that has taken to hot pursuit of personal pleasure and short cuts to success.

On a job application one question read, "Have you ever been arrested?" The applicant printed the word *No* in the space. The next question was a follow-up to the first. It asked, "Why?" Not realizing he did not have to answer this part, the honest and rather naïve applicant wrote, "I guess it's because I never got caught."

A Jeff Danziger cartoon shows a company president announcing to his staff, "Gentlemen, this year the trick is honesty." From one side of the conference table, a vice president gasps, "Brilliant." Across the table, another VP mutters, "But so risky!"

In a cartoon in the *New Yorker,* two clean-shaven middle-aged men are sitting together in a jail cell. One inmate turns to the other and says: "All along, I thought our level of corruption fell well within community standards."

The White House, the Pentagon, Capitol Hill, the church, the sports arena, the academy, even the day care center have all been hit hard by scandal. In every case, the lack of credibility can be traced back to the level of integrity of the individuals within those organizations and institutions.

A person with integrity does not have divided loyalties (that's duplicity), nor is he or she merely pretending (that's hypocrisy). People with integrity are "whole" people; they can be identified by their single-mindedness. People with integrity have nothing to hide and nothing to fear. Their lives are open books. Senior Editor of *Christianity Today* magazine, V. Gilbert Beers, says, "A person of integrity is one who has established a system of values against which all of life is judged."

Integrity is not what we do so much as who we are. And who we are, in turn, determines what we do. Our system of values is so much a part of us we cannot separate it from ourselves. It becomes the navigating system that guides us. It establishes priorities in our lives and judges what we will accept or reject.

We are all faced with conflicting desires. No one, no matter how "spiritual," can avoid this battle. Integrity is the factor that determines which one will prevail. We struggle daily with situations that demand decisions between what we want to do and what we ought to do. Integrity establishes the ground rules for resolving these tensions. It determines who we are and how we will respond before the conflict even appears. Integrity welds what we say, think, and do into a whole person so that permission is never granted for one of these to be out of sync.

Conflict breeds despair because it divides a whole person into fragments. Integrity binds our person together and fosters a spirit of contentment within us. It will not allow our lips to violate our hearts. When integrity is the referee, we will be consistent; our beliefs will be mirrored by our conduct. There will be no discrepancy between what we appear to be and what our family knows we are, whether in times of prosperity or adversity. Integrity allows us to predetermine what we will be regardless of circumstances, persons involved, or the places of our testing.

Integrity is not only the referee between two desires. It is the pivotal point between a happy person and a divided spirit. It frees us to be whole persons no matter what comes our way.

"The first key to greatness," Socrates reminds us, "is to be in reality what we appear to be." Too often we try to be a "human doing" before we have become a "human being." To earn trust a leader has to be authentic. For that to happen, one must come across as a good musical composition does—the words and the music must match.

If what I say and what I do are the same, the results are consistent. For example:

I say to the employees: "Be at work on time."	I arrive at work on time.	They will be on time.
I say to the employees: "Be positive."	I exhibit a positive attitude.	They will be positive.
I say to the employees: "Put the customer first."	I put the customer first.	They will put the customer first.

If what I say and do are *not* the same, the results are inconsistent. For example:

I say to the employees: "Be at work on time."	I arrive at work late.	Some will be on time, some won't.
I say to the employees: "Be positive."	I exhibit a negative attitude.	Some will be positive, some won't.
I say to the employees: "Put the customer first."	I put myself first.	Some will put customers first, some won't.

Eighty-nine percent of what people learn comes through visual stimulation, 10 percent through audible stimulation, and 1 percent through other senses. So it makes sense that the more followers see and hear their leader being consistent in action and word, the greater their consistency and loyalty. *What they hear, they understand. What they see, they believe!*

Too often we attempt to motivate our followers with gimmicks that *are short-lived and shallow. What people need is not a motto to say, but a model to see.*

The CREDIBILITY ACID TEST

The more credible you are the more confidence people place in you, thereby allowing you the privilege of influencing their lives. The less credible you are, the less confidence people place in you and the more quickly you lose your position of leadership.

Many leaders who have attended my conferences have said to me, "I hope you can give me some insights into how I can change my company." My response is always the same: My goal is to inspire you to change; if that happens, the organization will also be changed. As I have said time and time again, everything rises and falls on leadership. The secret to rising and not falling is integrity. Let's look at some reasons why integrity is so important.

Leadership functions on the basis of trust.

Dwight Eisenhower said: "In order to be a leader a man must have followers. And to have followers, a man must have their confidence. Hence, the supreme quality for a leader is unquestionably integrity. Without it, no real success is possible, no matter whether it is on a section gang, a football field, in an army, or in an office. If a man's associates find him guilty of being phony, if they find that he lacks forthright integrity, he will fail. His teachings and actions must square with each other. The first great need, therefore, is integrity and high purpose."[1]

Pieter Bruyn, a Dutch specialist in administration, holds that authority is not the power a boss has over subordinates, but rather the boss's ability to influence subordinates to recognize and accept that power. He calls it a "bargain": Subordinates tacitly agree to accept the boss as boss in return for being offered the kind of leadership *they* can accept.

What does Bruyn's theory boil down to? Quite simply the manager must build—and maintain—credibility. Subordinates must be able to trust that their boss will act in good faith toward them.

Too often people who are responsible for leading look to the organization to make people responsible to follow. They ask for a new title, another position, an organization chart, and a new policy to curtail insubordination. Sadly they never get enough authority to become effective. Why? They are looking to the outside when their problem is on the inside. They lack authority because they lack integrity.

Only 45 percent of four hundred managers in a Carnegie-Mellon survey believed their top management; a third distrusted their immediate bosses. With so much depending on credibility and trust, someone in every organization must provide the leadership to improve these numbers.[2]

Cavett Roberts said: "If my people understand me, I'll get their attention. If my people trust me, I'll get their action." For a leader to have the authority to lead, he needs more than the title on his door. He has to have the trust of those who are following him.

Integrity has high influence value.

Emerson said, "Every great institution is the lengthened shadow of a single man. His character determines the character of the organization." That statement "lines up" with the words of Will Rogers who said, "People's minds are changed through observation and not argument." People do what people see.

According to 1,300 senior executives who responded to a recent survey, integrity is the human quality most necessary to business success. Seventy-one percent put it at the top of a list of sixteen traits responsible for enhancing an executive's effectiveness.[3]

Regrettably we also forget the high influence value of integrity in the home. R. C. Sproul, in his book *Objections Answered*, tells about a young Jewish boy who grew up in Germany many years ago. The lad had a profound sense of admiration for his father, who saw to it that the life of the family revolved around the religious practices of their faith. The father led them to the synagogue faithfully.

In his teen years, however, the boy's family was forced to move to another town in Germany. This town had no synagogue, only a Lutheran church. The life of the community revolved around the Lutheran church; all the best people belonged to it. Suddenly, the father announced to the family that they were all going to abandon their Jewish traditions and join the Lutheran church. When the stunned family asked why, the father explained that it would be good for his business. The youngster was bewildered and confused. His deep disappointment soon gave way to anger and a kind of intense bitterness that plagued him throughout his life.

Later he left Germany and went to England to study. Each day found him at the British Museum formulating his ideas and composing a book. In that book he introduced a whole new worldview and conceived a movement that was designed to change the world. He described religion as the "opiate for the masses." He committed the people who followed him to life without God. His ideas became the norm for the governments of almost half the world's people. His name? Karl Marx, founder of the Communist movement. The history of the twentieth century and perhaps beyond was significantly affected because one father let his values become distorted.

Leaders are to live by a higher standard than followers.

This insight is exactly opposite of most people's thoughts concerning leadership. In a world of perks and privileges that accompany the climb to success, little thought is given to the responsibilities of the upward journey. Leaders can give up anything except responsibility, either for themselves or their organizations. John D. Rockefeller Jr., said, "I believe that every right implies a responsibility; every opportunity, an obligation; every possession, a duty." I often use the diagram below when teaching this principle.

Too many people are ready to assert their rights, but not to assume their responsibilities. Richard L. Evans, in his book *An Open Road,*

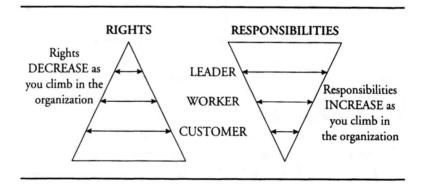

said: "It is priceless to find a person who will take responsibility, who will finish and follow through to the final detail—to know when someone has accepted an assignment that it will be effectively, conscientiously completed. But when half-finished assignments keep coming back—to check on, to verify, to edit, to interrupt thought, and to take repeated attention—obviously someone has failed to follow the doctrine of completed work."

Tom Robbins said, "Don't let yourself be victimized by the age you live in. It's not the times that will bring us down, any more than it's society. There's a tendency today to absolve individuals of moral responsibility and treat them as victims of social circumstance. You buy that and you pay with your soul. What limits people is lack of character." When the character of leaders is low, so are their standards.

*Our tendency is to work harder on
our images than on our integrity.*

Image is what people think we are. Integrity is what we really are.

Two old ladies were walking around a somewhat overcrowded English country churchyard and came upon a tombstone. The inscription said: "Here lies John Smith, a politician and an honest man."

"Good heavens!" said one lady to the other. "Isn't it awful that they had to put two people in the same grave!"

All of us have known those who were not the same on the outside as they were inside. Sadly many who have worked harder on their images than on their integrity don't understand when they suddenly "fall." Even friends who thought they knew them are surprised.

In ancient China the people wanted security against the barbaric hordes to the north, so they built the great wall. It was so high they believed no one could climb over it and so thick nothing could break it down. They settled back to enjoy their security. During the first hundred years of the wall's existence, China was invaded three times. Not once did the barbaric hordes break down the wall or climb over it. Each time they bribed a gatekeeper and then marched right through the gates. The Chinese were so busy relying on walls of stone they forgot to teach integrity to their children.

Use these questions to determine when you are image-building instead of integrity-building:

Consistency: Are you the same person no matter who you are with? Yes or no.

Choices: Do you make decisions that are best for others when another choice would benefit you? Yes or no.

Credit: Are you quick to recognize others for their efforts and contributions to your success? Yes or no.

Thomas Macauley said, "The measure of a man's real character is what he would do if he would never be found out." Life is like a vise; at times it will squeeze us. At those moments of pressure, whatever is inside will be found out. We cannot give what we do not have. Image promises much but produces little. Integrity never disappoints.

Integrity means living it myself before leading others.

We cannot lead anyone else further than we have been ourselves. Too many times we are so concerned about the product we try to shortcut the process. There are no shortcuts when integrity is involved. Eventually truth will always be exposed.

Recently I heard of a man who interviewed a consultant to some of the largest U.S. companies about their quality control. The consultant said, "In quality control, we are not concerned about the product. We are concerned about the process. If the process is right, the product is guaranteed." The same holds true for integrity; it guarantees credibility.

When the *Challenger* exploded, America was stunned to discover Quality Control had warned NASA that the space shuttle was not fully prepared to go. But production said, "The show must go on!" *Crash,* just like many leaders.

I remember hearing my basketball coach, Don Neff, repeatedly emphasize to our team, "You play like you practice; you play like you practice." When we fail to follow this principle, we fail to reach our personal potentials. When leaders fail to follow this principle, eventually they lose their credibility.

A charismatic personality will draw people;
only integrity will keep them.

Recently I had dinner with Fred Smith. This wise businessman shared with me the difference between being clever and being credible. He said that clever leaders never last. That statement reminded me of the words of Peter Drucker. His closing remarks to about forty pastors gathered to discuss important issues in the church were, "The final requirement of effective leadership is to earn trust. Otherwise there won't be any followers. To trust a leader, it is not necessary to agree with him. Trust is the conviction that the leader means what he says. It is a belief in something very old-fashioned called 'integrity.' A leader's actions and a leader's professed beliefs must be congruent or at least compatible. Effective leadership—and again this is very old wisdom—is not based on being clever; it is based primarily on being consistent."[4]

Leaders who are sincere don't have to advertise the fact. It's visible in everything they do and soon becomes common knowledge to everyone. Likewise, insincerity cannot be hidden, disguised, or covered up, no matter how competent a manager may otherwise be.

The only way to keep the goodwill and high esteem of the people you work with is to deserve it. No one can fool all of the people all of the time. Each of us, eventually, is recognized for exactly what we are—not what we try to appear to be.

Ann Landers said, "People of integrity expect to be believed. They also know time will prove them right and are willing to wait." Integrity is lasting.

Integrity is a victory, not a gift.

Integrity is not a given factor in everyone's life. It is a result of self-discipline, inner trust, and a decision to be relentlessly honest in all situations in our lives. Unfortunately in today's world of quick fixes and easy believism, strength of character is a rare commodity. As a result, we have few contemporary models of integrity. Our culture has produced few enduring heroes, few models of virtue. We have become a nation of imitators, but there are few leaders worth imitating.

The meaning of integrity has been eroded. Drop the word into conversations in Hollywood, on Wall Street, even on Main Street, and you'll get blank stares in return. For most Americans the word conjures up ideas of prudishness or narrow-mindedness. In an age when the meanings of words are squeezed into the speaker's mold, marble values such as integrity can be pulverized overnight.

Integrity is antithetical to the spirit of our age. The overarching philosophy of life that guides our culture revolves around a materialistic, consumer mentality. The craving need of the moment supersedes consideration of values that have eternal significance.

After a sting operation to uncover graft, U.S. Attorney Rudolph Giuliani made the following statement. "On 106 occasions, bribes were offered or discussed. On 105 of those occasions, the public official involved accepted the bribe. And on the other occasion, he turned it down because he didn't think the amount was large enough."[5]

When we sell out to someone else we also sell out ourselves. Hester H. Cholmondelay underscores this truth in his short poem.

JUDAS

Still as of old
Men by themselves are priced—
For thirty pieces Judas sold
Himself, not Christ.

Billy Graham said, "Integrity is the glue that holds our way of life together. We must constantly strive to keep our integrity intact."

"When wealth is lost, nothing is lost; when health is lost, something is lost; when character is lost, all is lost."[6]

You will only become what you are becoming right now.

Though you cannot go back
and make a brand new start, my friend.
Anyone can start from now
and make a brand new end.[7]

To build your life on the foundation of integrity, take the following mirror test written by Edgar Guest. It is called "Am I True to Myself?"

I have to live with myself, and so
I want to be fit for myself to know,
I want to be able, as days go by,
Always to look myself straight in the eye;
I don't want to stand, with the setting sun,
And hate myself for things I have done.
I don't want to keep on a closet shelf
A lot of secrets about myself,
And fool myself, as I come and go,
Into thinking that nobody else will know
The kind of man I really am;
I don't want to dress up myself in sham.
I want to go out with my head erect,
I want to deserve all men's respect;
But here in the struggle for fame and pelf
I want to be able to like myself.
I don't want to look at myself and know
That I'm bluster and bluff and empty show.
I can never hide myself from me;
I see what others may never see;
I know what others may never know,
I never can fool myself, and so,
Whatever happens, I want to be
Self-respecting and conscience free.

Next, take the Mentor Test. It asks, "Am I true to my leader?" Joseph Bailey interviewed more than thirty top executives. He found that all learned firsthand from a mentor.[8] Ralph Waldo Emerson said, "Our chief want in life is somebody who shall make us what we can be." When we find that person, we need to check our growth on a regular basis, asking, "Am I totally availing myself of the teaching I am receiving?" Taking shortcuts in this process will hurt both your mentor and you.

Finally, take the Masses Test. It asks, "Am I true to my followers?" As leaders, we quickly understand that wrong decisions not only adversely affect us, but they affect those who follow us. However, making a bad decision because of wrong motives is totally different. Before reaching for the rein of leadership we must realize that we teach what we know and reproduce what we are. Integrity is an inside job.

Advocates of the significance of modeling dependability before followers, James Kouzes and Barry Posner report in their book, *The Leadership Challenge,* that followers expect four things from their leaders: honesty, competence, vision, and inspiration.[9]

Write out what you value in life. A conviction is a belief or principle that you regularly model, one for which you would be willing to die. What are your convictions?

Ask someone who knows you well what areas of your life they see as consistent (you do what you say) and what areas they see as inconsistent (you say but don't always live).

Reflecting on the *Integrity* of My Leadership

1. How deep are my personal roots regarding integrity?

2. To what degree will I walk away from a deal, sever a relationship, or take a risk for my integrity? How have I performed in the past in this area?

3. To paraphrase a verse from the Book of Job, "My integrity is mine, and no one can steal it or take it. I have to voluntarily give it up." Do I agree or disagree?

4. How do I teach a younger generation of leaders about integrity?

Notes

1. Dwight D. Eisenhower, *Great Quotes From Great Leaders,* ed. Peggy Anderson (Lombard: Great Quotations, 1989).

2. CCM *Communicator,* newsletter of the Council of Communication, Spring 1988.

3. Joint study by Korn/Ferry International, New York, 1985.

4. Peter Drucker, *Management, Tasks, Responsibilities and Practices* (New York: Harper & Row, 1974).

5. *Newsweek* Magazine, 24 August 1987, 11.

6. Anonymous, quoted by Ted W. Engstrom in *Integrity* (Waco: Word, 1987).

7. Richard Kerr for United Technologies Corp., *Bits and Pieces,* March, 1990.

8. Joseph Bailey, "Clues for Success in the President's Job," *Harvard Business Review,* 1983.

9. James Kouzes and Barry Posner, *The Leadership Challenge* (San Francisco: Jossey-Bass, 1987).

Seasons

Just as each year has its seasons, so the life of every leader goes through seasons of leadership.

S OMETIMES IT TAKES SOMEONE like Hans Finzel to state the obvious and put it to work. That's exactly what he does in "Life Cycles of Leaders," from his book *Empowered Leaders.* In this chapter he uses the life of the apostle Paul to examine the seasons of a leader's life. The first season is that of the start-up years, which are followed by the middle years, the maturing years, and finishing well. Finzel identifies the elements that make each life stage unique and warns against the dangers that can derail our leadership during those times.

Finzel cites real-life examples, references Scripture, and quotes sources from Bill Cosby to Søren Kierkegaard to illustrate his points and bring them home. The result is a deeply personal and rich analysis of the trajectory of a leader's life, and insight that can help us not only to be more effective but also to understand our situation better, no matter what stage we're in. It's true that other writers have approached this topic in another manner, dividing the seasons differently or labeling them in some other way. For us, the details of divisions and labeling are not what's important. What matters is

My burning passion is to have success at the other end of the flight, fulfilling God's objectives for me and accomplishing all that He intended me to do while on this earth.

that leadership looks different depending on where you are in life, and there are different challenges, struggles, and rewards along the way—the primary purpose of which is to remind us that God is our power and our strength.

Finzel is the executive director of CBI, an international mission agency, and spent ten years in Vienna conducting leadership training in Eastern Europe. We hope you will find this selection helpful in your own journey to the finish line—and that it will help you finish well.

Life Cycles *of* Leaders

Seasons *in a* Life *of* Leadership

• • •

Hans Finzel

On a recent visit to the beautiful city of Rome, I received a fresh and deep impression about the apostle Paul. Seeing what conditions he faced at the end of his life made me appreciate all that much more that he finished well. Every leader I talk with readily admits that they earnestly want to finish well. We want it and Paul showed how it is done.

Though Paul's leadership was well known throughout the ancient church in and around Rome, I am not sure how many people who visit Rome today have any idea who he was, although he was one of the church's greatest leaders. Traces of him are scarce in modern-day Rome.

Any visitor to Rome learns immediately that St. Peter's Church is at the center of the city's attractions. Like magnets, the Vatican, St. Peter's Basilica, and the beautiful museums that surround it draw millions to this ancient city each year. I visited Vatican Square, toured St. Peter's Cathedral, and spent half a day in the Vatican Museum. I was especially impressed by the works of Michelangelo in the Sistine Chapel. However, what inspired me most about my visit to Rome happened after I left those great buildings and that rich history. As impressive as they are, there was something more special in store.

On an obscure side street a few kilometers from the Vatican, there is a small building thought to house the prison cell where Paul spent his final days. Whether it is actually his prison cell or not is of course debatable. We climbed down into this cramped hole beneath the ground and spent about a half-hour in the dark cell. It was cold, damp, and musty. A small grate in the ceiling allowed a little daylight to shine through.

Historians agree that Paul probably lost his life around A.D. 67 when Nero ruled.

As I sat on that cold stone floor, I imagined what it must have been like for Paul in those last days. If this wasn't the exact room, it had to be just like it. What a way to spend your final weeks. As we stood in the cell and talked, drinking in the story that the stones could tell if they spoke, we noticed that only a few visitors climbed down into the cell with us. This was in stark contrast to the thousands who waited in line to enter the Vatican Museum not far away. The streets above were filled with tourists who were flocking to St. Peter's Cathedral, but only occasionally did someone stop long enough to even peer through the grate down into the cell. I thought to myself, "Here is where the man who wrote the greatest portion of the New Testament spent his last days. The greatest missionary and church planter of the first century died here. Wouldn't more people want to feel what it was like for him?" Obviously the answer is no. Most people visiting Rome today do not list Paul's cell as one of their top ten tourist sites. But for me it ranked as the number-one spot in Rome.

The words Paul wrote in his prison cell in those last days filled my heart as I contemplated his lifetime contribution to the church. He had sacrificed a great deal, but the reward was worth it. This passage came to my mind: "For I am already being poured out like a drink offering, and the time has come for my departure. I have fought the good fight, I have finished the race, I have kept the faith. Now there is in store for me the crown of righteousness, which the Lord, the righteous Judge, will award to me on that day—and not only to me, but also to all who have longed for his appearing" (2 Tim. 4:6–8).

Here is where he finished well. I silently prayed to the Lord, "That's what I want to do somewhere, someday Lord—to finish well as Paul did, but hopefully, however, not in a cell like this." Paul had made it to the end of his life and he knew it. He had a bumpy start, he learned much about maturity in his middle years, he accomplished incredible tasks during the height of his missionary ministry, and he was now showing what it meant to finish well. Could he have written what he wrote without the painful experiences he went through? I doubt it. We have the glib saying in our modern culture, "No pain, no gain." But Paul wrote the original bestseller on gain through pain centuries ago. As he was defending his apostleship to the Corinthian church, against his own personal desire, he took the time to summarize some of the costs he had to pay as a great leader.

> Are they servants of Christ? . . . I am more. I have worked much harder, been in prison more frequently, been flogged more severely, and been exposed to death again and again. Five times I received from the Jews the forty lashes minus one. Three times I was beaten with rods, once I was stoned, three times I was shipwrecked, and I spent a night and a day in the open sea. I have been constantly on the move. I have been in danger from rivers, in danger from bandits, in danger from my own countrymen, in danger from Gentiles; in danger in the city, in danger in the country, in danger at sea; and in danger from false brothers. I have labored and toiled and have often gone without sleep; I have known hunger and thirst and have often gone without food; I have been cold and naked. Besides everything else, I face daily the pressure of my concern for all the churches. Who is weak, and I do not feel weak? Who is led into sin, and I do not inwardly burn? If I must boast, I will boast of the things that show my weakness. (2 Cor. 11:23–30)

Paul was a survivor; He finished well. He used his tough experiences to defend his apostleship. Paul's trials were an integral part of how God used Paul; they helped to validate his leadership over the long haul. Those trials were part of the cost of being all he needed to be as God's man in the hour in which God called him to lead. Perhaps it was because Paul had such experiences of suffering that he was able to end his game so victoriously.

Who ever said finishing well gets easier the closer you get to the end?

How much did the hardships in Paul's life condition him for the end game? The great price he paid for his leadership role was to end his life in that dark, damp, lonely prison cell.

J. Oswald Sanders wrote of the price of leadership: "No one need aspire to leadership and the work of God who is not prepared to pay a price greater than his contemporaries and colleagues are willing to pay. True leadership always exacts a heavy toll on the whole man, and the more effective the leadership is, the higher the price to be paid."[1]

Paul paid that price and concluded his life with a sterling testimony. From his early days as a zealous missionary to the final days of his apostolic leadership, the seasons of his life serve as examples to us.

A final lesson we need to observe in the pursuit of effective leadership is to recognize that leadership has its seasons. Since our goal is to finish well, then we must traverse each stage of life intact. Unfortunately this doesn't always happen. Steve Farrar has observed that it is the *rare* man who finishes strong, it is the *exceptional* man who finishes strong, and it is the *teachable* man who finishes strong.[2]

Yet many around us have made it to the finish line successfully. This chapter examines the seasons of leadership and key issues we need to master in order to reach that goal line of finishing well. Paul gives us lessons of hope along the way—he made it under the worst of circumstances.

Just as each year has its seasons, so the life of every leader goes through seasons of leadership. We begin with the early start-up years of youthful enthusiasm and faith, followed by the stretching middle years that can make or break us, and then the rewards of heightened effectiveness in the maturing years of ministry. We'll take a look at all three of these times of the life of a leader and some of the signposts along the way that can help us navigate them successfully. No matter when God decides it is time for us to finish our journey on earth, we should be wanting to end well. This chapter concludes with a discussion of the barriers and hallmarks of finishing well.

The START-UP YEARS

Nothing is quite so refreshing to an older leader as to see the youthful zeal and spark of a young leader launching out with idealism and energy. Our early experience in ministry can be like the launching of a rocket. The trouble is, not all those rockets stay in orbit. And some young leaders don't last beyond their start-up years.

I have loved rockets and space exploration all my life, having been infected at an early age by my father who spent his career building missiles. During the final desperate years of World War II, my dad and his boss, Wernher von Braun, and several thousand German scientists and engineers were busy at a secret rocket installation in northern Germany, developing, testing, and building the first intercontinental missile, known as the V-2.

As the war was winding down, von Braun made a decision to flee to the Western front, purposely, to be captured by the Americans. In the summer of 1945 the United States captured him and a hundred other men, including my dad, and brought them to America. With them they shipped dozens of the V-2's, which were later fired in the White Sands desert in New Mexico. The U.S. Government wanted to learn all they could about building rockets from this bank of immigrants. Within two years the wives and children joined their husbands and fathers in Texas and the United States space program was about to be born.

The problem with those early rockets was that many started with an impressive launch only to end up nose down in the sand. They were duds. After my parents moved to Huntsville, Alabama, where I grew up and where NASA got its start, there were many disappointing days in the early years of the race to the moon when the rockets would fail. The funny thing about a dud is that you never really knew it was one as it sat on the launching pad. It looked good, but so many things could go wrong. A certain number of every batch of rockets they built in those years were duds.

I don't want to end up like one of dad's dud rockets, with my nose down in the sand, expended, useless, and a huge disappointment to those who were counting on me. My burning passion is to have success at the other end of the flight, fulfilling God's objectives for me and accomplishing all that He intended me to do while on this earth. That thought brings me right back to Paul and his words in prison: "Not that I have already obtained all this, or have already been made perfect, but I press on to take hold of that for which Christ Jesus took hold of me. Brothers, I do not consider myself yet to have taken hold of it. But one thing I do: Forgetting what is behind and straining toward what is ahead, I press on toward the goal to win the prize for which God has called me heavenward in Christ Jesus" (Phil. 3:12–14).

The best way to finish well is to *begin with the end in mind.* We all know of Paul's very dramatic beginning to his ministry. On the way to Damascus, where he planned to arrest every Christian he could find, he was stopped in his tracks, confronted with a vision of the Lord Jesus Christ. After walking blind for three days—it took a lot to get Paul's attention!—he received God's call for ministry through the words of Ananias: "But the Lord said to Ananias, 'Go! This man is my chosen instrument to carry my name before the Gentiles and their kings and before the people of Israel. I will show him how much he must suffer for my name'" (Acts 9:15–16).

Hearing God's call on his life, Paul did take off like a rocket in his zeal to be a diligent worker in this new harvest field. His early progress was truly remarkable for a young man fresh into the ministry. He is every mentor's dream come true. "Yet Saul *grew more and more powerful* and baffled the Jews living in Damascus by proving that Jesus is the Christ" (9:22, italics added).

But there needed to be a proving and growing time for Paul. This time of deepening began when believers sent him back home to Tarsus, to spend some time growing up in the faith outside the limelight of ministry (9:30; Gal. 1:1–2:1). This same experience of having a quiet period for growth and development is common among other great biblical leaders. It happened to Joseph, Moses, and David, to name a few. Jesus Himself had a proving and developing time as an adult, before beginning his lifework at thirty years of age. Similar growth is needed by many young zealous leaders.

Two years after Paul's conversion, he dropped out of sight for what became known as the silent years he spent in Tarsus. Peter became the focus of the Book of Acts until Paul resurfaced in Acts 13, years later. From A.D. 36 to about A.D. 46, Paul was maturing and growing in his faith privately in a part of the story that is not revealed to us. In fact he received a second call when the maturing and testing time was over, a call for ministry. "While they were worshiping the Lord and fasting, the Holy Spirit said, 'Set apart for me Barnabas and Saul for the work to which I have called them'" (13:2).

The first call of Paul in Acts 9 was to ministry in general, followed by a maturing time. But now in Acts 13 he was ready to be set apart for specific public ministry, and the pressure cooker began. What did God accomplish in Paul during those quiet years? Although we don't know for sure, I believe Paul was learning at least four things. First, he learned the power of *prayer,* how to draw strength from his new Lord and Commander. He needed to draw strength from his vertical relationship with God before he engaged in horizontal ministry to men and women.

Second, he learned *patience,* how to wait on God till He gives the signal to "go." Action-oriented Paul had to learn to let His new Chief be the Initiator of his ministry activities.

Third, he learned the *promises of God* in the Scriptures and how they related to his calling. He knew the Old Testament as well as any good Pharisee, but no doubt he studied it afresh with new eyes after his conversion and call to ministry.

Fourth, he learned the importance of a *proven character.* Certainly God was working in Paul's heart to break him of some of his bad pharisaic habits and to build in him the character he needed to lead the church through its great expansion period.

In November 1996 *Christianity Today* celebrated its fortieth anniversary by devoting an issue to "Up & Comers." Recognizing the passing of the baton from the World War II era of leaders to the next generation, *Christianity Today* editors wrote, "In this issue we look to those 40 and under who are now taking the reins of leadership. All are bright, talented visionaries and doers, and each seeks the Spirit's leading."[3]

It was a great issue, and I couldn't help but think statistically about these fifty promising young faces that filled their pages. Where will they be twenty years from now? I hope *Christianity Today* does a twenty-year follow-up, and I hope the report is a good one. It was an encouraging thing to see such promising talent and energy taking over leadership in evangelicalism. These men and women are truly starting with big impact!

The MIDDLE YEARS

Leaders in their middle years—in their forties—are about twenty years out with twenty left to go. These years are much like the middle of a marathon. Remember the marathon I mentioned running while living in Vienna [talked about earlier in his book]? I did actually complete the twenty-six miles to the finish line, thanks to Donna who would not let me give up. Without question, the middle was the hardest. Beginning was euphoric, and the end was pure adrenaline as I saw the finish line within view. But in the middle I got tired and discouraged and almost gave up hope that I would have what it would take to finish. I felt like quitting; I felt that completing the race was just not worth the sacrifice. And I looked at all those people on the sidelines; they were content to be spectators. Why wasn't that good enough for me?

In the middle years of Paul's ministry he was busy about his missionary journeys. He was a hardworking man. And like Paul, in our middle years we have to work the hardest as leaders. Usually the greatest weight of what we will ever bear will be on our shoulders by then. Several times Paul revealed the passion of his heart that was driving him forward to fulfill his vision. "We proclaim him, admonishing and teaching everyone with all wisdom, so that we may present everyone perfect in Christ. To this end I labor, *struggling with all his energy, which so powerfully works in me*" (Col. 1:28–29, italics added).

It is important to note that although Paul *was* a hardworking, driven man, he was constantly aware of his complete and utter dependence on the power of the Lord Jesus Christ. He did not attempt great things for God on his own. This cannot be emphasized strongly enough. If Paul had forged ahead in these middle years as a missionary, church planter, and writer on his own strength alone he would have burned out and given up. Instead he drew on the deep well of the energy and power of his Lord, fully aware that his work was God's work. We can step ahead in our middle years as leaders only if we know we are walking in complete dependence on the leading and strength of our Lord.

Was Paul successful in these middle ministry years? Of course. Forming a riot to get rid of Paul and his companions, unbelievers in Thessalonica said, "These who have turned the world upside down have come here too" (Acts 17:6 NKJV). What greater compliment could anyone have paid them?

Something seems to happen to people in their forties, something we label "the midlife crisis." Call it what you will, it's a time when we realize we are probably living our dreams at the present time. We know who we are and sense our weaknesses more than ever.

No matter what we may at one time have hoped and dreamed we would become, what we are now is most likely what we will be to the end.

During these days we must learn to be content with where God has planted us. The disillusionment and disparity between the early dream and the present reality can throw the midlife leader into a crisis. During these years it is easiest to let our guard down and decide that the race to the end just might not be worth it.

Looking at issues in the middle of life, Bob Buford challenges us to "go for the gold" in the second half of life, not giving up on our dreams and ambitions.

The game [of life] is won or lost in the second half, not the first. It's possible to make mistakes in the first half and still have time to recover, but it's harder to do that in the second half. In the second half, you should at long last know what you have to work with. And you know the playing field—the world you live in. You have experienced enough victory to know how hard the game is most of the time, yet how easy it is when the conditions are just right.

Some people never get to the second half; a good many don't even know it exists. The prevailing view in our culture is that as you close out your fortieth year or so, you enter a period of aging and decline. To pair age with growth seems a contradiction of terms. This is a myth I refuse to believe.[4]

Many people have accomplished great feats in their latter years of life. However, midlife is a time of soul-searching and also a time when we come face to face with the physical limitations of our own mortality. Our hair begins to fall out, our teeth give out, our bodies are slowing down, our shapes are changing, and we wonder if we still have the appeal and attractiveness we had in our youth.

Outward success can be our greatest enemy in the middle years. At this most successful time, we leaders are often the most vulnerable. If you read Gordon MacDonald's book, *Rebuilding Your Broken World*,[5] written after the great failure he faced in his personal life, you'll find he candidly describes the events leading to his own moral failure in the pastorate. His greatest enemy was the pressurized demands of his great success. He looked great on the outside but was decaying on the inside. Pressure stretched him too thin for his own good.

In a recent article MacDonald discusses what he calls "the seven deadly siphons" that cause us to lose enthusiasm for ministry as our spiritual passion runs dry. In my midlife experience I have struggled on each of these battlefields; what he is saying rings hauntingly true to life.

The Seven Deadly Siphons

1. Words without actions (talking a good spirituality without real-life practice in private).
2. Busyness without purpose (the lazy shallow river of busyness).

3. Calendars without a Sabbath (a filled-up calendar with no margin planned for quiet and reflection).

4. Relationships without mutual nourishment (acquainted with too many and intimate with no one).

5. Pastoral personality without self-examination (healing others without genuine self-evaluation).

6. Natural giftedness without spiritual power (allowing your natural gifts to carry you will eventually catch up with you as you run out of soul power).

7. An enormous theology without an adequate spirituality (a giant view of God and His work but a pea-sized personal spirituality).[6]

How do we push on to be effective in the middle years? What can we do to prevent the hollow drift into motion without inner substance? One answer is to refine our purpose and focus in life. In the second half it is imperative to write down your life dreams, your purpose, your mission statement. You may have done it early on in your career, but now in the middle years you need to take a hard look at the second half based on what you learned in the first. Peter Drucker points out things that will help in that pursuit: "*What have you achieved?* (competence). What have you learned that you are good at, and how can you build on your strengths to continue to contribute as a leader? *What do you care deeply about?* (passion). What is it that motivates you and satisfies you at the end of a week?"[7]

Buford calls this revised concentration the finding of the one thing in the box that you should focus on for your second half. Caring enough to keep going and growing in the second half takes more effort than in the first. Vaclav Havel said of this pursuit, "The real test of a man is not when he plays the role that he wants for himself, but when he plays the role destiny has for him."[8] Søren Kierkegaard said, "The thing is to understand myself, to see what God really wishes me to do . . . to find the idea for which I can live and die."[9]

The early years of our careers and ministry seem to be wrapped up in fulfilling other people's expectations.

Sooner or later a leader wakes up and realizes that he can never meet everyone's expectations and that he must quit worrying about what other people think.

This reminds me of what Bill Cosby says: "I don't know the key to success, but the key to failure is trying to please everybody."

Coming to this realization, a better approach is to (a) focus on what God wants as the ultimate contribution of my life, even if that means a radical change for my life, and (b) focus on what my relationship is with the most important people in my life: my Lord, my wife, my children. All those others who want a chunk of me come and go, but my personal relationship with God and my connection to my family is with me forever. Again quoting Bob Buford, "One of the most common characteristics of a person who is nearing the end of the first half is that unquenchable desire to move from *success* to *significance*. After a first half of doing what we're supposed to do, we'd like to do something in the second half that is more meaningful—something that raises above perks and paychecks into the stratosphere of significance."[10]

In thirteen years Peter Lynch took Fidelity's Magellan Fund from 20 million to 14 billion dollars. No one has had a more successful career on Wall Street. Yet at age forty-six he blew the whistle. His goal was to gain greater control over his own life. He explained, "My life was like a hot fudge sundae: how much can you handle without getting a stomachache?" He now stays at home each morning until the children are off to school and works four days a week—two for charity and two for Fidelity. The fifth day each week is spent with his wife!

Sure, you probably don't have responsibility for 14 billion dollars, but Lynch's choice does provide a great lesson of looking at life in a fresh way as we approach the second half of life. Although we may not have the freedom to shorten our work schedule to one like Peter has, each of us has the power to give our family more of ourselves and our time.

I began this section on the middle years with the illustration of running the Vienna Marathon. I said, "Donna would not let me give up." That was literally true! She and a friend took public transportation all over Vienna (with our son in a stroller), literally chasing me by following a map I had drawn with estimates of when I would be at various places on the marathon run. At each checkpoint, she would be waiting for me with cheers and smiles and words of encouragement; then I would have a new burst of energy to keep going. Just as in that marathon, Donna in these middle years is right there with me, cheering me on and believing in me. But beyond cheering me, she is an integral part of our team. Together, we are seeking to navigate and finish well the marathon God has set before us.

The MATURING YEARS

Prime Minister Golda Meir, one of the founders of the modern state of Israel, once said, "Old age is like a plane flying through a storm. Once you're aboard, there's nothing you can do."[11] But actually there is one thing that can be done: *Don't give up.* It's never too late to get a new lease on life. William James once stated that after age thirty people become like plaster, unwilling to change. But he is wrong, because many people have made major contributions after age fifty. It was after age fifty that Ray Kroc bought a couple of hamburger stands from the McDonald's brothers. After age fifty Dwight L. Moody founded Moody Bible Institute, and after age fifty Billy Graham spoke to the most people ever at any one time in his years of crusade evangelism.

One of America's most dramatic stories of starting life over again in the second half is that of John D. Rockefeller. At age fifty-three he was a miserable, paranoid billionaire. He was unable to sleep, felt unloved as a person, and lived in constant fear of his life. Having contracted a rare disease, he learned that the doctors had given up on him and said he had only a year to live. As he faced eternity and eternal issues, he decided to change his way of thinking about money. All his life up to that point he had hoarded money and his life was oriented inwardly. But then he established the Rockefeller Foundation and began giving away large portions of his money. His focus of philanthropy was on hospitals, medical research, education, and churches. Rockefeller received a new lease on his life, his health improved, and he lived to age ninety-eight. He went beyond selfishness and self-centeredness and began to focus on what he could do to help others.

The best way to view life in the maturing years of leadership is to focus in on the issues of finishing well. And this is a fitting conclusion to our study of effective leadership.

FINISHING WELL

"A tree is best measured when it's down." So goes an old woodsman's proverb. And how true this is of men and women. How will we know until it is all over whether they finished well?

In contrast to the failed voyage of the *Titanic,* a young "leader" that sank the first time out, there is a great warship of America's past that not only succeeded in all its dangerous voyages but was recently brought back to life after being out of commission for over a century. The *USS Constitution* ruled the seas for the United States Navy in the eighteenth century. No wonder, after being mothballed for over a century, the government poured millions into her restoration. This ship never lost a battle and went down in history as one of the navy's finest leaders. She finished so well they brought her back to life!

So in 1997 America's oldest battleship was relaunched. No living human being on planet earth had ever seen the *USS Constitution* sail, since it was drydocked 116 years ago. The scene can only be described as majestic, as this warship from a bygone era set sail from the Charleston (Mass.) Naval Yard. In the tradition of bringing back a bygone piece of American history, veteran newscaster Walter Cronkite became the official commentator of this cruise that took the newly restored and refitted two-hundred-year-old ship from Boston's outer harbor on a five-mile cruise off the coast of Marblehead. Twelve million dollars were spent to restore it, down to the finest detail. This was done to celebrate the two-hundredth anniversary of its original commissioning.

Old Ironsides, as the ship was affectionately known, was relaunched near its original launch site when it was first put out to sea in 1798. She was constructed of timbers felled from Maine to Georgia, armed with cannons, cast in Rhode Island, held together by copper fasteners made by Paul Revere, and, as such, is truly a national treasure.

Leadership is a lot like *Old Ironsides.* The apostle Paul was like that old ship—a survivor who was victorious in every battle he fought. He made it to the end, as recorded in one of the Scriptures' greatest displays of victory. The passion he showed toward the end of his life is compelling. On his way to meeting the fate that awaited him in Jerusalem, he gave a farewell speech to the Ephesian elders—a speech that summed up the passion of his heart. "And now, compelled by the Spirit, I am going to Jerusalem, not knowing what will happen to me there. I only know that in every city the Holy Spirit warns me that prison and hardships are facing me. However, I consider my life worth nothing to me, if only I may finish the race and complete the task the Lord Jesus has given me—the task of testifying to the gospel of God's grace" (Acts 20:22–24).

Then while in prison Paul wrote some of his most insightful and moving letters. In his letter to the Philippians, he shared the passion of his life that would not abate: "Brothers, I do not consider myself yet to have taken hold of it. But one thing I do: Forgetting what is behind and straining toward what is ahead, I press on toward the goal to win the prize for which God has called me heavenward in Christ Jesus. All of us who are mature should take such a view of things. And if on some point you think differently, that too God will make clear to you. Only let us live up to what we have already attained" (Phil. 3:13–16).

Even when in prison, Paul did not let up on his preaching. His readers may have reacted the way we should today. If he could have this kind of attitude in his prison cell, what is my excuse?

What will they say at your retirement party? What will your kids write on your tombstone? What will your friends remember about you?

The older I get, and the longer I watch the leadership game, the more concerned I am with simple fundamentals like finishing well.

I used to want to be a man known for great accomplishments— a person of notable deeds and ideas that rocked the planet. But now I would settle for this epitaph, "He was a good and godly man, loved his family deeply, and finished well."

The last couple of years I've spoken at retirement dinners for several individuals who have finished well. Each time I get this opportunity, my mind begins to fixate on this topic of finishing well. I've had the privilege in each of these instances to be able to say enthusiastically that the person has indeed finished well.

Recently a couple in their seventies (who could best be described as in their "convergence years") shared with some of our leadership team the lessons they have learned in their distinguished career in Christian leadership. As I introduced them, I admonished our young leaders to listen carefully to them. We've gotten hung up in our culture on worshiping youth and sidelining our elders. Somewhere along the way we have forgotten that eldership in the New Testament was connected to age. We can't go to a local Christian bookstore and buy the kind of wisdom that comes from years of experience. We can't download from an Internet site the maturity that can only be learned in the school of long and disciplined experience. How refreshing it was to have this couple in these final years of their active ministry share from their spiritual depths the lessons they've learned along the way on the road to spiritual resiliency. It was deep, rich, and satisfying. I think our young leaders at this seminar were surprised at how much they learned from these seasoned leaders.

There comes a time in every leader's life when he realizes it is time to back off. Moses certainly understood when it was time to pass the torch to Joshua. Though God clearly told Moses it was time for a leadership transition, the time is not always so clear-cut for us. Lyle Schaller says that most people stay in leadership positions too long, as opposed to leaving prematurely. A corollary to that principle is that if you stay too long, you can do more damage than if you leave too soon. We need to be sensitive to not overstay our welcome when it is time to step aside for the next generation or the next appointed person.

When it is time for transition in the leadership life cycle, it is important for all parties involved to deal from a position of grace and humility. I'll always be thankful to Warren Webster, whom I succeeded, for the gracious way in which he stepped down and made way for my presence in our organization. During the last two years of his leadership, especially when it became known that our board of directors had chosen me to succeed him, he did all he could to promote me and to step aside and to make way for me.

One of the great final acts of a good leader is to create a smooth leadership transition to his or her successor.

Many leaders have failed in this critical final leadership challenge. They have been in control so long that it is difficult for them to give the reins to someone else. How could anyone possibly do as good a job or know as much as they do?

One way of knowing that it is time to step down is when you realize privately that you may no longer have what it takes to lead effectively. Keeping your job may be best for you, but you must ask, What is best for the organization? If you are a pastor, is it better for the church that someone else takes over who can take the ministry to new places, with different giftedness than your own? We need to approach our jobs from the first day we take over as a leader with the attitude that we are not irreplaceable. The cause can and will go on without us. While we are leaders, we want to make the maximum contribution and do the best job we can before the Lord. But when it is time to go on, we need to realize we are only humans and that God will raise up the next person in His time.

When we know it's time to leave and we can sense that our leadership contribution is winding down, we need to face that final transition head-on. In the spirit of Moses' passing the mantle to Joshua, we need to ask God to give us the grace to bless and empower those who will follow us in leadership.

> Then Moses went out and spoke these words to all Israel: "I am now a hundred and twenty years old and I am no longer able to lead you. The LORD has said to me, 'You shall not cross the Jordan.' The LORD your God himself will cross over ahead of you. He will destroy these nations before you, and you will take possession of their land. Joshua also will cross over ahead of you, as the LORD said." . . . Then Moses summoned Joshua and said to him in the presence of all Israel, "Be strong and courageous, for you must go with this people into the land that the LORD swore to their forefathers to give them, and you must divide it among them as their inheritance. The LORD himself goes before you and will be with you; he will never leave you nor forsake you. Do not be afraid; do not be discouraged." (Deut. 31:1–3, 7–8)

We need to use grace and kindness as we relate to our older leaders when they reach the point in their lives where they are no longer effective. In their golden years they can make a great contribution in mentoring, counseling, writing, and teaching. That final transition is a move from direct leadership to indirect influence, or stated another way, from the work of doing leadership to the mentoring and sharing role of teaching about leadership.

The final stage of a life well lived for the Lord is what some call "the afterglow years." I like that term because it expresses the lives of leaders today like Billy Graham, Henry Blackaby, or Elizabeth Elliott, who glow in the fruit of a life lived in faithfulness to the Master. Paul had such an afterglow time during his last years in Rome while he was under house arrest. "For two whole years Paul stayed there in his own rented house and welcomed all who came to see him. Boldly and without hindrance he preached the kingdom of God and taught about the Lord Jesus Christ" (Acts 28:30–31).

IT COMES DOWN *to* CHARACTER

In the introduction to the second edition of their landmark book, *Leaders: The Strategies for Taking Charge,* Bennis and Nanus observe, "Although a lot of executives are derailed (or plateaued), for lack of character or judgment, we've never observed a premature career ending for lack of technical competence. Ironically what's most important in leadership can't be easily quantified."[12]

Even these writers in the secular world know that character is a key issue for effective lifelong leadership. In fact they admit that the longer they study effective leaders, the more they have seen that character is the defining issue. Another person who has studied hundreds of leaders over a lifetime is Bobby Clinton. In his research he has found six barriers to finishing well.[13]

First, he says, is *finances.* As leaders grow in their influence and the amount of money they are responsible for, greed and mismanagement can easily creep in and compromise an effective leader. Examples are Gideon's golden ephod and Ananias and Sapphira.

Second is *power.* With the growth of power comes the subtle temptation to abuse it. Privileges come with a rise in perceived status, which can easily become abusive. An example is Saul's usurpation of the priestly privilege. Abraham Lincoln said, "Nearly all men can stand adversity, but if you want to test a man's character, give him power."

Third is *pride.* We must maintain a healthy respect for who we are and what we have accomplished, but we must not allow successes to go to our heads. God is the One who is to be given credit for anything good that comes from our ministries.

Fourth is *sex.* This one needs no elaboration and has been a key test of leadership from day one. Joseph did it right; David did it wrong.

Fifth is *family.* Tension and trouble in a leader's home can result in his or her ministry being destroyed. This can be between husband and wife, parents and children, or even between siblings.

Sixth is *plateauing.* Some leaders experience a growing dryness and dullness in their ministry. If this is not countered with a lifelong learning attitude and with spiritual renewal, plateauing will reduce the leader's effectiveness. This hardening can even lead to rebellion and disobedience, as in the case of Saul.

We've looked at the negatives; now let's focus for a moment on the positives. Again I am indebted to Bobby Clinton, who has done extensive research on leaders who finish well. In studying the lives of hundreds of Christian leaders who have finished well, he has isolated these recurring threads throughout all their lives.[14]

LEADERS WHO FINISH WELL

First, *they maintain a vibrant relationship with God.* Our relationship with God is first in our priorities for lifelong effective leadership. Accept no substitutes—they won't work.

Second, *they maintain a lifelong posture of learning and growing.* Leaders are learners. Never develop the attitude that you have arrived and that you can rest. Have the passionate attitude Paul had about maturity and Christlikeness, "This one thing I do."

Third, *they exhibit a Christlike character, the fruit of the Spirit.* Lifelong leaders who finish well exhibit the fruit of the Spirit throughout their lives. People who know them in private acknowledge that "what you see is what you get."

Fourth, *they live out their convictions in real life.* Effective leaders walk the walk; they don't just talk the talk.

Fifth, *they leave behind one or more ultimate contributions.* Those who have finished well have left behind a significant contribution to the church. It may not be known by others, but there is a lasting contribution to God's work.

Sixth, *they walk with a growing sense of destiny.* Those who make it well to the end have a sense of God's call on their lives throughout their lives. They are convinced that God has a plan for their lives, and they are determined not to falter in seeing that plan through to the end.

General Douglas MacArthur gave one of history's most famous retirement speeches at the end of his fifty-two-year military career.

Speaking to the United States Congress on the day of his retirement, he bade farewell with these words:

> I am closing my 52 years of military service. When I joined the Army even before the turn of the century, it was the fulfillment of all my boyish hopes and dreams. The world has turned over many times since I took the oath on the Plain at West Point, and the hopes and dreams have long since vanished. But I still remember the refrain of one of the most popular barracks ballads of that day which proclaimed most proudly that "Old Soldiers Never Die; They Just Fade Away." And like the old soldier of that ballad, I now close my military career and just fade away—an old soldier who tried to do his duty as God gave him the light to see that duty. Good-bye.[15]

What a great way to finish well! There is nothing wrong with fading away into faithful retirement if you are able to look back and say, "I finished well." In his book *The Life God Blesses,* Gordon MacDonald has an excellent chapter entitled, "What Kind of Old Man Do You Want to Be?" Gordon's ten points of the effective older person are appropriate for this chapter on finishing well. Hopefully these ten will be the trademarks of all our lives in our older years: showing gratitude, having an enthusiastic interest in the accomplishments of the younger generation, keeping our minds sharp and agile, thinking in macroterms (seeing the big picture), never really retiring, still loving our spouses dearly, even romantically, not trying to hold on to institutional power, knowing how to pray, and not being afraid of death.[16]

One final thing to note about finishing well. We need to make sure our last will has a testament in it. Most people include in their wills only what actually is least important, the disposition of their earthly goods. Years ago people would actually take the time to make a testimony, and that old practice deserves a comeback. When your heirs sit together in the lawyer's office to hear the reading of your will, you will have one last opportunity to tell a captive audience what has mattered most to you in this life. Will it only include your jewelry, stocks, home, and savings? Or will you include something like this, which Donna and I have written?

Our Last Will and Testament

Of all the things we valued in this earthly life, our personal salvation in Jesus Christ was that of most value. Your mother and I met at Columbia Bible College, whose motto was, "To know Him and to make Him known." That is why we went to CBC, and had we not had that commitment we would never have met nor would we have become one in marriage and family. You, our children and grandchildren, have grown out of our love and commitment to one another and our common bond in Christ. Our testimony is this, that Jesus Christ is the Lord and Savior of our lives. He is the heart of our family, and without Him we could have done nothing! Our greatest desire is that each of you will also know Him and allow Him to lead you all the days of your lives.

When we were married in 1975, at Judson Baptist Church in Oak Park, Illinois, we chose Ephesians 3:20–21 as our "marriage verse": "Now to him who is able to do immeasurably more than all we ask or imagine, according to his power that is at work within us, to him be glory in the church and in Christ Jesus throughout all generations, for ever and ever! Amen."

You would make us the happiest and most fulfilled if after we are long gone these words from the apostle John would ring true all your lives: "I have no greater joy than to hear that my children are walking in the truth" (3 John 4).

Much more could be said on this topic, which is as complex as the world in which we live. As we keep the main things the main things, the comforting thing to remember is that we serve the God of grace and mercy. He has chosen to use us, His imperfect vessels, in the great adventure of accomplishing His perfect will on planet Earth. To serve as a leader in that quest can be a profoundly rewarding pursuit.

Reflecting on the *Seasons* of My Leadership

1. Which leadership season am I currently going through?
2. How did I do in previous seasons?
3. Who have I seen lead successfully through all the seasons of life?
4. What am I doing to finish well in life?

Notes

1. J. Oswald Sanders, *Spiritual Leadership* (Chicago: Moody, 1969), 169.
2. Farrar, *Finishing Strong* (Multnomah Publishers, Inc., 2000), 8.
3. "Up & Comers: Fifty Evangelical Leaders Forty and Under," *Christianity Today,* 11 November 1996, 20.
4. Bob Buford, *Halftime* (Grand Rapids: Zondervan, 1994), 20–21 (italics his).
5. Gordon MacDonald, *Rebuilding Your Broken World* (Nashville: Nelson, 1988).
6. Gordon MacDonald, "The Seven Deadly Siphons," *Leadership* (winter 1998), 31.
7. Peter Drucker, quoted in Buford, *Halftime,* 123.
8. Vaclav Havel, quoted in Buford, *Halftime,* 23.
9. Søren Kierkegaard, quoted in Buford, *Halftime,* 61.
10. Buford, *Halftime,* 84 (italics his).
11. Golda Meir, quoted in *Great Quotes from Famous Leaders,* 55.
12. Bennis and Nanus, *Leaders: The Strategies for Taking Charge* (HarperBusiness, 1997).
13. Bobby Clinton, "Finishing Well: The Challenge of a Lifetime" (Pasadena, Calif.: Barnabas Resources, 1994), 8–9.
14. Ibid., 13–14.
15. Douglas MacArthur, quoted in Bobby Clinton, "The Mantle of the Mentor" (Pasadena, Calif.: Barnabas Resources, 1993), 1.
16. MacDonald, *The Life God Blesses,* 98–110.

Character

When God gets hold of a company president, a department manager or a shift supervisor, that person has to remove some things from his life, add some things and leave some things alone for his leadership to be all that God wants it to be.

A FTER READING THIS FAR, YOU'VE probably figured out what this book is about: it's an attempt to look at leadership through the eyes of faith, to marry and intertwine those two topics. With that goal in mind, we're ending with an article we wrote for the *Life@Work* journal that asks what difference it makes when a leader embraces faith in Christ.

The title of the article, which is about the apostle Paul, asks a question: "Does a changed heart produce a changed leader?" The answer is both yes and no. It goes without question that no one who genuinely encounters Christ can come out of that experience unchanged, and Paul's encounter with the Messiah is one of the most dramatic events recorded in Scripture. He embraced the Lord, dropped his murderous campaign against Christians, and dedicated his life to spreading the gospel message. Those are some dramatic changes.

But in other ways he stayed the same. The same forceful zeal that had driven him in his Judaism also marked his missionary campaigns. He remained a tentmaker and supported himself throughout his

Entrepreneurs,
pastors, physi-
cians, corporate
executives and
ministry founders
are notorious for
building an
environment that
creates a messiah
effect for them.
In this situation,
followers develop
a fixation on the
leader's strengths
and personality.

ministry. Many aspects of his leadership style and personality remained. The difference is that all these things were channeled into the cause of Christ, who transformed Paul into the person he was created to be from the beginning.

Character encompasses all these things: our goals and values, our personality, and the extent to which we allow God to mold us. This can be seen not only in Paul but also in other biblical leaders, whose "report cards" we've included in a table at the end of the chapter. In the end, leadership is not really about style but about character, and the lessons from Scripture teach us that better than any other source.

Before *and* After

Does *a* Changed Heart Produce *a* Changed Leader?

• • •

Stephen R. Graves & Thomas G. Addington

The organization was well-established. Well-respected. Rich in corporate culture and history. It had faced numerous cutthroat challenges over the years, but it always had survived, thanks to strong, committed leadership. But the competitor it faced now was far more serious. In fact, if given half a chance, it had the potential to steal the entire market.

One young leader wasn't about to let that happen. Trained by the best minds in the industry, this aggressive individual had been rapidly scaling the organizational ladder under the careful guidance of the existing leadership team. They knew the kind of leader their organization would need to succeed in the future, and this young man had all the right qualities.

He was fiercely loyal to the organization and its corporate culture. He was forceful, passionate and dogmatic. He did whatever it took to overcome obstacles, even if he had to destroy his rivals in the process. He thrived on the road—in fact, it was while traveling that he achieved some of his greatest successes. And he wasn't about to let some upstart competitor steal his organization's glory.

Then, one day, he saw the light.

His world did a one-eighty.

His path made a sharp U-turn.

Life as he knew it turned upside-down.

He was on his way to a key assignment in another city when he met Christ.

The experience changed his life to the very core, although it didn't change *everything* about him. He was still the same leader. He still had the same intense focus. The same dogged determination. The same insatiable drive to succeed. The same aggressive, Type-A personality.

There was, however, a huge difference. After his experience with Jesus, he went through a shocking career transition—he said good-bye to the position he had held and joined the leadership team of the upstart competitor.

This young leader wasn't climbing the corporate ladder at Microsoft, Wal-Mart or General Electric when he met Christ. He was on the road to Damascus, armed with arrest warrants for followers of The Way. His name when he encountered the light of Christ? Saul. His name after his life had been transformed by Christ? Paul. As in "The Apostle." As in one of the founding fathers of the Early Church. As in the author of more than half of the New Testament.

Paul, who has been described by Biblical scholars as the most outstanding and commanding personality the Christian faith has produced, dominates the New Testament in much the way that Moses dominates the Old. "In many ways, he stands as the outstanding example of leadership—with the exception of our Lord Himself," writes Kenneth O. Gangel in *Lessons in Leadership from the Bible* (BMH Books, 1980). "And in the sense of leadership being reproductive, there is no person in either the Old or the New Testaments who offers us a greater model of building one's life into others for the cause of Christ than does this complex man from Tarsus."

But who was Paul? And what lessons on leadership does his transformed life hold for the 21st century businessperson?

A NEW MISSION

Paul was born a Roman citizen, probably into an influential Jewish family in the distinguished city of Tarsus. As a boy, he was immersed in the curriculum of the synagogue school; during his teenage years, he studied under the noted scholar, Gamaliel. According to Gangel, "he was trained to be a rabbi and apparently excelled many of his peers, entering the defense of the Hebrew faith and persecution of Christians with great zeal."

It is in this setting that Paul—then called Saul—makes his first appearance in Scripture. Acts 7:58 indicates that the witnesses who stoned Stephen laid their clothes at Saul's feet before carrying out their dirty business. This action, along with the note in Acts 8:1 that Saul gave approval to Stephen's death, "indicates that this young man had already attained a position of importance in the battle against the young church at Jerusalem," writes D. Edmond Hiebert in *Personalities Around Paul* (Moody Press, 1973). "He promptly demonstrated his native leadership ability by personally pressing the persecution that arose against the church upon the death of Stephen."

After his dramatic conversion, Saul spent several years in obscurity, being discipled by other believers. But although he had switched sides and was now working to grow the church instead of destroy it, his personality and leadership style were unchanged. To be sure, some of his rough edges were knocked off, and his people skills improved as he matured in his relationship with Jesus. But God had called Paul to lead one of the greatest international expansion efforts ever undertaken, and many of the traits that made him so good at persecuting the church were the same traits that helped him succeed in his new leadership role.

Paul, though short and balding, was "one of those arresting, magnetic personalities that inevitably produces a polarizing effect upon those around them," Hiebert writes. "Men could not remain neutral toward him. When confronted with his dynamic, disciplined, decisive character, they were compelled to react. They were either strongly repelled by him or strongly drawn to him. Paul was both fiercely hated and devoutly loved."

His burning desire to communicate was one of the most important ingredients of his leadership, writes Gangel. In *St. Paul, the Traveller and the Roman Citizen* (Baker Book House, 1962, reprint edition), W. M. Ramsey writes that Paul gestured frequently while speaking, and his fixed, steady gaze—a marked feature in his personality—was one source of his influence over the people with whom he associated.

Paul was a professional tentmaker before he encountered Christ, and he remained one afterwards. Even as the leader of the rapidly growing organization that was the early church, he was self-reliant and he retained a real sense of individuality.

When it came to his personal brand of leadership, Paul was a launcher. A vision caster. A networker. A risk-taker. He was a mentor, but he wasn't particularly personable. He was direct, to the point, confrontational. Whatever he did—from killing Christians to mentoring young pastors—he did with passion. His reputation and personality were well known among the early believers, so it's no wonder his conversion had such a whiplash effect on the church. Imagine the hushed conversations behind locked doors: "How do we know it's not just a ploy? How do we know his conversion isn't just a way for him to infiltrate our ranks and eventually turn on us? How do we know he's for real?"

Despite these doubts, Paul's sincerity and newfound faith quickly became evident to everyone who met him. He was as mission-driven after his conversion as he was before; he just had a new mission. And he had all the tools he needed: natural wirings and gifts, a huge vision and an incredible market opportunity.

TACKLING ISSUES

So he went about his work, establishing and developing churches throughout the Mediterranean region. But he didn't ride into town, hold a three-day seminar at the downtown convention center, attend a reception in his honor and fly off to his next destination. He invested himself in each community, often spending months helping believers become grounded in their faith and instilling in them the same kind of mission focus that he had.

At Corinth, a thriving commercial center along one of the Roman Empire's most vital trade routes, Paul founded a church in the spring of A.D. 52 and spent 18 months there. Several years after he left, however, he received reports of deep problems in Corinth—problems that had caused the believers there to lose sight of their mission. So, troubled about what he had heard, Paul wrote them a letter and confronted the issues that had surfaced. The material in I Corinthians is not theoretical. It's a personal letter from a leader to a group of followers. It's like Jeff Bezos writing an intimate instructional memo to his forces at Amazon.com, or like Jack Welch confronting organizational problems in a personal note to his colleagues at General Electric.

Paul knew these people. He had led them on a daily basis for months. He knew their strengths and their weaknesses. Above all, he knew how far they had come during his time with them. And that's why he was frustrated when he heard that they had been quarrelling among themselves and bickering about who was the better leader— Paul or Apollos, another early church leader who was known for his great oratorical skills. So in I Corinthians 3:1–9, he tackles the issue in his usual direct style. He tells the people they are worldly and immature, he reprimands them for choosing favorites, and he sets the record straight about the true force behind any growth.

"For when one says, 'I follow Paul,' and another, 'I follow Apollos,' are you not mere men?" he writes. "What, after all, is Apollos? And what is Paul? Only servants, through whom you came to believe—as the Lord has assigned to each his task. I planted the seed, Apollos watered it, but God made it grow. So neither he who plants nor he who waters is anything, but only God, who makes things grow. The man who plants and the man who waters have one purpose, and each will be rewarded according to his own labor." (I Corinthians 3:4–8)

As a whole, I Corinthians is not a letter about Paul's leadership style. It's about issues. But the first few verses of the third chapter offer a clear picture of Paul's personality and philosophy of leadership at that point in his life. The concepts are buried in the issues, but closer examination reveals what Paul really thinks about leading people. In fact, if Paul the Apostle had been invited to speak on leadership at a Ken Blanchard seminar, a Willow Creek convention or a Harvard Business School conference around the same time he was composing I Corinthians, it's conceivable that his message would have come straight out of this passage.

A Lesson *from a* Cover Story Leader

Here, then, is Paul's take on what a great leader looks like, based on his first letter to the Corinthians and on his own life after he met Christ.

Great leaders have a healthy sense of selflessness.

"What, after all, is Apollos? And what is Paul? Only servants, through whom you came to believe. . . ." (I Corinthians 3:5a)

Like most good leaders, Paul had a healthy self-image, and he didn't minimize the fact that he played a key role in the growth and development of the church at Corinth and elsewhere. But he didn't lord his apostleship over anyone, and he didn't get a big head about what he was doing. He had that vitally important sense of selflessness.

Make no mistake—Paul was not a passive, quiet leader whose personality made it easy for him to serve selflessly. He was as much a three-green-light, go-get-'em type of person as there's ever been. He had to figure out selflessness just like everyone else—it didn't come naturally. He had to work on developing humility and a servant heart.

In *Leadership by the Book* (Waterbrook Press, 1999), Ken Blanchard, Bill Hybels and Phil Hodges talk about selflessness as it relates to keeping one's ego in check. "An emphasis on obedience to a higher mission and a set of values, which Jesus lived, requires keeping one's ego under control," says one of the main characters in the book. "A big ego can't coexist with a servant heart because it puts concern for self ahead of service to others and pleasing God. You start thinking that the sheep are there for the benefit of the shepherd. And that mind-set soon begins to negatively impact the rest of your life. . . .

"Leaders with servant hearts by definition have *genuine humility* . . . but they also have confidence. They don't think less of themselves, they just think about themselves less. Their egos don't *Edge God Out*. In fact, their primary concern is for spiritual significance rather than earthly success."

But did Paul really fit this description? After all, wasn't he the guy who, in the very same letter, urged the Corinthians to imitate him? (I Corinthians 4:16) He must have thought pretty highly of himself to be able to say that. The answer lies in a correct understanding of what it means to be ego-less. Some may think that being ego-less means that a person minimizes his role as a leader or has a lack of confidence about what he does. But that's not it at all. The key has to do with motivation—ego-less leaders aren't in it for themselves.

Paul may have been accused of being ego-driven when he told his followers to imitate him, but he really wasn't. He wasn't full of himself; he simply wanted to give them an example or a model of how they should act as followers of Christ. His instruction to the Corinthians wasn't driven by self. In fact, Paul's other writings indicate that he was committed to getting rid of self in his efforts to become more like Christ. If nothing else, that only made him more worthy of imitating.

Great leaders don't intentionally create messiah effects.

"For when one says, 'I follow Paul,' and another, 'I follow Apollos,' are you not mere men?" (I Corinthians 3:4)

This is a tricky point because the characteristics that often are found in good leaders—charisma, a strong personality, etc.—often are the very same characteristics that cause employees to worship the leaders and put them on pedestals. One well-known example is Steve Jobs, head of Apple Computer, who was once described by *Salon* as "a manipulative cult-of-personality leader."

Entrepreneurs, pastors, physicians, corporate executives and ministry founders are notorious for building an environment that creates a messiah effect for them. In this situation, followers develop a fixation on the leader's strengths and personality. At the same time, they completely ignore the leader's weaknesses, either because they don't want to see them or they lack the ability to recognize them. This is a dangerous situation because it can lead to severe disillusionment among the followers if the leader falls. It's also dangerous because it can give the leader more power than he or she can handle. As British statesman Lord Acton once said, "All power corrupts and absolute power corrupts absolutely."

Some leaders—including many who firmly believe they are called to take on the world, revitalize their company or transform their industry—are quite unintentional about creating messiah effects. Other leaders, however, create messiah effects intentionally. Their whole reason to be in leadership is to offset neurotic issues deep in their soul. They need the constant admiration of people below them, and they have to surround themselves with people who make them feel secure. It's what we call the "crooked-stick complex." The only way some people will ever be a straight stick is to constantly surround themselves by sticks that are even more crooked. Instead of measuring themselves to straighter sticks, they constantly compare themselves to people who are less qualified and less competent. Organizational leadership provides the perfect environment for this—it makes it easy to measure across and down, not up.

Great leaders, on the other hand, surround themselves with people who will force them to measure up, to constantly improve. For example, when we formed Cornerstone Group, our consulting firm, we knew we were teaming up with another individual who would serve as a straight stick. We didn't form partnerships with someone weaker in every area so that we would always feel affirmed and needed. We chose to partner with each other because we knew we had different strengths, and we counted on the other person to help us improve, not to make us look good.

Great leaders see their leadership as one piece of a bigger process.

"The man who plants and the man who waters have one purpose. . . ." (I Corinthians 3:8a)

Most corporate leaders know the importance of their leadership—otherwise, they probably wouldn't be where they are. By itself, their leadership is a big deal, but it's also part of a bigger picture. Paul had a healthy sense of this idea. He knew he played a key role in the expansion of the church, but he also realized it was only a part of the huge process that had begun when Jesus returned to heaven.

Unlike some newly appointed CEOs of today, Paul didn't try to discount or erase the work that had been done by the leaders who had come before him. Nor did he have the false notion that his leadership would never end; that's why he was so committed to developing young leaders such as Timothy. He recognized that he was one link in the chain—an important link, to be sure, but only one link nonetheless.

A modern-day example of this kind of thinking is David Glass, the recently retired CEO of Wal-Mart Stores Inc. Glass joined the retail chain during the mid 1970s and worked with Sam Walton, the company's legendary founder, for several years before succeeding him as chief executive in 1988. Rather than try to outdo Walton, copy his unique leadership style or make drastic changes in the company, Glass instead worked to build upon and improve the retailing empire that Walton had created. And he did just that. From a national chain with annual sales of $16 billion in 1988, Wal-Mart grew to an international force with sales of $165 billion in the fiscal year that ended Jan. 31, 2000.

Although Glass's achievements are many, he didn't hold on to his position tightly or think that he was the only person who could make it grow in the future. Just the opposite, as he indicated in a speech published in Wal-Mart's latest annual report. "One of my principal responsibilities as CEO has been to build the next generation of management so this company can rise to the next level of success," he said.

Glass stepped down in January [2000] so that the next generation, led by new President and CEO Lee Scott, could pick up where he left off, just as Glass had done after Walton more than a decade earlier. Unfortunately, it's a lack of this sense of continuity and process that disqualifies many leaders from seeing themselves and their roles correctly. As our good friend Tom Muccio, Procter & Gamble's vice president for customer business development worldwide, once said, "Leadership is a set of responsibilities, not a job that you hang on to."

Hans Finzel helps put this in perspective in *Empowered Leaders* (Word, 1998). "We need to approach our jobs from the first day we take over as leader with the attitude that *we are not irreplaceable,*" he writes. "The cause can and will go on without us. While we are leaders, we want to make the maximum contribution and do the best job we can before the Lord. But when it is time to go on, we need to realize we are only humans and that God will raise up the next person in His time."

Great leaders recognize that there is a God component
and a people component to all success.

"I planted the seed, Apollos watered it, but God made it grow." (I Corinthians 3:6)

Sometimes leaders perpetuate the belief that it's their formula or plan that has caused their organization to grow; they fail to acknowledge that factors like timing, market conditions and environment also play a role. Not Paul. He made a huge distinction between his role and the outcome, which was growth. And he couldn't have been clearer if he had painted his message on his forehead: "I planted the seed, Apollos watered it, but God made it grow." (I Corinthians 3:6) In other words, there are some elements of success that lie outside of us—elements that frequently are stirred in from above. For followers of Christ, the key to keeping this in perspective lies in understanding the headship of Jesus—He is the vine; we are merely the branches, and apart from Him we can do nothing. (John 15:5)

TAKING STOCK

A quick review of the life and work of Paul the Leader reveals that when he met Christ, he left some things behind, he added some things, and he kept some things. The same is true for leaders today. When God gets hold of a company president, a department manager or a shift supervisor, that person has to remove some things from his life, add some things and leave some things alone for his leadership to be all that God wants it to be.

In Paul's case, he left behind his selfishness—the idea that the world revolved around him. He wasn't a grossly immoral person, but he obviously left behind his immoral behavior of jailing and killing believers. When it came to addition, Paul added Jesus Christ as his model. It didn't happen overnight, but as he matured in his faith, he added relational skills and his emotional intelligence improved, as evidenced by his initially rocky relationship with John Mark. (Acts 15:37; Colossians 4:10; II Timothy 4:11) His growing commitment to relationships also is noticeable in the tender tone of some of his other letters, particularly Philippians.

In the final analysis, however, Paul kept far more than he added or left behind. He remained cause-driven. He kept his mission focus. He kept a sense of not wanting to inappropriately depend on others. He kept his attitude of doing whatever it took to accomplish his work. And he kept his personality.

The difference was that after Paul met Christ, these attributes were transformed by the power of God's love and grace. "A natural leader by any measure," writes Sanders, "Paul became a great spiritual leader when his heart and mind were captured by Jesus Christ." That's why he could confidently instruct the believers at Rome—and followers of Christ in the 21st century—to "not conform any longer to the pattern of this world, but be transformed by the renewing of your mind. Then you will be able to test and approve what God's will is—His good, pleasing and perfect will."

That, in a nutshell, should be the goal of any godly leader.

TABLE 16.1. *Biblical Leadership: A Report Card*

Examples of leadership in action fill the pages of Scripture. Some leaders were highly effective throughout their lives, while some did better during certain phases. This chart grades Biblical personalities on their performance during four key phases of leadership. The Scripture references included with each entry are not comprehensive; they merely serve as a starting point for further study.

TABLE 16.1. *Biblical Leadership: A Report Card, continued*

Leadership actions	*"A" rating*	*"C" rating*	*"F" rating*
Responding to the call to lead	Noah (Gen. 6:8–22) Abraham (Gen. 12:1–4) Shammua, Shaphat, Caleb, Igal, Joshua, Palti, Gaddiel, Gaddi, Ammiel, Sethur, Nahbi, Geuel (Numbers 13:1–24) Samuel (I Samuel 3) Saul (I Samuel 9–10) Elisha (I Kings 19:19–21) Hosea (Hosea 1:2–3) Isaiah (Isaiah 6:1–8) Esther (Esther 4) Jesus (Mark 14:32–36) Philip (Acts 8:26–40)	Moses (Exodus 3–4) Gideon (Judges 6:11–40)	Balaam (Numbers 22–24) Korah, Dathan, Abiram (Numbers 16:1–35) Jonah (Jonah 1)
Leading well	Joseph (Genesis 39–47) Moses (Exodus through Deuteronomy) Bezalel and Oholiab (Exodus 35:30–39:43) Joshua (Joshua 1–24) Caleb (Numbers 13:30) Deborah (Judges 4–5) Samuel (I Samuel 4–12) David (II Samuel 5–10) Abigail (I Samuel 25) Uriah (II Samuel 11:6–13) Solomon (I Kings 2:13–4:34) Uzziah (II Chronicles 26:1–15) Josiah (II Chronicles 34–35) Daniel (Daniel 1–6) Ezra (Ezra 7–10) Nehemiah (Nehemiah 1–13) Esther (Esther 5–7)	Aaron (Exodus 32) Miriam (Exodus 15:20–21; Numbers 12) Samson (Judges 14–16)	Pharaoh (Exodus 5–12) Nadab and Abihu (Lev. 10:1–5) Shammua, Shaphat, Igal, Palti, Gaddiel, Gaddi, Ammiel, Sethur, Nahbi, Geuel (Numbers 13:26–33) Phinehas and Hophni (I Samuel 2:12–36) Saul (I Samuel 13–15) Absolom (II Samuel 15–17) Rehoboam (I Kings 12:1–24; 14:21–31; II Chronicles 10–12) Ahab (I Kings 16:29–33) Jezebel (I Kings 19:1–2)

TABLE 16.1. *Biblical Leadership: A Report Card, continued*

Leadership actions	"A" rating	"C" rating	"F" rating
	John the Baptist (Matthew 3:1–16; Mark 1:1–8; Luke 3:1–19) Jesus (The four Gospels) Peter (Acts 2:14–4:31) Paul (I Corinthians 3:4–8) Priscilla and Aquila (Acts 18:24–26)		Athaliah (II Kings 11:1–3; II Chronicles 22:10–12) Manasseh (II Kings 21:1–18) Herod (Matthew 2:1–18) Pilate (John 18:29–19:22)
Maintaining spiritual vitality	Joseph (Genesis 39) Moses (Exodus, Numbers, Deuteronomy) David (Psalms) Hosea (Hosea 1–3) Jeremiah (Lamentations) Daniel (Daniel 1–6) Jesus (Matthew 4) Paul (Philippians 4:4–13)	Thomas (John 20:24–29)	Samson (Judges 14–16) Saul (I Samuel 18–19) Solomon (I Kings 11:1–13) Joash (II Chronicles 24:17–27) Uzziah (I Chronicles 26:16–23) Jonah (Jonah 4) Judas (Acts 1:15–19)
Passing the baton	Moses (Numbers 27:12–23; Deuteronomy 31:1–8) Joshua (Joshua 24:31) Elijah (II Kings 2:1–14) John the Baptist (John 1:19–36) Jesus (Matthew 28:16–20) Paul (I Timothy 6:11–21)		Eli (I Samuel 2:12–36) Saul (I Samuel 18:1–16)

Reflecting on the *Character* of My Leadership

1. How has my leadership changed through the years?

2. Twenty years from now, will I be scored as a successful leader or a failure?

3. Buy a journal and sit down a few times over the next few weeks. Pour yourself a hot cup of your favorite coffee and craft a few statements on leadership. Write a profile of the kind of leader you would like to be if only you had the strength and skills. Write down a series of prayers. Isolate six key concepts from this book that you want to absorb into your daily practice of leadership.

Conclusion

In wrapping up this book, we would like to spend some time think-ing about a passage near the end of the book of Hebrews. The writer of this New Testament epistle makes an interesting reference to lead-ers as he presents his concluding exhortations to the readers of his mes-sage. He makes this direct and bold statement: "Remember your leaders. . . . Consider the outcome of their faith and imitate their faith" (Hebrews 13:7). There are three admonitions in this verse that war-rant our attention as we wrap up these thoughts on leadership.

The first is the command to remember our leaders. If we think about all the individuals who have played that role in our lives, that's a lot of people. In the beginning our parents were our leaders; then our leader circle grew to include coaches in Little League and on the soccer field, Girl Scout troop leaders, Sunday school teachers, teach-ers throughout elementary school and high school, professors and advisers in college, mentors, employers, other work associates, parents of friends, pastors. Most likely, the list is long.

Why does the writer of Hebrews ask us to remember these people? One reason is to experience—and, where appropriate, express—a sense of gratitude and appreciation for the investment our leaders made in our lives. Although this idea is not explicitly stated in this verse, the importance of gratefulness is a theme that runs throughout the Bible. It's mentioned repeatedly as a mark of the nation of Israel's faithfulness to God in the Old Testament, and New Testament writers regularly express thanks for the way the churches care for one another and seek to work out their faith. Remembering someone with gratefulness and appreciation keeps our perspective right; it helps us realize anew that our success doesn't originate with us—it's the result of God's provision and other people's willingness to help us along the way.

Once we've remembered our leaders and given thanks for who they are and what they've done, the next step is to consider the outcome of their way of life. The Greek word that is translated as *consider* here actually means "to weigh the results." In other words, we're to hit the "replay" button, play back a video of that person's life, and examine how it ended and what happened as a consequence. Abraham Lincoln said that you shouldn't measure a tree until after it's fallen. The best time to measure someone's influence is after he or she has completed life. That doesn't mean we can't recognize a leader's contribution while that person is alive, it simply means there is a ripple effect to influence.

Interestingly, the writer of Hebrews tells us to consider the outcome not just of a leader's life but of his or her *way* of life. How did this person traffic up and down the roads of life? What were the patterns that came through again and again? This admonition carries the implication that we're not just talking about public endeavors but also the private sphere—home and family, personal relationships, ethical motivations. The apostle is saying, "Listen: remember your leaders, bring them up one by one in the front of your mind, examine who they were and how they 'did life' on a daily basis, and take a look at the results." We are to be cautious and not too quick to give away the trophy and attach the medal until we have sifted and filtered a person's actions and way of life.

If, after this process, someone has proven to be a worthy leader by meeting the criterion of achieving positive, godly results, then our job is one of imitation. How do we do this? Sure, we can read the books and listen to the seminar presentations, but if we really want to learn about a person's way of life, why not spend a summer with him? Why not do an internship or sabbatical under him? Why not sit down with that person and pick her brain, find out what's in her heart, observe how she interacts with the people who come in and out of her life? Seeing the person's leadership in action will give us a much broader foundation on which to base our imitation.

Finally, it's important to note that the writer of this verse does not say to imitate leadership. He says to imitate faith. The leaders whose writings we have included in this book have all, in one way or another, provided an angle to better understand the life of faith. The kind of leader we're trying to identify and celebrate in this book is one who is both spiritually bent and able in business. Someone who has hit on an aspect of convergence in faith and leadership and communicated it in a startlingly clear manner. That mind-set was the fuel that propelled us down this journey, and that is the source of motivation and strength we hope you take with you on your journey toward better leadership and greater faith.

Additional Reading

We know that there are two kinds of learners: readers and listeners. If you're a listener like our friend Ken Blanchard, this reading list might not be for you. You'll need to go to seminars, listen to books on tape, and talk with people over coffee. But if you are a reader, we invite you to dive into this list and work your way through some of these excellent suggestions. The list includes some of our favorites and those of our friends Alan Nelson and Howard Hendricks, to whom we extend a sincere thank you.

At first we were going to put together a standard bibliography that included every bit of publication information. Then we realized that in today's information society, if you have the title and the author's name, you can find any book—maybe even a used or discounted copy. So that's the way we created this reading list, to be as user-friendly and efficient as possible. If there's a book you think we missed, be sure to let us know. Send an e-mail to sgraves@lifeatwork.com or taddintgon@lifeatwork.com. We'd love to see your list.

1. *The Book of Leadership Wisdom,* by Peter Krass.

2. *Built to Last: Successful Habits of Visionary Companies,* by James C. Collins and Jerry I. Porras.

3. *The Center for Creative Leadership Handbook of Leadership Development,* by Cynthia O. McCauley, Russ S. Moxley, and Ellen Jan Velsor (eds.).

4. *Certain Trumpets,* by Garry Wills.

5. *The Charismatic Leader,* by Jay Alden Conger.

6. *Churchill on Leadership,* by Stephen F. Hayward.

7. *Credibility,* by James M. Kouzes and Barry Z. Posner.

8. *Dedication and Leadership,* by Douglas Hyde.

9. *Deep Change,* by Robert E. Quinn.

10. *Developing the Leader Within You,* by John C. Maxwell.

11. *The Drama of Leadership,* by Patricia Pitcher and Henry Mintzberg.

12. *The E Myth Revisited,* by Michael E. Gerber.

13. *The Effective Executive,* by Peter F. Drucker.

14. *The Empowered Leader,* by Calvin Miller.

15. *Empowered Leaders: The Ten Principles of Christian Leadership,* by Hans Finzel.

16. *Encouraging the Heart,* by James M. Kouzes and Barry Z. Posner.

17. *Executive EQ,* by Robert K. Cooper and Ayman Sawaf.

18. *Faith in Leadership,* by Robert J. Banks and Kimberly Powell (eds.).

19. *Feeding and Leading,* by Kenneth O. Gangel.

20. *The Fifth Discipline,* by Peter M. Senge.

21. *The Five Temptations of a CEO,* by Patrick M. Lencioni.

22. *Five-Star Leadership: The Art and Strategy of Creating Leaders at Every Level,* by Patrick L. Townsend and Joan E. Gebhardt.

23. *A Force for Change,* by John P. Kotter.

24. *The Founding Fathers on Leadership,* by Donald T. Phillips.

25. *The Genius of Sitting Bull,* by Emmett C. Murphy and Michael Snell.

26. *Good to Great,* by James C. Collins.

27. *Great Leaders of the Christian Church,* by John D. Woodbridge.

28. *Growing Leaders by Design: How to Use Biblical Principles for Leadership Development,* by Harold L. Longenecker.

29. *Handbook of Leadership Development,* by Center for Creative Leadership.

30. *The Heart of an Executive,* by Richard D. Phillips.

31. *The Heart of Godly Leadership,* by Hudson T. Armerding.

32. *A Higher Standard of Leadership,* by Keshavan Nair.

33. *How to Speak, How to Listen,* by Mortimer J. Adler.

34. *Images of Organization,* by Gareth Morgan.

35. *In the Name of Jesus,* by Henri J. M. Nouwen.

36. *Increasing Your Leadership Confidence,* by Bobb Biehl.

37. *The Inner Work of Leadership,* by Barbara Mackoff and Gary Wenet.

38. *Insights on Leadership,* by Larry C. Spears.

39. *Integrity of Heart and Skillfulness of Hands: Biblical and Leadership Studies in Honor of Donald K. Campbell,* by Charles Dyer and Ray Zuck (eds.).

40. *Jesus CEO,* by Laurie Beth Jones.

41. *Jesus on Leadership,* by C. Gene Wilkes.

42. *John Stott: The Making of a Leader,* by Timothy Dudley-Smith.

43. *The Leader of the Future: New Visions, Strategies, and Practices for the Next Era,* by Frances Hesselbein, Marshall Goldsmith, and Richard Beckhard (eds.).

44. *Leader to Leader,* by Frances Hesselbein and Paul M. Cohen (eds.).

45. *The Leader Within,* by Howard Haas with Bob Tamarkin.

46. *Leaders,* by Harold Lawrence Myra (ed.).

47. *Leaders on Leadership: Wisdom, Advice, and Encouragement on the Art of Leading God's People,* by George Barna.

48. *Leaders: The Strategies for Taking Charge,* by Warren Bennis and Burt Nanus.

49. *Leadership,* by James MacGregor Burns.

50. *Leadership,* by Charles Swindoll.

51. *Leadership and the New Science,* by Margaret J. Wheatley.

52. *Leadership and the One Minute Manager,* by Ken Blanchard.

53. *The Leadership Challenge: How to Keep Getting Extraordinary Things Done in Organizations,* by James M. Kouzes and Barry Z. Posner.

54. *The Leadership Engine: How Winning Companies Build Leaders at Every Level,* by Noel M. Tichy.

55. *Leadership for Dummies,* by Marshall Loeb and Stephen Kindel.

56. *Leadership for the 21st Century,* by Joseph C. Rost.

57. *Leadership in Organizations,* by Gary A. Yukl.

58. *Leadership Is An Art,* by Max De Pree.

59. *Leadership Jazz,* by Max De Pree.

60. *The Leadership Lessons of Jesus: A Timeless Model for Today's Leaders,* by Bob Briner and Ray Pritchard.

61. *Leadership Lessons of Robert Lee,* by Bill Holton.

62. *Leadership—Magic, Myth, or Method?* by J. W. McLean and William Weitzel.

63. *Leadership Without Easy Answers,* by Ronald A. Heifetz.

64. *Leading Change,* by John P. Kotter.

65. *Leading Change,* by James O'Toole.

66. *Leading Minds: An Anatomy of Leadership,* by Howard Gardner and Emma Laskin.

67. *Leading People,* by Robert H. Rosen.

68. *Leading Without Power,* by Max De Pree.

69. *Leading Your Ministry,* by Alan E. Nelson.

70. *Learning to Lead,* by Jay Alden Conger.

71. *Learning to Lead,* by Fred Smith.

72. *Lincoln on Leadership,* by Donald T. Phillips.

73. *The Making of a Leader,* by J. Robert Clinton.

74. *The Management Methods of Jesus: Ancient Wisdom for Modern Business,* by Bob Briner.

75. *The Managerial Mystique,* by Abraham Zaleznik.

76. *Managing Our Work,* by John W. Alexander.

77. *Managing People Is Like Herding Cats,* by Warren Bennis.

78. *The Master Plan of Evangelism,* by Robert E. Coleman.

79. *Mentoring: Learning How to Learn from Others,* by J. Robert Clinton and Paul D. Stanley.

80. *Mind of a Manager, Soul of a Leader,* by Craig R. Hickman.

81. *Nehemiah: Becoming a Disciplined Leader,* by Gene Getz and Bruce Wilkinson.

82. *The New Leader,* by Myron Rush.

83. *On Becoming a Leader,* by Warren Bennis.

84. *On Becoming a Servant Leader,* by Robert K. Greenleaf.

85. *On Leadership,* by John W. Gardner.

86. *Overcoming the Dark Side of Leadership: The Paradox of Personal Dysfunction,* by Gary McIntosh and Samuel D. Rima, Sr.

87. *Patton on Leadership,* by Alan Axelrod.

88. *Paul the Leader,* by J. Oswald Sanders.

89. *The Power of Followership: How to Create Leaders People Want to Follow, and Followers Who Lead Themselves,* by Robert E. Kelley.

90. *The Power of Servant Leadership,* by Robert K. Greenleaf.

91. *The Power of Vision,* by George Barna.

92. *Principle-Centered Leadership,* by Stephen R. Covey.

93. *Psychology for Leaders,* by Dean Tjosvold.

94. *Real Power,* by Janet O. Hagberg.

95. *Rediscovering the Soul of Leadership,* by Eugene B. Habecker.

96. *Reflections on Leadership,* by Larry C. Spears.

97. *Seeker and Servant,* by Robert K. Greenleaf.

98. *Selling the Invisible,* by Harry Beckwith.

99. *The Seven Habits of Highly Effective People,* by Stephen R. Covey.

100. *The 7 Levels of Change,* by Rolf Smith.

101. *Spiritual Leadership,* by J. Oswald Sanders.

102. *Stewardship,* by Peter Block.

103. *They Smell Like Sheep: Spiritual Leadership for the 21st Century,* by Lynn Anderson.

104. *Thriving on Chaos,* by Tom Peters.

105. *The Timeless Leader,* by John K. Clemens and Steven Albrecht.

106. *The Top Ten Mistakes Leaders Make,* by Hans Finzel.

107. *Transforming Leadership: A Christian Approach to Management,* by Richard Higgingson.

108. *The 21 Indispensable Qualities of a Leader,* by John C. Maxwell.

109. *The 21 Irrefutable Laws of Leadership,* by John C. Maxwell.

110. *Values-Driven Leadership: Discovering and Developing Your Core Values for Ministry,* by Aubrey Malphurs.

111. *What Leaders Really Do,* by John P. Kotter.

112. *Who's in Charge,* by Leith Anderson, Jack Hayford, and Ben Patterson.

113. *Why You Can't Be Anything You Want to Be,* by Arthur F. Miller.

114. *The Will to Lead,* by Marvin Bower.

The Editors

Stephen R. Graves and *Thomas G. Addington* have been business part-
ners and friends for over a decade. For the last twelve years, they have
been exploring how to blend business excellence with biblical wisdom
through consulting, teaching, mentoring, and writing around the
world. This mission statement, originally scratched out on a breakfast
napkin early one morning twelve years ago, has been their "never lost"
system as they have journeyed through a variety of entrepreneurial
endeavors and experiments. They founded Cornerstone Group Consulting and the *Life@Work* journal; speak regularly in business, ministry, and academic settings; publish frequently; serve on national
boards; and are active in coaching leaders toward the finish line. Both
have an earned doctorate, both are deeply devoted to their families,
and both love the never-ending challenge of meshing real life with the
message of Jesus.

About Cornerstone Group

For over twelve years, Cornerstone Group has been helping leaders and organizations navigate their way to success. We have provided assistance at every stage of the development bell curve: the exciting, confident "go go" stage; the reflective, cautious "slow go" stage; and the discouraging, confusing "no go" stage. Each stage of organizational life produces its own unique set of challenges and opportunities. Whether you are a small or large nonprofit, a family business going through transition, or a medium-sized company trying to move to the next level, we can provide a valuable helping hand. Our list of clients is impressive; our reputation is rich, and our approach is refreshing.

What We Do Best
- Identify "what's broken"
- Grow business into mass retail
- Construct a compelling future vision
- Align boards and organizations
- Coach leadership transitions
- Advise senior leaders
- Make plans happen
- Create leadership teams
- Expand into international markets

CORNERSTONE GROUP

The Art of Change

Contact us and let us send you a brochure and talk about a free White Board Session (taddington@cornerstoneco.com or (479) 236-0665/ sgraves@cornerstoneco.com or (479) 236-0664).

Index

Behind the Bottom Line:

Powering Business Life with Spiritual Wisdom

Stephen R. Graves and Thomas G. Addington

$19.95 Hardcover

ISBN: 0787964670

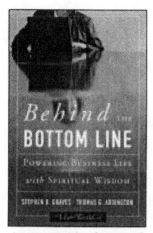

How does someone in business understand the spiritual implications of the central dimensions of work life? In this latest book from the editors of the *Life@Work* journal, business consultants Stephen R. Graves and Thomas G. Addington share a wealth of spiritual wisdom on topics that their research indicates are at the cutting edge of the growing spirituality at work movement. Business leaders are searching for ways to make the workplace friendly toward spirituality, and no authors are better equipped than these to tackle hot-button issues such as business ethics, ambition, change, influence, entrepreneurship, innovation, failure, and strategy.

Graves and Addington take the twenty central themes of business life and bring powerful, life-changing spiritual insights to bear. Each chapter builds on an issue of *Life@Work*, blending the best of biblical wisdom with business excellence. The twenty topics address readers in a practical, thoughtful way to show them the relevance and importance of the spiritual to the issues and concerns of business life.

STEPHEN R. GRAVES is cofounder of Cornerstone Group, a consulting firm specializing in change management and strategy for both non-profit and for-profit organizations around the world. He is also cofounder of the influential journal *Life@Work*. Graves is considered a hardcore businessman and a rock-solid theologian. He has a doctorate from Dallas Theological Seminary and lives in Fayetteville, Arkansas, with his wife and three children.

THOMAS G. ADDINGTON is cofounder of Cornerstone Group and *Life@Work*. He was formerly a professor at the University of Alabama-Huntsville and the University of Arkansas. Addington is an expert in organizational analysis, strategic planning, and persuasive communication strategies. He holds a doctorate in communication from Penn State University and lives in Fayetteville, Arkansas, with his wife and their three children.

[Price subject to change]

Printed in the United States
67659LVS00005B/58